—FAVORITE—
EASY~TO~MAKE
TOYS

—FAVORITE—
EASY~TO~MAKE
TOYS

SEDGEWOOD PRESS

Published by Sedgewood Press

For Sedgewood Press
Editorial Director: Jane Ross
Supervising Editor: Gale Kremer
Production Manager: Bill Rose

Produced for Sedgewood Press by
Marshall Cavendish House
58 Old Compton Street
London W1V 5PA

For Marshall Cavendish
Consultant Editor: Virginia Colton
American Editors: Eleanor Van Zandt
and Andrew Kemp
House Editor: Yvonne Deutch
Designer: Caroline Dewing

First printing 1982

© Marshall Cavendish Limited 1982

Library of Congress Cataloging in
Publication Data
1. Non-fiction
2. Crafts
LCCN 81-71013

Distributed in the Trade by:
Van Nostrand Rheinhold Company

ISBN 0-442-28022-2

Printed in The United States of America

Introduction

Making hand-crafted toys for your children is part of the fun of being a parent; they are also perfect – and warmly personal – gifts from a loving aunt, uncle or grandparent. *Favorite Easy-To-Make Toys* is a fairy-tale collection of some fifty wonderful projects – including soft toys to sew, knit and crochet, imaginative toys to make from wood, and a mixed-media group that you put together from odds and ends of everyday materials.

Any child whose Mom and Dad are blessed with nimble fingers is fortunate indeed. For the not-so-expert grown-ups (and that includes most of us), we've provided comprehensive know-how sections so beginners can tackle the techniques involved in any project in the collection.

With a well-stocked bag of fabric scraps, some bits of yarn and leftover decorative trimmings, you can create some marvelous characters. With the easy-to-follow step-by-step instructions you get clear, detailed diagrams and inspiring full-color illustrations, so you can't go wrong. Most of the wooden toys, too, are made with scraps – in this case odd pieces of lumber. For guidance, there are simple-to-use trace patterns.

Favorite Easy-To-Make Toys is a truly varied collection, with something to delight any youngster in your life. There are all sorts of dolls and doll clothes; huggable crocheted bunnies, lambs and dolls; a sensational knitted lion, and a most unusual doctor and nurse team to knit for budding young medics. There are hand and finger puppets for every kind of playacting, plus a revival of a good, old-fashioned idea – a teach-me rag book to help a child learn to manage buttons and snaps and such all by himself.

As for cost, these toys are anything but expensive to make. For example, with a few empty thread spools and some fabric scraps, you can create the most adorable tiny Victorian four-poster bed literally for just a few cents.

You'll never regret a minute of the time spent on these delightful toys. You may even enjoy the project as much as the child does the toy – and that is saying a great deal.

Contents

SOFT TOYS

In the following pages you'll find a colorful selection of delightful soft toys to sew, knit and crochet. Children regard these cuddly playmates as very special friends – they are taken to bed, hugged, squeezed and kept close by as constant companions. Any one of these adorable characters will make a perfect gift for your child.

Basic know-how

Sewing techniques

Basic sewing tools
pins
tailor's chalk (for marking around
    patterns)
needles in a range of sizes for plain
    sewing and embroidery
    tape measure
scissors, including small size for
    clipping seams and large for
    cutting out
iron and ironing board
sewing machine (useful for most
    of the sewing projects)
pinking shears (useful for making
    decorative edges on felt toys and
    for neatening seams)

Basic sewing
Layouts
Some of the projects in this book
have a layout diagram included.
This shows how to arrange the pattern pieces on the fabric most economically. Study this and arrange
your pattern pieces in the same way.
Mark around all pattern pieces with
tailor's chalk.

Making a graph pattern
Graphs are a way of giving readers a
full-sized pattern by first scaling it
down to fit onto the pages of a book.
The graph lines serve as a guide,
enabling you to enlarge the pattern
to the original size—or another size
if you prefer. You will need to work
on a flat surface such as a table,
using a pencil, ruler, and sheets of
either graph paper or dressmaker's
pattern paper, which is already
drawn up into squares. You can rule
the squares yourself, but this requires accuracy and is rather
tedious.

To draw up the pattern, first check
the scale given with it; this might
say, for example, "each square
equals 1in," but the scale will vary
with the project. To copy a pattern,
say for the bodice of a doll's dress,
start at the top left-hand corner of
the diagram. Count the squares to
the lower point of the neckline and
mark this point on paper. Now
measure distance of upper point of
neck from side and top of paper and
mark it. Connect the two points,
copying the neck curve. Draw the
remainder of the pattern to scale
similarly. Copy all pattern pieces in
the same way. Always check that
pieces fit together well before cutting them out in fabric. You might
have to make small adjustments.
Identify every pattern piece—back,
front, and so on. Also mark in any
detail such as center back or front.

Changing the size of a pattern
It is a simple matter to make a graph
pattern larger or small than the sizes
given.

If you want to make the pattern
twice as large, simply interpret the
1in grid as being a 2in grid, for
example, and plot the graph onto 2in
squares. Similarly, you can make it
$1\frac{1}{2}$ times larger by using a $1\frac{1}{2}$in grid,
or smaller by reducing the size of
the squares. One word of warning,
however; the seam allowance gets
enlarged or reduced in the same proportion, and if you do not take the
new seam allowance the toy will be
out of proportion. A way of overcom-

ing this is to draw in the stitching
line on the pattern given in the book
and use this line—not the cutting
line—when drawing the new pattern. Then add the normal seam
allowance to each piece.

Cutting out
If the fabric is creased, press it
carefully before cutting.

Note if any of the pattern pieces
have a left and a right side. If you are
cutting out on a single layer of
fabric, you must first place the pattern with its right side facing
upward; after cutting, turn it over
and cut a second piece with the
wrong side of the pattern facing
upward.

Seams
Seams can be either hand- or
machine-sewn.

To sew a plain seam, place the
pieces of fabric to be joined with
right sides facing each other, unless
otherwise directed, and with edges
even. Pin at the ends, at any notches,
at the center, and then at regular
intervals in between. Baste (make
large, temporary running stitches)
along the line that will be the seam.
This is a given distance from the
edge of the fabric, usually from $\frac{1}{4}$ to
$\frac{5}{8}$in for toys. Place the fabric under
the presser foot with the edges to the
right and stitch along the seamline.
A stretch machine stitch is useful for
toys. If you are sewing the seam by
hand, use small backstitches.

French seam
1. With WS facing, pin, baste and

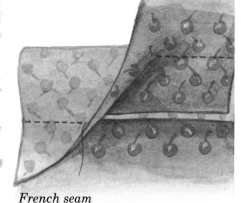

Plain seam

French seam

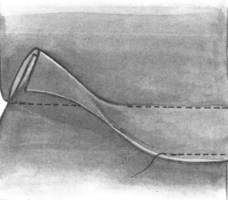

Flat fell seam

1. *Glass safety eyes positioned correctly onto fabric.*

r.s. w.s.

2. *Eye made from plastic button.*

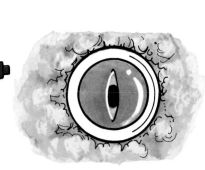

3. *Eye made from felt pieces.*

machine-stitch the edges together about $\frac{1}{4}$in from the seamline. Press as stitched.

2. Trim the seam allowances to $\frac{1}{8}$in of the stitching and press the seam open.

3. Next turn the RS of the fabric together, fold on the stitched line and press.

4. Baste, then machine-stitch along the seamline.

Press as stitched.

Flat fell seam

1. Start by forming a plain seam.

2. Press the seam open and trim one of the allowances to half the original width.

3. Press the other allowance over the trimmed one and fold under the edge $\frac{1}{8}$in. On curved seams clip into the turned edge just short of the fold at even intervals.

4. Pin, baste and then machine-stitch near the fold through all thicknesses.

Cutting and sewing felt

Felt is very easy to handle. As it does not fray, it need not be hemmed, and seams do not need finishing. Also, it has no wrong side. However, it is not hard-wearing.

Cutting and sewing fur fabric

Fur fabrics have woven or knitted backings. In either case, lay the fabric pile side down, checking that the pile is running in the same direction on all pieces. Cut one layer at a time, using sharp scissors and taking care not to cut the pile.

Stitch with a strong needle, using synthetic thread, which has some elasticity. Separate hairs of pile before stitching. After stitching, use a pin to ease out pile along the seams.

Stuffing

The material generally used for stuffing soft toys is polyester fiberfill. It is washable and packs easily to give a smooth surface. An alternative is foam pieces. These, too, are washable, but they can produce a lumpy finish unless the fabric is very firm. Foam pieces are best used for large toys, which would require vast quantities of polyester stuffing.

A large knitting needle is useful for pushing the stuffing into place. Fill the narrowest parts first and also the parts farthest from the opening. Make sure that the toy is evenly stuffed, especially if made in a stretch fabric. When the stuffing is completed, slipstitch the opening edges together with the seam allowances turned in. Fasten off securely.

Safe toys

For young children make sure that the toys you make are free from anything that could cause injury. Substitute embroidered eyes for buttons and do not include anything with wire in it.

Features

Special glass safety eyes can be bought from most craft and hobby suppliers. Follow the manufacturer's instructions carefully when inserting them (fig. 1). Avoid glass eyes with wire stems. These can be easily pulled out by a determined child.

Make eyes from buttons (fig. 2) or a series of shapes in felt of different size and color to suggest iris, pupil, etc. Place them on top of each other in graduating sizes and move the pieces around until you obtain the desired expression (fig. 3).

Noses are often attached after the toy has been stuffed and sewn up. Noses can be round, oval, or triangular. If a round shape needs stuffing, cut it double the required finished size and overcast around the outside edge. Place the stuffing in the middle and pull up the thread tightly. Fasten off securely. Slipstitch it to the face so that the drawn-up edge is not showing (fig. 4). For a flat nose draw the shape required on a piece of thin cardboard. Cut out and place it on the felt. Cut around the shape leaving at least $\frac{1}{2}$in extra all around. Overcast the edges and pull thread up evenly and tightly all around the cardboard. Fasten off securely. Slipstitch it to face on the wrong side (fig. 5).

Whiskers can be bought or made with transparent synthetic thread. The simplest way of attaching them is to cut a whisker double the length required, fold it in half, and sew it to the face across the center crease of whisker (fig. 6). However, these can be pulled out easily and it is safer to attach them in the following way, before the toy is stuffed. Cut a long piece of synthetic thread and tie two knots in it, spacing them the same distance apart as that required between the whiskers. From the wrong side of the face thread the two ends of the synthetic thread through to the right side with a needle, leaving the knots on the wrong side of the face. Work a few stitches on the wrong side of the face to hold the whiskers in place (fig. 7). To add character, thread the whiskers through small black felt dots to

11

4. *Making a stuffed nose*
5. *Making a flat nose*
6. *Attaching folded whiskers to face*
7. *Attaching whiskers with knots*
8. *Small felt dots placed on whiskers*
9. *How to make a tongue*

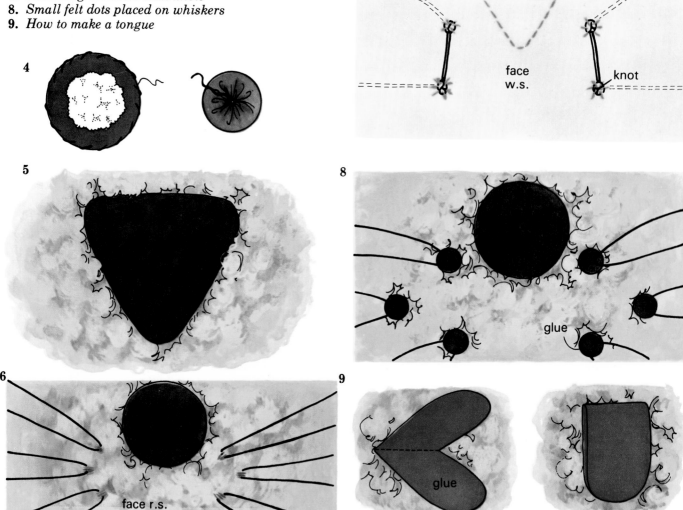

which you have previously applied a dot of glue to the underside. Then push the dots onto the face (fig. 8).

To make a toy animal's tongue, use colorfast felt or leather. Cut double the length required and fold in half. Open the tongue out and place it on the face, right sides together; then backstitch it in place along the fold. Apply fabric glue to the ends of the tongue and press them together (fig. 9).

Rag dolls' faces
Faces tend to be flat, so it is best to aim for stylized features rather than realism. Felt circles make effective eyes and embroidery can be added.

Hair is usually made from yarn and can be styled in various ways. You can get a frizzy effect if you unravel the yarn first. Or use a mohair-type yarn.

Machine-stitched patchwork
Decide on the size of the squares or rectangles to be used, allowing $\frac{3}{8}$in seam allowances. Patchwork is used for the toys on pages 74–77.

Choose the fabric pieces to be used in the design—they should be the same weight, thickness, and washability. Press fabrics.

Working along the straight grain of the fabric, draw each patch accurately on the wrong side of fabric, using a ruler and pencil, or a sharp white crayon for dark fabrics. When cutting a large number of patches of equal size it is helpful to make a template from stiff cardboard or plastic. Include seam allowances and mark and cut out accurately using sharp scissors.

When you have cut the required number of patches, you can begin to plan the exact design of the

patchwork and to build up the required pattern.

Placing right sides together and taking $\frac{3}{8}$in seam allowance, machine-stitch the patches together into a strip the required length (fig. 1). When you have enough strips to make the required width of fabric, press all the seams open.

Placing right sides together, machine-stitch the strips together, taking $\frac{3}{8}$in seam allowance. When you have finished, press seams open and tie off and cut the ends of thread.

To give extra strength to the fabric, you can carefully topstitch the patchwork on the right side, working close to the seams as shown in fig. 2.

Hand-sewn patchwork
This method is suitable for those without sewing machines.

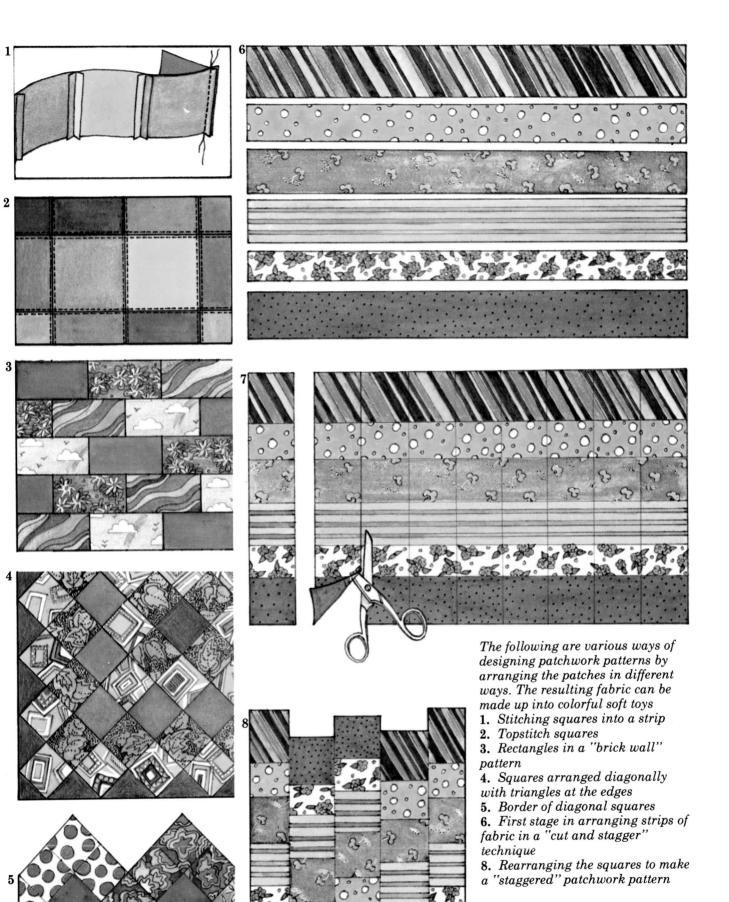

The following are various ways of designing patchwork patterns by arranging the patches in different ways. The resulting fabric can be made up into colorful soft toys

1. Stitching squares into a strip

2. Topstitch squares

3. Rectangles in a "brick wall" pattern

4. Squares arranged diagonally with triangles at the edges

5. Border of diagonal squares

6. First stage in arranging strips of fabric in a "cut and stagger" technique

8. Rearranging the squares to make a "staggered" patchwork pattern

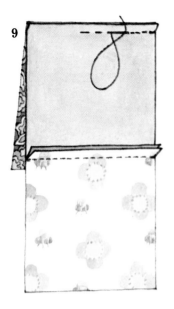

9

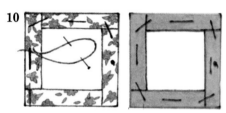

10

11

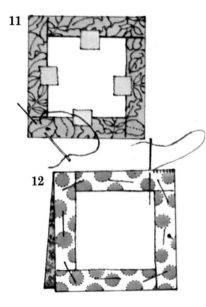

12

9. *Sewing patches together by hand with a running stitch*
10. *Many people like to use paper patches to provide support when they are doing hand-sewn patchwork. Here the patch is shown basted to the paper*
11. *If using fine fabrics, stick edges of paper with masking tape and baste corners through the seam allowances*
12. *Overcasting the patches together*

Join the patches as you would for machine patchwork. Cut out the number of patches required, then place patches together, right sides facing, and join them carefully with a small running stitch (fig. 3). Join the patches into strips, press seam allowances to one side, and join the strips together. Do not press seams open, as this will put too much strain on the running stitch.

Hand and embroidery stitches

Backstitch
Bring the thread through on the stitching line, then take a small backward stitch through the fabric. Bring the needle through again a little in front of the first stitch. Then take another stitch, inserting the needle at the point where the first stitch came through.

Buttonhole stitch
Work from right to left forming a tiny loop at the top of each stitch. Do not pull stitches too tight.

Blanket stitch
The thread loops underneath the needle, which lies vertically.

Chain stitch
Work from right to left, making a chain of loops on the right side of the fabric. The needle returns to the place where it came out, the thread looping under it.

Lazy daisy (detached chain)
Each stitch is held down separately with the working thread. Finish a line of chain stitch in this manner.

French knots
Bring the thread through the fabric, hold it down with the left thumb, and wind the needle around it (a). Insert the needle beside the point where it emerged and pull through (b).

Overcasting
Used on raw edges to prevent fraying and sometimes to join pieces. Working from either direction, make diagonal, evenly spaced stitches over edge of fabric.

Running stitch
Weave needle in and out of fabric before pulling through. Several stitches can be made on needle at the same time. Draw up stitches if gathers are required. Large running stitches are used for basting.

Satin stitch
Work straight stitches closely together across the required shape. Stitches should be of even tension and not too long.

Slipstitch
Working from right to left, take a stitch through fabric and then pass it through the turned-in edge.

Stab stitch
Worked from right to left. Push needle down vertically, pull needle through on underside. Then push needle up vertically and pull through on upper side. Stitches should be very small.

Stem stitch
Work from left to right, taking regular, slightly slanting stitches along the line of the design.

Cross stitch
For an even appearance, work one row below another. Make sure that all stitches have the top thread slanting in the same direction. Work the first diagonal stitch all along a row, then work back along the row adding the second stitch. Stitches should form a perfect square.

Catch stitch (herringbone stitch)
Work from left to right, taking a small horizontal stitch in the upper layer and then a small horizontal stitch in the lower layer diagonally as shown. Do not pull stitches too tight.

Split stitch
This stitch looks rather like chain stitch and is ideal for outlining. It can also be stitched in curving and spiral lines in close fillings as well as in straight lines.

As diagram shows, make a new stitch and bring the needle through again halfway along the stitch just made, splitting the thread into equal halves. The stitches can be gradually increased or decreased in length to fill the shape, but each should be brought up close to the center of the one before. When you are working curves use shorter stitches.

Backstitch

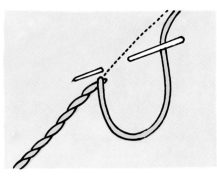

Stem stitch

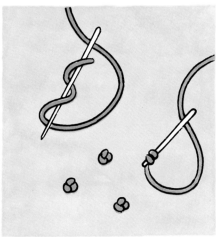

French knots

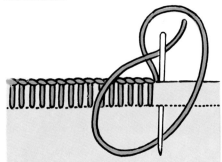

Buttonhole stitch

Overcasting

Cross stitch

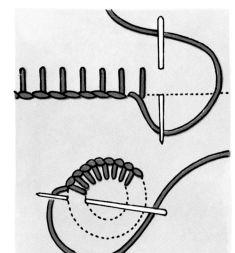

Blanket stitch

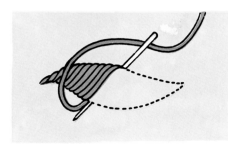

Satin stitch

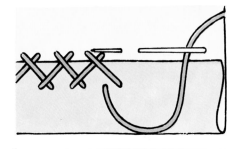

Catch stitch

Chain stitch

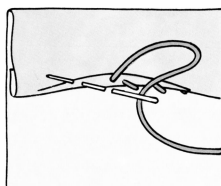

Slipstitch

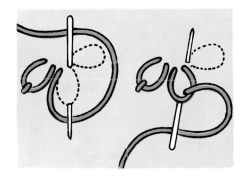

Lazy daisy stitch

Stab stitch

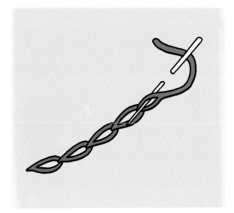

Split stitch

Knitting techniques

Apart from the knitting instructions themselves, patterns usually contain basic information under several different headings so that you can see at a glance such details as size and materials needed. Read through the instructions before you begin work, in order to check that you have everything you need. You will also get an idea of the way the pattern is worked.

Gauge

The gauge of a knitted fabric describes its elasticity and the tightness of its stitches. It is expressed in terms of the number of rows and stitches that are worked over a given measurement. Work a test piece of knitting to check your gauge; it can be adjusted by using a different-sized needle. Since the yarns specified are general classifications, rather than brand names, the gauge will vary somewhat. However, it is not as important as when making a garment, for which you need a precise gauge for a perfect fit. Gauge here acts as a general guide.

It is important to work the instructions in the order in which they are given. Asterisks (*) are often used to save repetition; in a pattern row an asterisk denotes that you should repeat the sequence of stitches from that point as instructed. A single or double asterisk at the beginning and end of a complete section of the pattern shows that a whole set of instructions is later repeated.

Finishing instructions tell you the order in which pieces should be sewn together and how to work any final edgings or trimmings.

Abbreviations

alt	alternate(ly)
approx	approximately
beg	begin(ning)
cont	continu(e)(ing)
dc	double crochet
dec	decreas(e)(ing)
foll	follow(ing)
hdc	half double crochet
inc	increas(e)(ing)
K	knit
K-wise	knit-wise
M1	pick up strand between needles and knit into back of it (called "make 1" or M1).
psso	pass slipped stitch over
P	purl
P-wise	purl-wise
rem	remain(ing)
rep	repeat(ing)
RS	right side
sc	single crochet
sl	slip
sl st	slip stitch
st(s)	stitch(es)
tbl	through back of loop(s)
tog	together
tr	triple
WS	wrong side
yo	yarn over needle, or hook

Yarns

The word "yarn" once meant only wool yarn, but now a wide range of synthetic yarns, which imitate wool is also available.

Casting on and binding off

All knitting begins with a row of loops being cast on to one needle, and subsequent rows are worked into these loops. At the end of a piece of work the knitted stitches are secured by binding off, so that they do not unravel.

Casting on

Two-needle method for a firm edge
1. Make a slip loop on the left-hand needle. Holding the yarn in your right hand, take up the second needle and insert it into the slip loop from front to back. Wind the yarn under and over the point of the right-hand needle.
2. Draw a new loop through the slip stitch; transfer this new loop to the left-hand needle and withdraw the right-hand needle.
3. Insert the right-hand needle from front to back between the two loops on the left-hand needle. Wind the yarn under and over the point of the right-hand needle and draw a loop through. Transfer the new loop to the left-hand needle. Always inserting the right-hand needle between the last two loops on the left-hand needle, continue in the same way until you have the number of stitches that you want cast on.

Binding off

1. With the yarn and needles in the usual working position, work the first two stitches so that they are transferred to the right-hand needle. Use the point of the left-hand needle to lift the first stitch worked over the second one and off the needle. This leaves one stitch on the right-hand needle.
2. Work the next stitch on the left-hand needle and repeat the process of lifting one stitch over another. Continue in this way until you have one stitch remaining on the right-hand needle. Secure this last stitch by breaking off the yarn about 4in from the knitting, drawing this through the stitch on the needle and tightening. Darn in the end when finishing the work. Binding off is usually done on a knit row, but the same principle applies when purling.

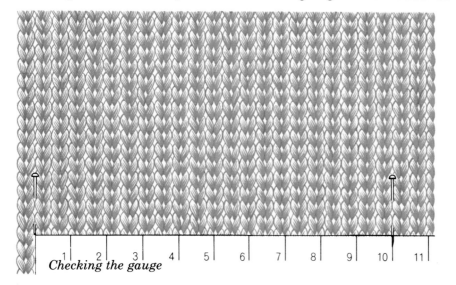

Checking the gauge

Slip loop

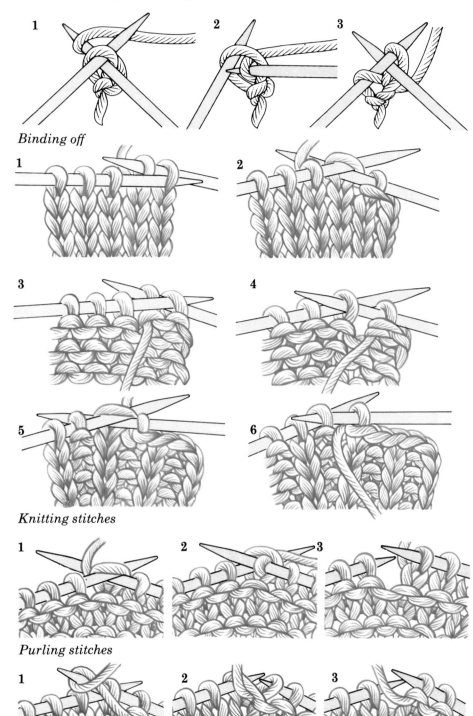

Casting on
2-needle method for a firm edge

1   **2**   **3**

Binding off

1   **2**

3   **4**

5   **6**

Knitting stitches

1   **2**   **3**

Purling stitches

1   **2**   **3**

Knitting and purling "tbl"

Basic stitches

Two simple stitches—knit and purl—are the basis of all the innumerable stitch patterns. The projects included in this book use very easy stitches.

Knitting stitches

1. Hold needle with cast-on stitches in left hand and insert free right-hand needle from front to back into first stitch on left-hand needle. Keeping yarn at back of work, wind it under and then over right-hand needle point.
2. Draw new loop through stitch on left-hand needle.
3. The new stitch remains on the right-hand needle and the one worked falls from left-hand needle. Work into each stitch in same way until you have transferred them all to right-hand needle.

Garter stitch (g st)

Garter stitch is simply knitting every stitch in every row, producing a horizontally ridged effect.

Purling stitches

1. Hold needle with cast-on stitches in left hand and insert free right-hand needle from back to front into first stitch on left-hand needle. Keeping yarn at front of work, wind it over and around right-hand needle point.
2. Draw new loop through stitches on left-hand needle.
3. The new stitch remains on right-hand needle and the one worked into falls from left-hand needle. Work into each stitch in same way until you have transferred them all to right-hand needle.

Knitting and purling "tbl"

To give a stitch a twisted appearance and make it firmer, you can knit through the back of the loop. Insert right-hand needle into back of stitch on left-hand needle, then knit in usual way.

To purl through the back of the loop insert right-hand needle through back of stitch on left-hand needle and purl in usual way.

Stockinette stitch

Knit and purl rows are worked alternately to produce a smooth fabric on the right side and a looped texture on wrong side.

Reverse stockinette stitch

The purl or "wrong" side of stockinette stitch is used as the right side.

Single rib

Knit one stitch and purl one stitch alternately across the first row. Keep the yarn at the back of the work when you knit a stitch, bring it between the stitches to the front when you purl a stitch, and take it to the back of the work for the next stitch. On the next and every subsequent row each stitch knitted in the previous row must be purled and each one purled must be knitted. To vary the pattern you can work a different number of stitches for the knit and purl ribs; for example, for double rib you knit two stitches and purl two stitches alternately. Another variation is to knit into knit stitches and purl into purl stitches on subsequent rows, thus producing a textured effect such as seed stitch.

Increasing and decreasing

This is used to shape the fabric as it is created. Doing this at the edge of a fabric alters the shape of the outline; doing it within the row will alter the flat shape.

Increasing one stitch

This can be worked anywhere in a row. Knit or purl into the stitch as usual, but do not let the loop fall from the left-hand needle.

Insert the right-hand needle into the back of this loop and knit or purl the same stitch again.

Making one stitch (M1)

This is worked within the body of the knitting rather than at the side edges. Use the right-hand needle to pick up the horizontal strand of yarn between the stitch just worked and the next stitch on the left-hand needle.

Place the strand on the left-hand needle to form a loop.

Knit into the back of the loop in the usual way so that the new stitch is twisted and does not leave a hole in the fabric. If the increase is on a purl row, pick up the strand of yarn in the same way and purl into it from the back.

Yarn over (yo)

The direction "yarn over" refers to

Increasing 1 stitch (inc 1)

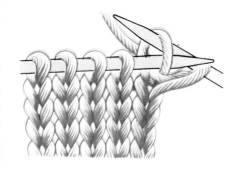

Making 1 stitch (M1)

1

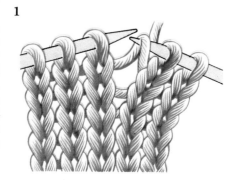

2

3

Yarn forward (yfwd)

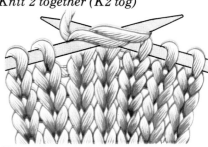

Yarn around needle (yrn)

Yarn over (yo)

Knit 2 together (K2 tog)

Slipped stitch decreasing (sl I, KI, psso)

several similar increasing techniques, all of which involve making an extra loop on the needle using the working yarn. The "yarn over" motion varies slightly according to the stitch just worked and the stitch to be worked next.

To increase a stitch between two knit stitches, bring the yarn forward under and then over the right-hand needle, and then knit the next stitch in the usual way.

To increase between a purl and a

knit stitch (the yarn being already at the front of the work), take the yarn over the top of the right-hand needle and knit the next stitch in the usual way.

To increase between two purl stitches (yarn being already in front), wind the yarn over the top of the right-hand needle and then under it to bring it forward again. Purl the next stitch as usual. The same method is also used for increasing between a knit and a purl stitch.

Grafting

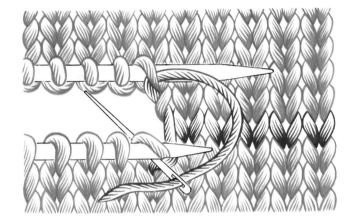

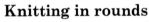

Knitting two stitches together

This decrease can be worked at either end of a row or at any given point. Simply insert the right-hand needle through two stitches instead of one and knit them both together in the usual way. The same procedure can be followed for purling two stitches together.

Slipped-stitch decreasing

When you are ready to work a decrease, slip the next stitch onto the right-hand needle without knitting it, then knit the following stitch. Using the point of the left-hand needle, lift the slipped stitch over the knit stitch and right off the right-hand needle.

Seams

When seaming knitting use a tapestry needle or yarn needle. Work backstitch between knitted stitches and avoid splitting the yarn. Sew firmly but not too tightly, without stretching knitting.

Place right sides together and work along the wrong side of the fabric about one stitch in from the edge. To secure the sewing yarn at the end, work one or two overcasting stitches.

Grafting

This is a method of joining two sets of stitches invisibly without first binding them off.
1. Do not bind off the stitches of the two pieces to be joined. Leave them on two needles, one behind the other, with both points toward the right and with wrong sides of fabric together. Check that there is an equal number of stitches on both needles.
2. Break off yarn from one section, leaving approximately three times the length of the edge to be grafted. Thread yarn into a tapestry needle.
3. Insert sewing needle K-wise through first stitch on back needle and pull yarn through; leave the stitch on the knitting needle. Repeat this action through the first stitch on the front needle, but slip this stitch off the knitting needle.
4. Insert sewing needle P-wise through next stitch on the front needle and pull yarn through. Leave this stitch on the knitting needle. Repeat this action through next stitch on the back needle, but let this stitch slip off the knitting needle.
5. Follow these steps in the order described until you use up all the stitches from both needles.

Knitting in rounds

To produce a narrow tubular fabric, use a set of four needles, pointed at both ends. Three needles are used to hold the fabric; the fourth is the working needle.

Casting on

Either cast all the stitches required onto one needle and then divide them equally among three needles, or cast them onto each of the three needles separately; leave the fourth needle free for working. Cast required number of stitches onto first, second, and third needles. Form the three needles into a triangle, making sure the stitches are not twisted around the needles or between the needles.

Working method

Use the extra needle to work all the stitches on the first needle, then the first needle to work the stitches on the second needle, and so on. Always pull the yarn tightly across the first stitch of each needle to avoid making a loose stitch. One round is complete when you have worked the stitches on all three needles. Marker loops in a contrasting color can mark the beginning of a new round.

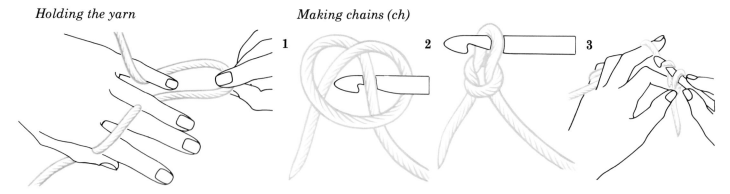

Holding the yarn   *Making chains (ch)*

Crochet techniques

Chains

1. Begin with a slip loop on the hook; make a loop about 4in from the end of yarn. Insert the hook behind the vertical strand as shown, then pull the ends of yarn to tighten the loop.
2. Hold the hook with the slip loop in your right hand and control the yarn with your left. Bringing the hook toward you, take it under and then over the top of the yarn in your left hand, so catching it in the curve of the hook; this is called "yarn over" (yo).
3. Holding the knot of the slip loop firmly between thumb and forefinger of your left hand, draw the yarn from back to front through the slip loop, so completing one chain. One working loop remains on the hook.
4. Repeat the actions in steps 2 and 3 until you have the length of chain needed.

Slip stitch (sl st)

This is a way of getting from one point in a row to another.
1. Insert the hook in the usual way into the next chain or stitch.
2. Wind the yarn around the hook from the back as shown.
3. Draw the yarn through the chain or stitch and loop on the hook; a single loop remains on the hook and one slip stitch is complete.

Single crochet (sc)

Make the required number of chains, plus one extra (the turning chain).
1. Insert the hook from front to back into the third chain from the hook; wind the yarn around the hook from the front to the back as shown, and draw a loop through the chain, so making two loops on the hook.
2. Wind the yarn around the hook

again and draw it through both loops on the hook; a single loop remains on the hook and one single crochet is complete.
3. Repeat steps 1 and 2 into each chain until you reach the end. Still holding hook in your right hand, turn the work from right to left so that the last stitch of this row becomes the first stitch of the next row.
4. For second and subsequent rows, make one turning chain to count as the first sc; work one stitch into each stitch in the previous row by inserting the hook under the two horizontal loops at the top of the stitch.

Half double crochet (hdc)

Make the required number of chains plus one extra (turning chain).
1. To work the first row, wind the yarn completely around the hook as in the diagram; insert the hook into the third chain from the hook and draw a loop through the chain, so making three loops on the hook.
2. Wind the yarn around the hook again and draw it through all three loops. A single loop remains on the hook, and 1hdc is complete.
3. Repeat 1 and 2 into each chain until you reach the end. Turn the work so that the last stitch of this row is the first stitch of the next.
4. To work the second and subsequent rows, make two turning chains to count as the first hdc; insert the hook under the two horizontal loops at the top of each stitch in the previous row.

Double crochet (dc)

Make the required number of chains plus two extra (turning chains).
1. Wind the yarn around the hook; insert the hook into the fourth chain from the hook and draw a loop through, so making three loops on the hook.

Slip stitch (sl st)

Single crochet (sc)

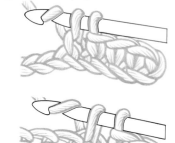

Half double crochet (hdc)

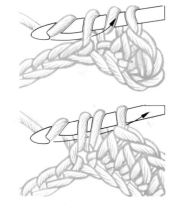

2. Wind the yarn around the hook and draw it through the first two loops on the hook, so leaving two loops on the hook.
3. Wind the yarn around the hook again and draw it through the remaining two loops; a single loop remains on the hook and one double crochet is complete.
4. Follow steps 3 and 4 of instructions for single crochet, but work three turning chains at the beginning of each new row.

Letter shapes

Learn some of the basic soft toy techniques by making these simple padded letters.

Finished size
Varies according to letter.

Techniques involved
Basic sewing skills; enlarging a design; stuffing.

Tools required
Basic sewing tools.

Materials
graph paper with 1in squares
scraps of felt or closely woven, firm fabric
sewing thread
synthetic stuffing

Select suitable letters (books, magazines, even cereal boxes are good sources) and enlarge them onto graph paper. The letters shown are about 5–6in tall. Cut out two shapes for each letter, then cut gusset strips for the letters. The strips should be as wide as the letter width (fig. 1).

It is easier to cut longer strips than necessary and trim them to fit as you sew. You will also need to cut small squares to close the ends of letters such as E, I, L, T, (fig. 2).

Some letters, such as B, D, and O, have inner gussets as well as outer ones. Some, such as M, C, and H, have only outer gussets.

Begin sewing by attaching a gusset edge to the outer curve of one letter piece. Start at any corner and work all around using a small glove stitch (fig. 3).

If the letter has sharp corners (M, N, T, for example), it is best to piece the gusset strip from corner to corner, as the stitching of these seams will give better definition to the letter shape (figs. 2 and 4). Where edges meet, overlap the ends slightly and then stitch together. Leave one square off to allow for stuffing later (if the letter has no square ends, leave a gap in the final seam). Now do inner curves in the same way. Join the second letter shape to the remaining edge of gusset strip. Fill the letter firmly with stuffing, then sew up the opening.

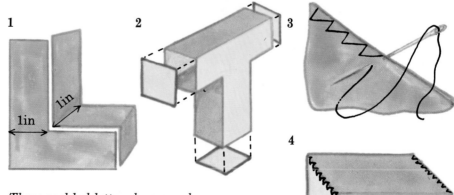

These padded letter shapes make learning the alphabet fun.
1. *Gusset and letter shape are equal in width.*
2. *The ends of certain letters must be closed with square shapes.*

3, 4. *For glove stitch bring the needle through the same hole twice to make neat corners.*

Finger puppets

Finger puppets are a good way to stimulate children's imaginations and let them act out their fantasies. These simple puppets are quickly made from little scraps of fabric and will provide hours of fun. They can also be adapted to make egg cozies—little covers to keep breakfast eggs warm.

Finished size
Varies according to puppet.

Techniques involved
Basic sewing; embroidery stitches.

Tools required
Basic sewing tools.

Materials
For each finger puppet, a 4in square
  of white felt (gray felt for dog)
scraps of pink and other colored felt
scraps of woven fabric
scraps of lace ½in and 2½ in wide for
  baby and granny
sewing thread
fabric glue
felt-tip markers or non-toxic crayons
small piece of copper wire for
  granny's glasses (draw these
  instead if the puppet is for a
  young child)
tracing paper

Father

Trace all pattern pieces for father, including the body shape and face.

Cut out two body shapes from white felt, a face from pink felt, and all other pieces from scraps of felt.

Place pants piece on one body piece and stitch down center and along top of pockets. Glue belt to top of pants and sew on suspenders with running stitches to cover the ends of the belt.

Using contrasting thread, embroider arms and shirt collar in backstitch and buttons in satin stitch.

Sew the body shapes together, leaving bottom end open. Glue on shoes to cover bottom of pants.

Draw the features on the face and glue face to head. Glue hair and mustache in place.

Mother

Trace pattern pieces for mother, including the body shape and face.

Cut out two body shapes from white felt. From pink felt cut out two hands and one face. Cut all other pieces from scraps of felt.

Sew the body shapes together, leaving bottom end open.

For the skirt, cut a piece of fabric 2½in deep and 6in wide. Join back seam and finish hem edge.

Run a line of gathering stitches ⅛in from waist edge, turning under raw edge at the same time.

Trace patterns

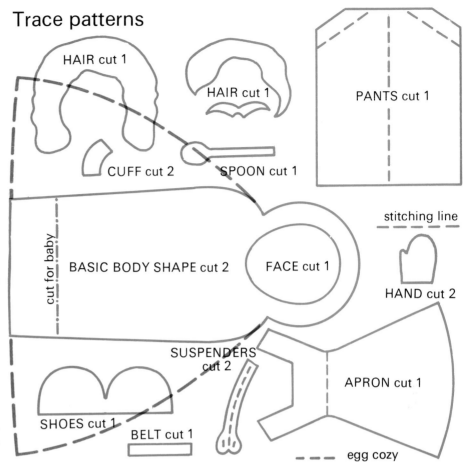

HAIR cut 1

HAIR cut 1

CUFF cut 2

SPOON cut 1

PANTS cut 1

stitching line

cut for baby

BASIC BODY SHAPE cut 2

FACE cut 1

HAND cut 2

SUSPENDERS cut 2

APRON cut 1

SHOES cut 1

BELT cut 1

egg cozy

Place skirt on puppet so that hem of skirt is level with open end of puppet, and pull up gathers to fit around waist. Sew skirt to body at waist, taking care not to sew the back and front of puppet together.

Sew apron to front of body across waistline. Glue straps to the shoulders.

Glue spoon to one hand. Glue wrist edges of hands to front of body at waist of skirt. Glue cuffs over the top of the hands.

Draw in features on face and glue face to head. Glue hair in place.

Granny

Trace all pattern pieces for granny including the body shape, face, and hands.

Cut two body shapes from white felt. From pink felt cut two hands and one face. Cut hair from gray felt.

Sew the body pieces together, leaving bottom end open.

For skirt, cut a strip of fabric 2½in deep and 4½in wide. Make skirt and attach as for mother.

Cut out the triangle for shawl from felt. Arrange shawl around granny's shoulders and, overlapping

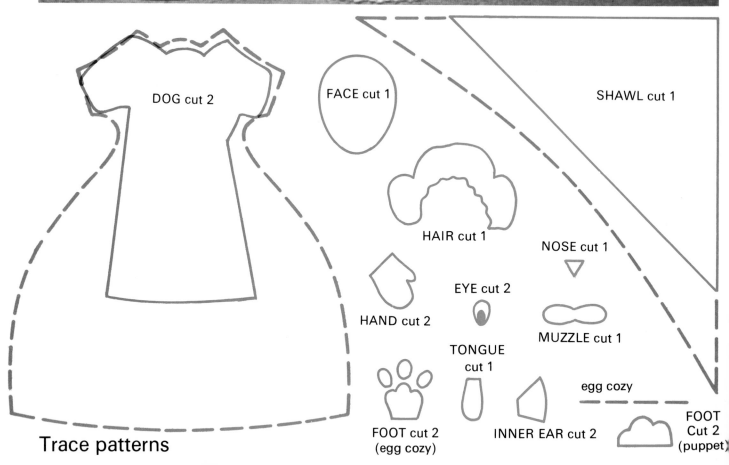

DOG cut 2

FACE cut 1

SHAWL cut 1

HAIR cut 1

NOSE cut 1

HAND cut 2

EYE cut 2

MUZZLE cut 1

TONGUE
cut 1

egg cozy

FOOT cut 2
(egg cozy)

INNER EAR cut 2

FOOT
Cut 2
(puppet)

Trace patterns

ends at front, catch-stitch to front of body.

For jabot, run a line of gathering stitches along the straight edge of a 1½in-long strip of ½in-wide lace. Draw up gathers, fold, and sew to front of body in neck of shawl, as shown (fig. 1). Turn in raw edges at top and sew in place.

For cuffs cut two pieces of the same lace 1¾in long. Join the cut ends of one piece. Make other cuff in the same way.

Attach these to body front at waist beneath edge of shawl. Insert a hand into each cuff and sew in place.

Shape a piece of copper wire around two matchsticks for glasses (fig. 2a). Push the ends through the felt face and flatten at the back (fig. 2b).

Draw in the features and glue face to the head.

Glue hair in place.

Baby

Trace pattern pieces for body shape, face, and hands, rounding off face as in photograph.

Cut out two body shapes from white felt. From pink felt cut out two hands and one face.

Cut a 3in strip of ½in-wide lace and gather along the straight edge. Pull up the gathers to fit around the head and baste to wrong side of one body piece.

Sew the two body pieces together, enclosing the gathered edge of the lace and leaving the bottom edge open.

Cut a 5½in strip of 2½in-wide lace. Join the two ends. Run a line of gathering stitches ½in from the straight edge. Insert puppet and pull up the gathers to fit around the neck. Sew dress to puppet on gathering line, taking care not to sew the back and front of the puppet together.

Draw in features on face and glue face to head. Sew wrist edges of hands to front of body through dress.

Dog

Trace pattern pieces for dog.

Cut out two body shapes, two feet, and all features from appropriate colored felt.

Sew the two body shapes together, leaving the bottom end open.

Draw pupil on each eye using a felt tip marker. Glue feet and features to front of body.

Matching egg cozies

It is easy to adapt these puppet designs to turn them into egg cozies to keep boiled eggs warm. Use a 8½in square of felt for each body. Use the alternative (red dotted) cutting line on the trace pattern for each body and for granny's shawl. Make the following alterations in the patterns for the various characters in order to use them as egg cozies.

Father

Center the trouser piece on one body piece and stitch down outer edges of trousers. When working the embroidery, outline the outer edge of arms (cutting line for puppet) as well as inner edge (fig. 3).

Baby

Cut a 9½in strip of 3½in-wide lace for the dress.

Granny and mother

Cut the strips of fabric for each skirt 2in deep and 9½in wide.

Mother

Work a line of backstitch to outline the outer edge of the arms, as for father, before assembling body.

Complete each of the cozies as for the puppets.

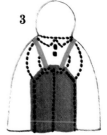

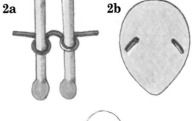

1. *Lace sewn in the neck of shawl.*
2a. *Shaping copper wire around matches.*
2b. *Wire flattened at back of face.*
3. *Pants positioned on egg cozy.*

Cat and dog

*These simple but unusual felt toys are made by hand from the
same basic pattern. They are 4 inches tall and are sewn together
using a close blanket stitch.*

Finished size
4in (height).

Techniques involved
Basic sewing skills; stuffing.

Tools required
Basic sewing tools.

Materials
For the dog:
tracing paper
12in square of brown felt
matching firm embroidery thread
scraps of white, black, and cerise
   felt
synthetic stuffing
fabric glue
For the cat:
tracing paper
8in square of orange felt
6in square of white felt
firm embroidery thread
scraps of green and black felt
whiskers cut from soft broom
synthetic stuffing
fabric glue

The dog

Trace the appropriate pattern pieces for the dog. From brown felt cut out two side body sections, one tail, an ear section, and an underbody, as directed. Mark in the darts on each side body section and sew them by hand on the wrong side.

Baste the two side body sections together along the top from A to B, wrong sides together. Sew with a small blanket stitch. Baste and blanket stitch the underbody to sides, matching points A and C. Leave the back of the animal open between B and C. Fold the tail in half lengthwise, wrong sides together. Baste and blanket stitch along the long edge. Stuff the tail, pushing the stuffing down with a knitting needle. Then stuff the body firmly, pushing the stuffing in with a pencil or knitting needle. Slipstitch the tail into the back opening, matching the tail seam to point B. Push more stuffing into the body if necessary. Then baste and blanket stitch opening.

Cut out circles of white and black felt for the eyes and nose, using small coins as patterns. From brown felt cut half circles for eyelids with a diameter slightly larger than the white circles. Glue on the nose, eyes, and then the eyelids as illustrated.

Backstitch the center of the ears

Trace patterns

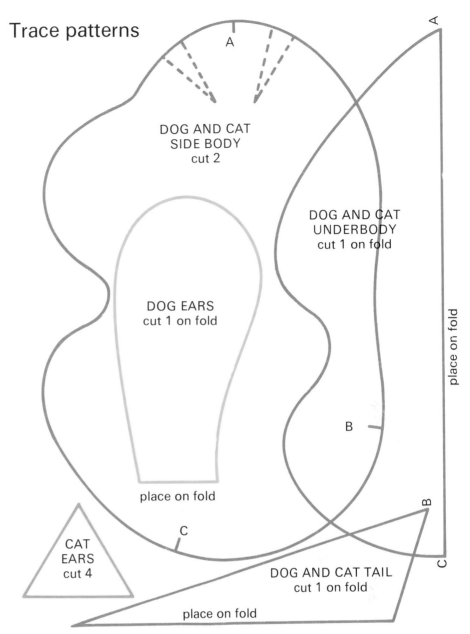

DOG AND CAT
SIDE BODY
cut 2

DOG AND CAT
UNDERBODY
cut 1 on fold

DOG EARS
cut 1 on fold

place on fold

place on fold

CAT
EARS
cut 4

DOG AND CAT TAIL
cut 1 on fold

place on fold

in place on the head, over the center seam. Bend each ear forward and secure the fold with a dab of glue (fig. 1). Cut a strip of cerise felt 11in × ⅜in and tie in a bow around the base of the tail. Or glue the bow.

The cat

Trace the appropriate pattern pieces for the cat. From orange felt cut out two side body sections, two ears, and one tail piece as directed. From white felt cut out two more ears and the underbody piece.

Make the body and tail following the instructions given for the dog.

Cut circles for the eyes in green felt, using a small coin as a pattern. Make a long straight stitch down the center of each circle with black

embroidery thread, then glue in place. Cut half circles for eyelids in orange felt, with a diameter slightly larger than the eyes. Glue in place, and then glue or sew the center of the bristle whiskers to the center of the cat's face, over the stitching. Sew the mouth with black embroidery thread, making three long straight stitches. Cut a small heart-shaped nose in black felt and glue.

Take one orange ear piece and one white one and blanket stitch them together along two sides. Sew the other two pieces together in the same way. Overcast to the head, above the eyes, along the third side.

Finally, cut a strip of green felt 11in × ⅜in and tie it around the base of the tail in a bow. Or glue the bow.

Animal hand puppets

These droll little creatures will take on a life of their own, once you've learned the simple technique of operating them. You can adapt the patterns to make other animals.

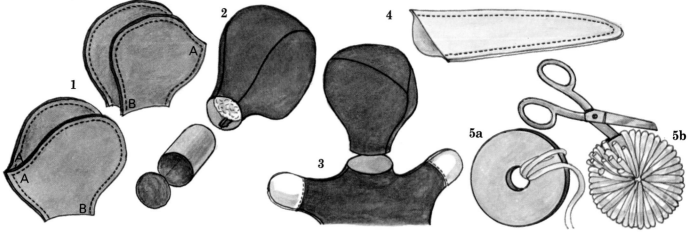

Finished size
Varies according to hand size.

Techniques involved
Basic sewing.

Tools required
Basic sewing tools.

Materials
For the cat:
tracing paper
24in square of black felt or
    patterned cotton fabric
scraps of white and colored felt for
    the muzzle nose, and eyes
a length of black yarn for the
    mouth
synthetic stuffing
1½in piece of a lin-diameter
    cardboard tube
sewing thread and white button
    thread
fabric glue
beeswax or candle wax
For the rabbit:
tracing paper
24in square of white felt
6in square of pink felt for inner ears
    and paw pads
7in square of blue felt for vest
scraps of gray and black felt for
    eyes
5in length of red ribbon for bow tie
scraps of black yarn for the paws
    and nose
white yarn for the tail
two circles of cardboard 2in in
    diameter

Cat

Trace the pattern pieces given and draw in the stitching lines; ¼in seam allowance is included. Label each piece with its name and the number to be cut out, and mark the straight of grain line.

Pin the pattern pieces to the fabric, placing them on the fold where indicated.

For a black cat, use black felt for all the body pieces including the tail, outer ears, and iris. Use white for eye whites and paws, muzzle, and

These toys have all the personality a child can give them.
1. *Head pieces sewn together.*
2. *Insert tube; add felt to seal in stuffing.*
3. *Inserting stiffened neck into body.*
4. *Inner ear stitched to outer ear.*
5. *Making a yarn pompon for tail.*

inner ears, and pink for the nose.

For a cat in cotton fabric, cut out the body, head, and tail in printed cotton, the paws, muzzle, eyes, outer and inner ears in colored felt and the nose in black felt.

Placing right sides together, sew the two back body pieces together along the center back seam.

Sew each felt paw piece to the corresponding front or back body piece, overlapping by about ¼in and top-stitching in place.

Placing right sides together, pin the front to the back, matching the paws and side seams. Stitch all around, leaving the bottom and neck open.

Trim the seam allowance neatly, snipping at curves, and turn body right side out.

Placing right sides together, fold the tail in half lengthwise. Stitch down the long edges and around the curved end, leaving the short straight end open. Trim and turn right side out.

Stuff the tail lightly and sew up the end.

Sew the tail firmly to the body across the back seam and level with the back legs.

Placing right sides together, pin the center gusset piece to the side head pieces, matching points A and B. Stitch gusset and chin seams, leaving the neck edge open (fig. 1). Trim and turn right side out.

Stuff the head well, but do not stuff the neck.

Insert the cardboard tube into the neck, and add more stuffing where necessary to make the head firm.

To prevent the stuffing from getting into the tube, cut a circle of felt a little larger than the diameter of the tube. Glue this to the stuffing above upper end of the tube (fig. 2).

Insert the stiffened neck into the body opening, overlapping edges by about ¾in (fig. 3) and slipstitch together.

If using cotton fabric, first turn in the neck edge of the body all around and baste with double thread.

Glue the inner ears to the outer ears. Fold a dart in the center of each ear and pin ears to head.

Now pin the white felt muzzle shape and the eyes in place so that you can adjust them if necessary to produce an effective cat-like expression.

Sew on the ears and the muzzle using contrasting thread and large stitches to achieve a furry effect.

Glue the black felt irises to the eye white, then glue the assembled eyes to the head.

Glue on the pink nose piece and embroider mouth, in black yarn.

Make whiskers by threading three lengths of white button thread through each side of the muzzle, taking a small stitch. Secure by knotting close to the muzzle; this makes six whiskers on each side. (The whiskers can be stiffened with beeswax or candle wax.)

Using black sewing thread, make three large stitches through each paw for claws.

Note: If you are using woven fabric, turn under and sew a small hem at the lower edge. Narrow elastic can be inserted through the hem to make the puppet fit neatly over the wrist.

Rabbit

Cut out the same basic pattern pieces as for the cat, but use the rabbit trace patterns for the ears, paws, pads, and eyes. Use pink felt for the inner ears and paw pads.

Make the rabbit body as for cat.

Sew pink inner ears to the outer white ears, so that the pink felt is taut while the white felt is loose and curved (fig. 4). This leaves a hollow center and will help to keep the ears upright.

After making and stitching the white paws, glue a pink pad on the front of each paw. Sew black claws as for the cat. Sew on the eyes.

Embroider the nose and mouth.

Make a pompon for a tail by winding white yarn around two cardboard circles with centers cut out (fig. 5a). Cut the yarn all around the outer edge (fig. 5b), and secure it firmly around the middle. Remove cardboard and sew pompon in place.

To make the simple felt vest, cut along the green lines marked on body pattern and cut out vest in blue felt.

Stitch the shoulder and side seams.

Slip the vest on the rabbit. Turn back the corners at the neck and sew down to form lapels.

Use the length of red ribbon to make a bow tie and sew it in place under the chin to complete the rabbit.

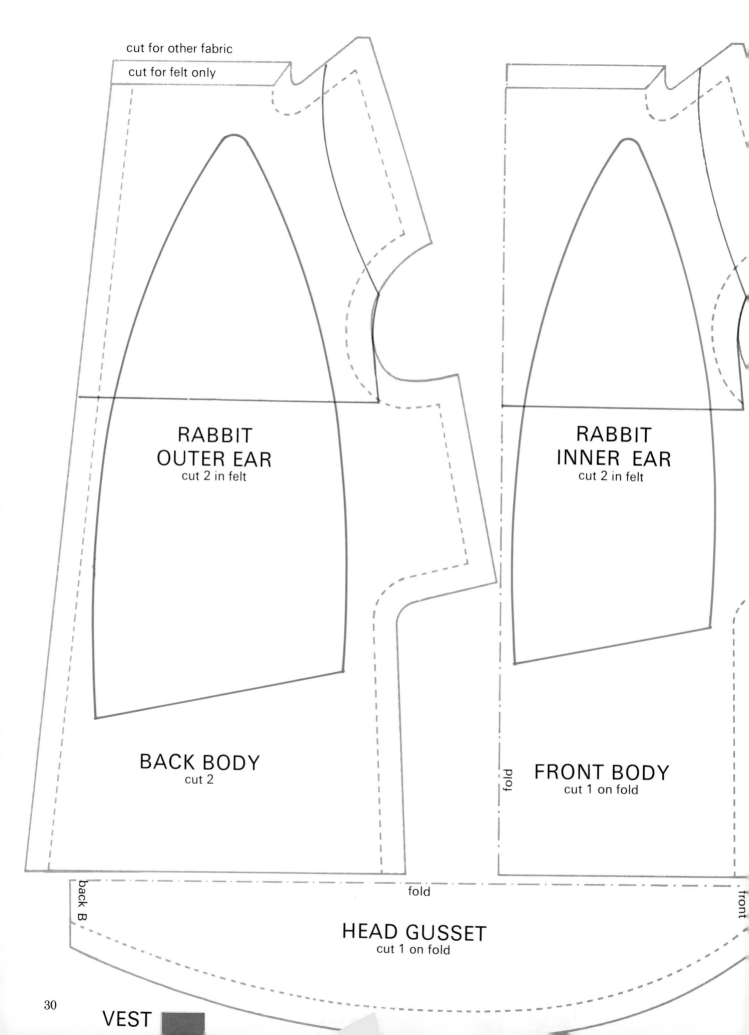

cut for other fabric

cut for felt only

RABBIT
OUTER EAR
cut 2 in felt

RABBIT
INNER EAR
cut 2 in felt

fold

BACK BODY
cut 2

FRONT BODY
cut 1 on fold

back B

front

fold

HEAD GUSSET
cut 1 on fold

30

VEST

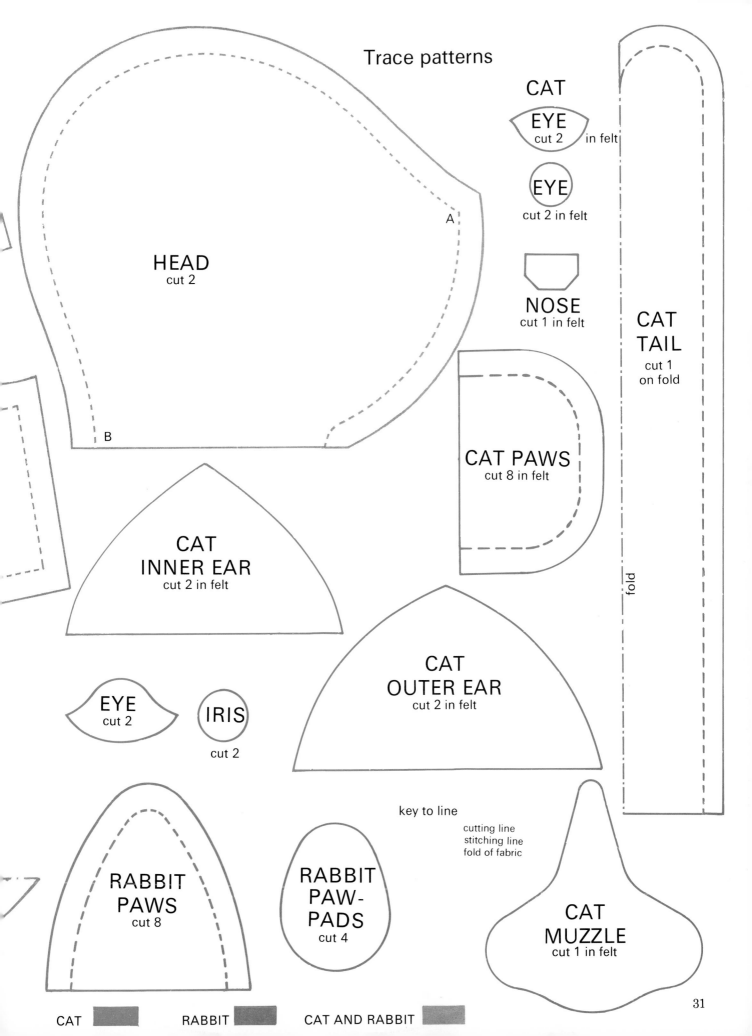

Trace patterns

HEAD
cut 2

A

B

CAT
EYE
cut 2 in felt

EYE
cut 2 in felt

NOSE
cut 1 in felt

CAT
TAIL
cut 1
on fold

fold

CAT PAWS
cut 8 in felt

CAT
INNER EAR
cut 2 in felt

EYE
cut 2

IRIS
cut 2

CAT
OUTER EAR
cut 2 in felt

key to line

cutting line
stitching line
fold of fabric

RABBIT
PAWS
cut 8

RABBIT
PAW-
PADS
cut 4

CAT
MUZZLE
cut 1 in felt

31

CAT   RABBIT   CAT AND RABBIT

Miniature dolls

This charming Turn-of-the-Century doll family—complete with governess—shows what you can achieve on a small scale. Each doll is made on a pipecleaner skeleton and none is taller than 7 inches. The clothes are very simple but hand-sewn together with meticulous care. You can adapt the patterns to make clothes of other periods.

Finished size
Varies from 6in to 7in (height).

Techniques involved
Basic sewing; embroidery stitches.

Tools required
Basic sewing tools.

Materials
tracing paper
embroidery thread
For the body:
3 pipecleaners
absorbent cotton
pink bias binding
small piece of pink felt or cotton for
    head
knitting yarn for hair
sewing thread
For clothes and accessories:
scraps of closely woven fabric (felt
    is ideal for shoes and some
    garments; patterns, if any, should
    be small)
narrow ribbon, lace, and other
    trimmings
short length of copper wire

The basic body

Join the pipecleaners together (fig. 1a). You can adjust arm and leg lengths by making an extra twist or two around the body.

Pad pipecleaner "skeleton" with absorbent cotton and wind sewing thread around it to keep it in place (fig. 1b).

Wind pink bias binding around the legs, arms, and body in overlapping layers (fig. 1b) and catch-stitch in several places to hold the layers in place, particularly at the ends of the arms.

Make a paper pattern for the head using the trace pattern given and cut out the two head pieces in pink felt or cotton fabric, adding ¼in seam allowance.

Sew the head pieces together, right sides facing, leaving the neck edge open. Trim the seams and turn right side out. Stuff the head with a little absorbent cotton, place it over the top of the pipecleaner ends, and continue to stuff until you have obtained a good head shape (fig. 1b). Catch-stitch the neck edge neatly to the body all around.

The mother

Make the body as described above. To create the S-line of Turn-of-the-Century fashion, pad the bust and seat with extra cotton.

Dress Cut out paper patterns for the skirt, bodice and sleeves from the trace patterns given. Check the length and width against the doll. Lay all the patterns on a double thickness of fabric and cut out, adding ¼in seam allowance. Placing right sides together, sew front bodice pieces to back bodice at shoulders and sides. Turn right side out.

Wrap a short piece of eyelet lace around the neck of the doll to form a high collar. This can be trimmed to ½in at the sides and back of the neck, but should be wide enough at the front to make a blouse front under the V-neck. If the trimming is already too narrow for this, sew a piece of white ribbon to the front of the doll's body before putting on the collar. Put the bodice on the doll. Turn in the neck and front edges and sew to doll along the folded edges.

Pull the sleeves onto the arms, turn under the top edges, and sew to bodice. Sew one or two layers of narrow lace trimming on to cover this stitching line.

To make the skirt, sew the back seam, right sides facing. Turn right side out. Put the skirt on the doll, turn in at the waist and sew to the bodice. Sew on one or two layers of narrow lace trimming to cover this stitching line.

Turn up and sew the skirt hem and the sleeve edges (unless you have managed to cut these edges on a selvage or have used non-fraying fabric).

Make the train from a piece of ribbon or lace about 4in square. Taper the ribbon or lace to 2in at the top and 4in at the bottom by folding in the sides by the required amount. Sew to the back of the skirt at the waist and sew down with a couple of stitches on each side of the train. A petticoat could also be made using the skirt pattern. Add lace trimming to the bottom edge for a feminine touch.

Hair Sew yarn to the head, starting at the top and working from the center part to the sides. Loop more yarn loosely at the sides and finish with a bun on top of the head. Embroider features on face of doll.

Hat This is not shown in the photograph. Make a frame out of pipecleaners with a 1in crown and approximately 2¼in brim (fig. 2). Cover the frame by winding brown ribbon or bias binding tape around it in layers lengthwise and catch-stitch in

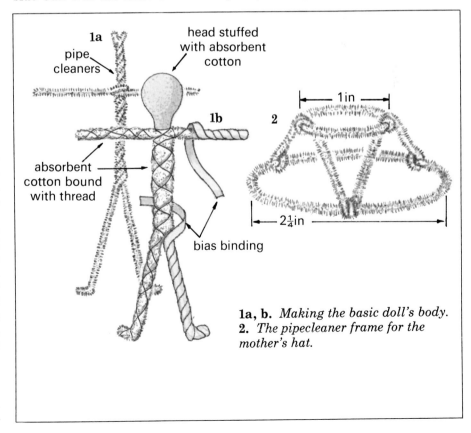

1a, b. *Making the basic doll's body.*
2. *The pipecleaner frame for the mother's hat.*

Trace patterns

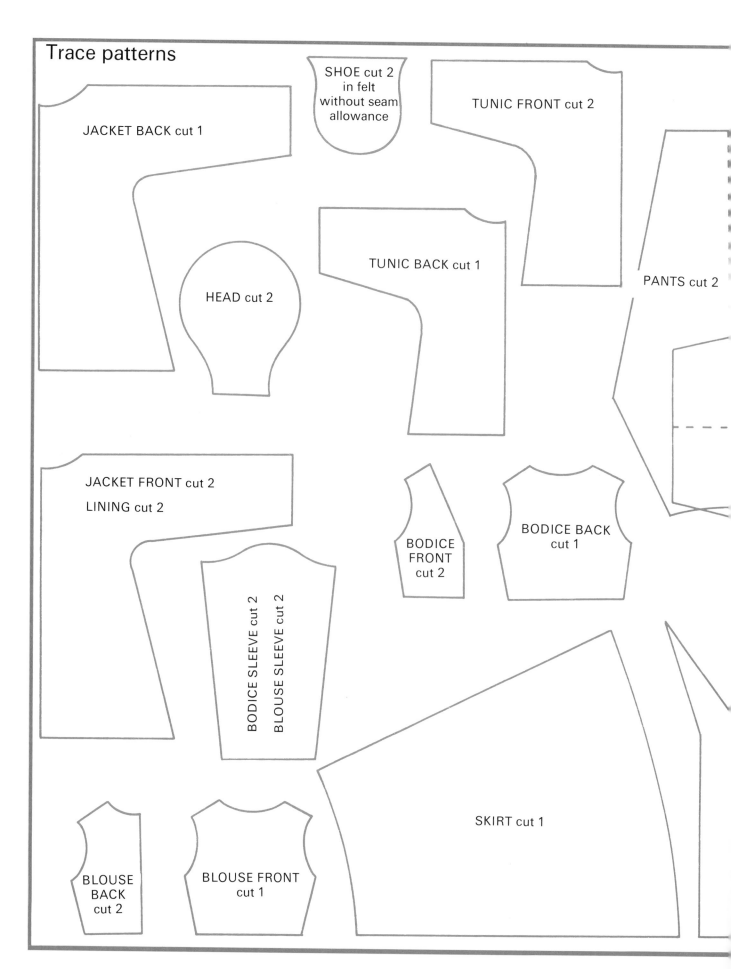

JACKET BACK cut 1

SHOE cut 2
in felt
without seam
allowance

TUNIC FRONT cut 2

TUNIC BACK cut 1

PANTS cut 2

HEAD cut 2

JACKET FRONT cut 2

LINING cut 2

BODICE
FRONT
cut 2

BODICE BACK
cut 1

BODICE SLEEVE cut 2
BLOUSE SLEEVE cut 2

SKIRT cut 1

BLOUSE
BACK
cut 2

BLOUSE FRONT
cut 1

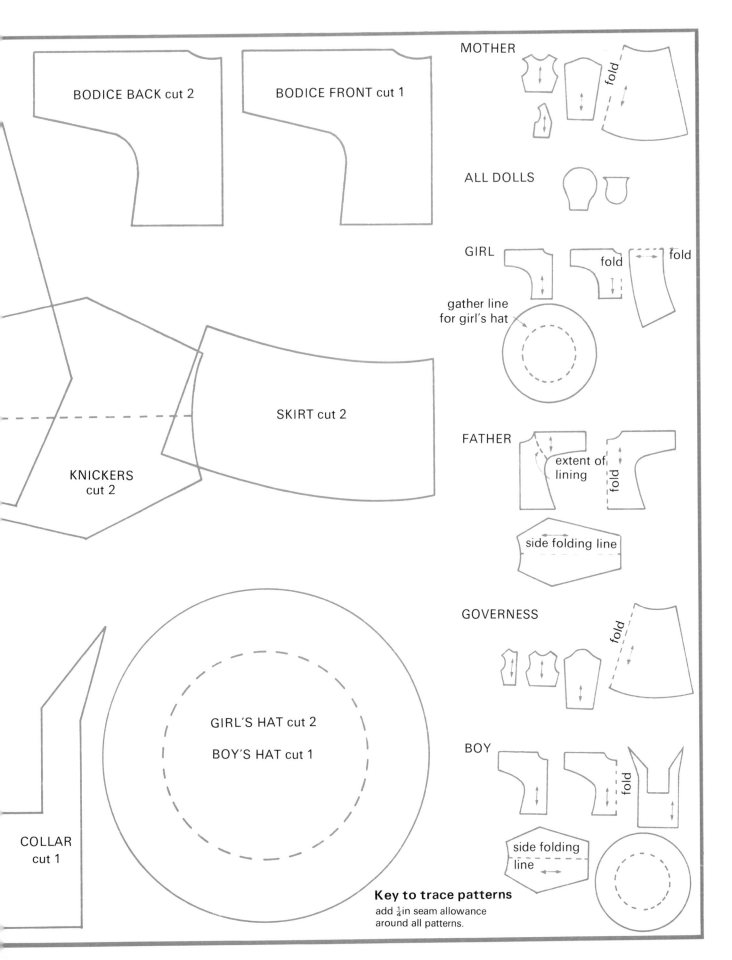

BODICE BACK cut 2

BODICE FRONT cut 1

MOTHER

fold

ALL DOLLS

GIRL

fold   fold

gather line
for girl's hat

KNICKERS
cut 2

SKIRT cut 2

FATHER

extent of
lining

fold

side folding line

GOVERNESS

fold

BOY

fold

side folding
line

GIRL'S HAT cut 2

BOY'S HAT cut 1

COLLAR
cut 1

Key to trace patterns
add $\frac{1}{4}$in seam allowance
around all patterns.

place at intervals around the frame.

Cut out two or three different sizes of colored felt circles, preferably with pinking shears. Arrange them around the hat in layers and sew on.

The hat can simply be pinned to the head, but if young children will be playing with the doll it should be sewn permanently in place.

The governess

Make body and skirt as for mother. Make the blouse from the appropriate patterns.

Put the skirt and blouse on the doll, sew up back overlap of blouse, turn in sleeve edges and hem by hand. Trim the sleeve edges with ribbon to indicate cuffs.

For a belt, sew a strip of felt at the waist; embroider a buckle.

Make the collar by wrapping a piece of white ribbon or binding around the doll's neck and sewing down at the back. Cut out a small felt bow and sew or glue it to the collar front.

Hair Sew knitting yarn to the head, working from front to back and finishing with a neat bun at the center back. Embroider features.

Make a pince-nez by bending copper wire to required shape and sewing in place between the eyes. Attach one side of the frame to a piece of black yarn or very narrow cord and tuck the other end into the belt.

The father

Make the body as already described, but slightly taller than that of the mother. Make paper patterns for pants and jacket, using trace patterns given. Check for size against the doll's body.

Lay all the patterns on a double thickness of fabric and cut out. Cut a sleeveless lining for the front of the jacket, using the jacket pattern up to the dashed line.

Pants Placing right sides together, join center front and center back seams.

Place pants so that front and back seams lie on top of each other and join inner leg seams. Trim seams and turn pants right side out.

Put the pants on the doll and sew to body at the waist, gathering in any surplus width. Turn under trouser hems and sew.

Jacket Placing right sides together,

sew front pieces to back piece at sides and shoulders. Turn right side out. Pin lining to front of jacket on each side, with right sides facing, and sew along shoulders and front edges. Trim seams and turn lining to inside of jacket. Make back collar by binding edge with matching ribbon or jacket fabric. Press flat.

Make the shirt collar with a small length of white ribbon or bias binding turned in at edges. Sew around the doll's neck, leaving a small gap at the front. Make a shirt front by sewing a piece of white ribbon to the front of the doll's body. For a cravat, tie a knot in black ribbon and sew in place on shirt neck.

Put the jacket on the doll. If the jacket is too wide at the back, it can be taken in by making a tuck at each shoulder.

Turn in the sleeve hems and sew. Turn back the lapels and catch-stitch in place. Details, such as felt or bead buttons, pockets and a breast pocket with handkerchief, may all be added if desired.

Hair Sew knitting yarn to head, starting at center front and working to sides and back. Begin with long stitches and build up with shorter ones. Embroider features, whiskers and mustache.

The girl

Make the body as already described, but about 1in shorter than that of the mother.

Make paper patterns for the bodice, skirt, and hat using trace patterns given and check against the doll for size. Lay them on double thickness of fabric and cut out.

Dress Placing right sides together, sew front bodice to back sections at sides and shoulders. Turn right side out. Turn in and sew neck edge. Put the bodice on the doll; turn in edges of back opening, overlap them and sew them down.

Sew side seams of the skirt, right sides facing. Turn right side out. Pin and sew skirt to bodice, making large pleats as you go. Turn up and sew sleeve edges and hem.

If the pleats stick out, sew them down.

Trim sleeves and neck with narrow lace and trim waist seam of skirt with narrow ribbon.

Hair Place lengths of yarn across head and sew them at the center to

form a part. Also anchor the strands at ear level. Embroider features.

Hat Placing right sides together, join edges of two round hat pieces, leaving a small gap.

Trim seam and turn right side out. Turn in edges of opening and overcast them together. Gather at line shown on trace pattern to fit head. Press edge of brim. Trim gathering line with ribbon. Attach to head as for mother's hat by pinning or sewing in place.

The boy

Make the body the same size as the girl doll. Make paper patterns for sailor outfit using trace patterns given and check against the doll for size. Lay patterns for tunic and knickers on double thickness of fabric (preferably white and navy as shown) and cut out.

Lay the patterns for hat and collar on a single thickness of navy blue fabric and cut out. It's a good idea to make the collar in felt to eliminate a hem. In this case omit the ¼in seam allowance.

Knickers Make these as you did the father's pants. The only difference is the length.

Sew the knickers to doll's legs, taking a tuck on the outside of each pants leg, and trim with a strip of blue felt or ribbon.

Tunic Make the tunic as you did the girl's bodice, but with the opening at the front.

Trim collar with a thin strip of navy felt or narrow ribbon and trim sleeve edges at wrist with two strips of navy felt or narrow ribbon. Trim the collar piece at the back and sides with a strip of white felt stitched in place near the edge.

Fasten collar piece at front by sewing to tunic at the point where the ties cross.

Hat Gather the circle of fabric at the edge so that it fits the head, and flatten the crown.

Sew a narrow band of felt around the edge of the opening, and sew this band to the head. Add two small strips of felt at one side of the head. Sew brim to head in one or two places to keep the crown flat.

Shoes

Make all the dolls' shoes from felt, using the trace pattern given. (No seam allowance is required.)

Poupard dolls

Originally a simple plaything—a wooden ball on a stick wrapped in swaddling clothes—the poupard (French for "baby doll") later became very elaborate. Nineteenth-century poupards were richly dressed and often equipped with music boxes or mechanisms for turning their sculpted wax heads. The ones shown here are simply constructed and trimmed with bells in the traditional manner. If making one for a small child, omit the bells and wire arms, and make sure that the paint for features is non-toxic.

Finished size
11in (height).

Techniques involved
Basic sewing; simple woodworking; painting.

Tools required
Basic sewing tools; hand drill with $\frac{1}{4}$in bit.

Materials
For doll:
a 1$\frac{1}{2}$in-diameter wooden ball for the head
a piece of $\frac{1}{4}$in dowel 10in long
scraps of knitting yarn for hair
scraps of pink yarn for the hands
chenille wire (pipecleaner) about 9$\frac{1}{2}$in long for the arms
a piece of unbleached muslin 6in × 4$\frac{1}{2}$in for the body covering
small pill box about 1$\frac{1}{2}$in deep and 1in in diameter
a little rice for a rattle
woodworking glue
enamel paints and brush, or felt-tip marker, for features

For the costume:
10in of 3in-wide eyelet lace
tracing paper
6in × 2in piece of cotton fabric for first underskirt
8in × 14in piece of silky fabric for the blouse and second underskirt
1$\frac{1}{4}$yd of $\frac{3}{8}$in-wide lace for trimming blouse and bonnet or cap
12in × 6in piece of velveteen or corduroy for skirt
1yd of $\frac{1}{4}$in-wide velvet ribbon
18in of $\frac{1}{4}$in-wide nylon ribbon
1yd of fine braid
about 7in × 6in piece of muslin for the bonnet or 5in square of cotton for the cap
5 jingle bells (optional—best omitted if doll is for a small child)

Assembling the doll

Drill a $\frac{1}{4}$in-diameter hole $\frac{1}{2}$in deep in the wooden ball. Glue the dowel rod in place (fig. 1).

Using enamel paint or felt markers, paint the features, either copying the ones shown in fig. 2 or designing your own.

Spread glue on the back of the head. Starting from the center, coil the knitting yarn around the head. The hair style can be elaborated by braiding some additional lengths of yarn, twisting the braid into a bun, and gluing it to the back of the head, as shown in fig. 3.

Make a small slit in the middle of the piece of muslin just large enough to slip over the dowel. Slip the material onto the dowel and up to the head, with the longer sides at the front and back.

To form the arms, take the chenille wire and, working from the center, twist it around the dowel just under the material. This will help to keep the material in place (fig. 4). Shape the arms and wind the ends of the chenille wire with a little pink yarn, then loop the ends of the bound chenille back and bind them to the arms to form the hands. Glue the arms in place on the dowel.

Make a hole in the center of the pill box lid and also in the base, just large enough to insert the dowel.

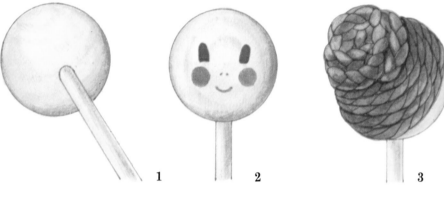

1 2 3

1. *The dowel glued in place.*
2. *Features can be painted or drawn with felt-tip markers.*
3. *The hair style can be as elaborate as you wish.*
4. *How to form the arms.*
5. *Unbleached muslin sewn over pill box.*

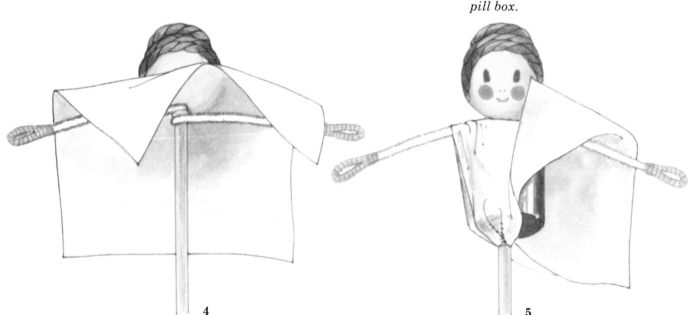

4 5

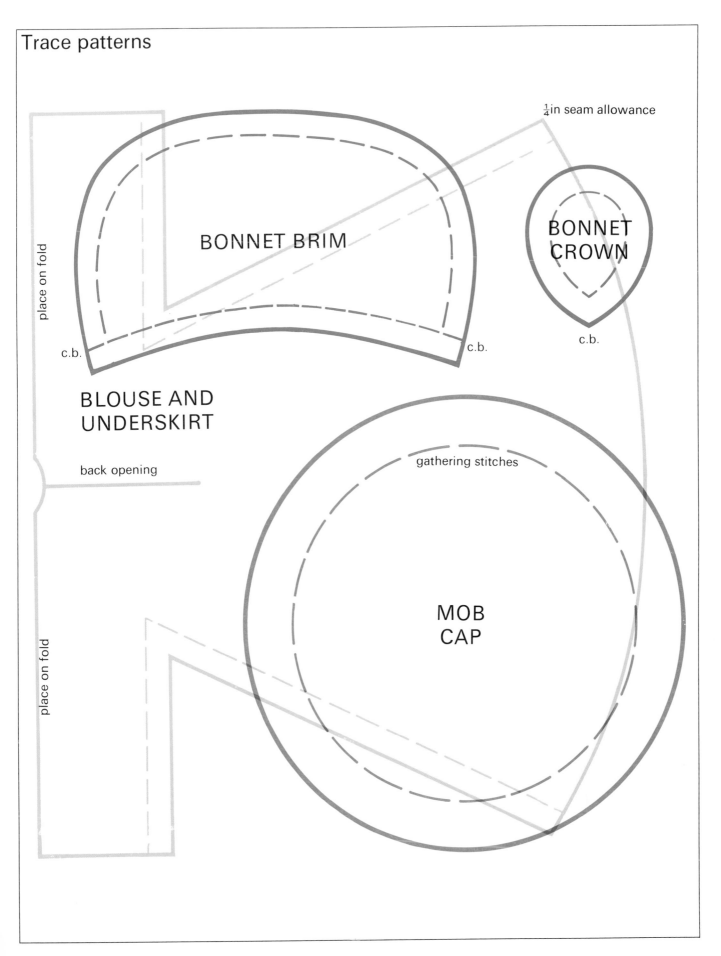

BONNET BRIM

BONNET CROWN

$\frac{1}{4}$in seam allowance

place on fold

c.b.

c.b.

c.b.

BLOUSE AND UNDERSKIRT

back opening

gathering stitches

MOB CAP

place on fold

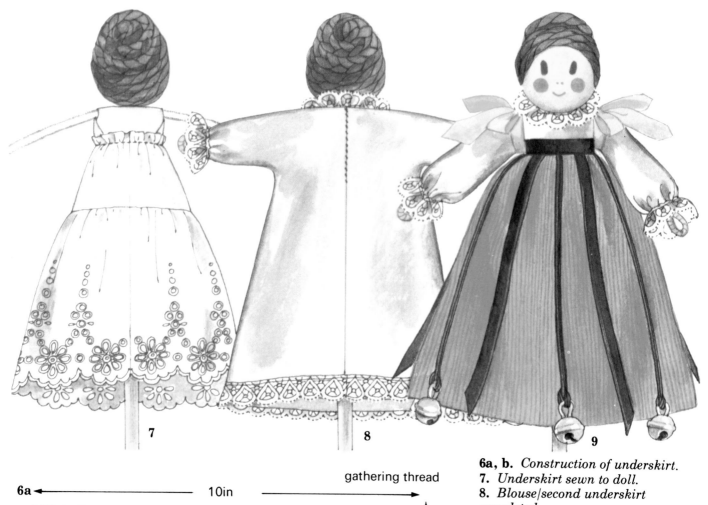

gathering thread

6a ←————— 10in —————→

back seam

eyelet lace

3in

6a, b. *Construction of underskirt.*
7. *Underskirt sewn to doll.*
8. *Blouse/second underskirt
completed.*
9. *The finished doll.*

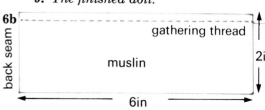

6b

back seam

gathering thread

muslin

2i

←————— 6in —————→

Slide the lid and then the box up the dowel, put some rice into the box, and glue on the lid. Glue the box to the chenille wire at the top of the dowel. Fold the material down around the box and sew it firmly in place (fig. 5).

Dressing the doll

For the underskirt, run a line of gathering stitches (fig. 6a) along top edge of the eyelet lace and gather up to fit one long edge of the cotton underskirt fabric. Pin and stitch together with right sides facing.

Run a line of gathering stitches along the top of the cotton fabric leaving a long thread (fig. 6b).

Placing right sides together, stitch the center back seam. Turn right

side out, draw up gathers at the waist and sew underskirt firmly to body of doll (fig. 7).

The blouse is cut full length to form a second underskirt. First cut out a paper pattern using the trace pattern given.

Fold the silky fabric in half to measure 8in × 7in. Place the pattern with the shoulder edges on the fold; pin in place and cut out. Cut an opening in the back at the neck edge large enough for the doll's head.

Stitch $\frac{1}{4}$in hems at the wrist and lower edges.

Placing right sides together, baste and stitch the side and sleeve seams.

Turn blouse right side out. Trim sleeves and hem with lace.

Put the garment on the doll and

slipstitch the back opening together, turning in the raw edges. Trim the neck with lace.

Run a gathering thread around the sleeves at the wrists and draw up to fit (fig. 8).

Cut the nylon ribbon in half; tie a piece around each arm at the shoulder, tie into a bow at the top of the shoulder, and sew it in place with tiny invisible stitches.

To make the overskirt, place the two short ends of the velveteen together with right sides facing and stitch to form the center back seam. (If the fabric you have chosen is stiff or thick, less width will be required in the skirt.)

Turn up lower edge and hand-hem.
Turn the skirt right side out and

run a line of gathering stitches along the top, leaving a long thread for finishing. Put the skirt on the doll, pull up the gathers to fit and sew firmly in place at the waist.

Cut five 5in lengths of velvet ribbon and five 5in lengths of braid. Sew a small bell to the end of each length of braid. Sew lengths of braid and ribbon alternately to the waist.

Cover the ends of the velvet ribbon and braid with another strip of velvet ribbon, forming a waistband.

Pull the ribbon tightly, covering all the raw edges, and sew firmly in place (fig. 9).

Trace bonnet and crown from trace pattern given. Fold the muslin in half to make an oblong 7in × 3in of double fabric. Place the brim and crown patterns on the muslin, pin, and cut out.

Turn in a ¼in hem along the long curved edge of each brim piece. Pin brim pieces together with wrong sides facing, and at the same time

insert a 9in length of lace trimming between the two curved brim edges. Topstitch the layers together by hand with small running stitches.

Baste the two crown pieces together, wrong sides facing. Starting at center back, hand-sew the brim to the crown with small running stitches, easing any fullness. Cover the raw edges with a double row of lace around the crown.

Place the bonnet on the doll's head. Sew the remaining piece of braid over the bonnet to form ties (fig. 10).

Alternatively, you can make a cap for the doll's headdress. Trace the cap pattern and cut it out in cotton. Sew a small hem around the outer edge and trim with narrow lace. Run a line of gathering stitches ½in away from the edge. Pull up gathers to fit the doll's head and fasten off securely.

Polystyrene dolls' heads

If you prefer, you can use high-density polystyrene balls to make heads for poupard dolls and other kinds of doll.

Materials
high-density polystyrene ball of a
 suitable size—1½in-diameter for
 the doll described here
orange stick
water-based paints: emulsion paint
 in flesh tone and poster colors or
 gouache for features
pencil
paintbrushes
Duco cement
yarn for hair (optional)

Decide on the type of face to be painted and make a working drawing, following fig. 11 for correct proportions.

Support the ball on an orange stick and paint it with an appropriate color emulsion base coat.

When the base coat is completely dry, lightly draw the features in pencil, then paint them, using a fine paintbrush and appropriate colors of poster paint or gouache. Allow to dry thoroughly.

Warning: Polystyrene is a flammable material and should be kept away from open flames.

10. *The finished bonnet.*

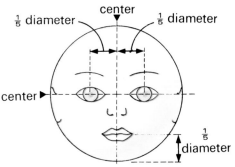

11. *The proportions of a doll's face.*

A collection of alternative heads for poupard dolls.

Rag doll

*Traditionally made from cast-off clothes and odds and ends
from the sewing basket, rag dolls are among the most endearing
of all toys. Make this appealing doll and delight a little girl.
Instructions for making the clothes are given on page 47.*

Finished size
24in (height).

Techniques involved
Basic sewing skills; enlarging a design; stuffing; embroidery stitches.

Tools required
Basic sewing tools.

Materials
tracing paper
¾yd closely woven cotton fabric 36in wide
1oz knitting worsted for hair
6in squares of brown and black felt
scraps of pink and white felt
pink embroidery thread
embroidery thread to match hair
sewing thread
2 tiny red buttons for shoes (use red felt circles for very small child)

Trace pattern pieces from those overleaf as directed. The finished doll is 24in tall. A seam allowance of ⅜in is included on the pattern where necessary. From cotton material cut one head front, two head backs, two body sections, two arms and two legs as directed. Cut all pieces on the straight of grain. Mark point and top of dart with single tailor's tacks.

Cut four shoe tops in black felt, two soles and two eye centers in brown felt, two eye whites in white and a mouth in pink.

Placing right sides together, baste and stitch head back sections from A to B. Trim seam, clip curve and press open. Placing right sides together, baste and stitch the dart in head front. Press dart to one side. Baste and stitch head front to head back, with right sides together and darts matching center back seam, easing where necessary. Trim seam and turn head right side out. Stuff firmly and overcast neck edges together.

To make hair, loop wool backward and forward across the head and backstitch to head along line of dart and down center back seam. Start stitching on face 1in below seamline (fig. 7) and continue to 1½in above neck edge at back. At the back of the head, pull strands evenly across head and backstitch to side seam at each side, beginning 1in above neck edge and finishing 1½in from center line of backstitching (fig. 8). Tie hair and trim ends.

Placing right sides together, baste

1

2

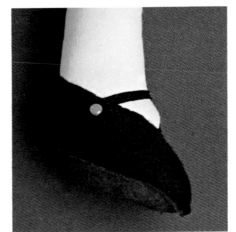
3

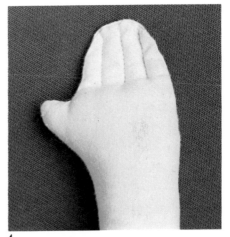
4

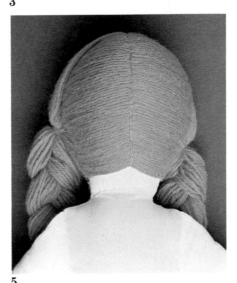
5

and stitch one arm on the stitching line. Trim, clip into angle of thumb, and turn right side out. Lightly stuff the hand and machine-stitch lines for fingers. Stuff arm firmly to within 1in of the top. Machine-stitch across the top ⅜in from the raw edge. Make the other arm in the same way.

Place two body sections with right

6

1. *Finished doll, undressed.*
2. *Doll's face (hair can be braided if you prefer).*
3. *Shoe with strap.*
4. *Lines of machine stitching for fingers.*
5. *Hair backstitched to center back seam.*
6. *The dressed doll.*

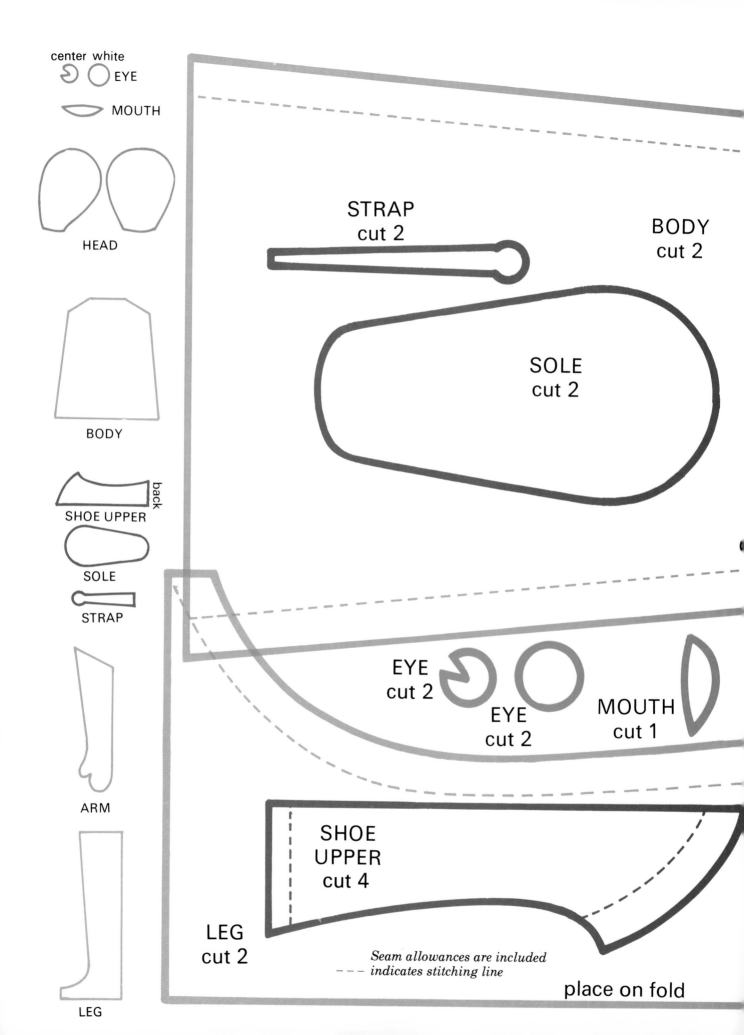

center white
EYE

MOUTH

HEAD

BODY

SHOE UPPER
back

SOLE

STRAP

ARM

LEG

STRAP
cut 2

BODY
cut 2

SOLE
cut 2

EYE
cut 2

EYE
cut 2

MOUTH
cut 1

SHOE
UPPER
cut 4

LEG
cut 2

Seam allowances are included
- - - indicates stitching line

place on fold

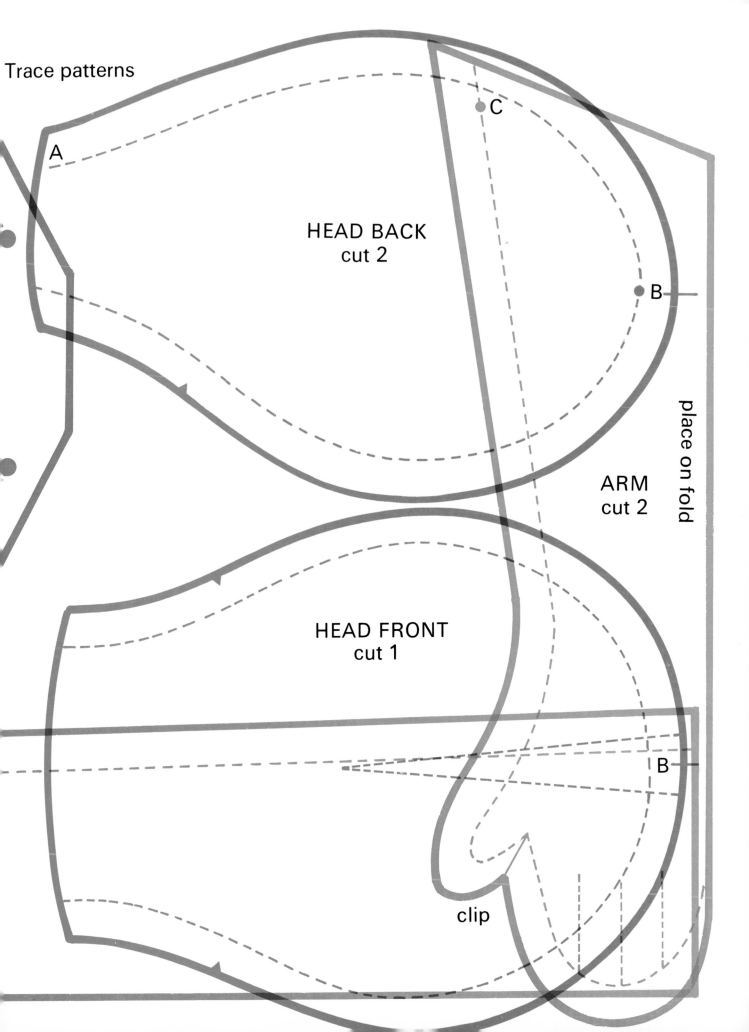

Trace patterns

A

HEAD BACK
cut 2

C

B

place on fold

ARM
cut 2

HEAD FRONT
cut 1

B

clip

sides together and one arm between them. Match raw edges and points C. Baste and stitch the side seam from C to bottom (fig. 9). Repeat with the other arm.

Stitch shoulder seams. Turn body right side out.

Turn in raw neck edge on body and insert head about $\frac{1}{2}$in into opening, matching side seams on head to shoulder seams on body. Baste and then overcast the body to the head (fig. 10). Stuff body firmly to within $1\frac{1}{2}$in of lower edge.

Turn in $\frac{3}{8}$in along the lower raw edge and close with basting.

Placing right sides together, stitch back seam of one pair of shoe tops $\frac{1}{4}$in from the edge. Press seam open and trim. Place upper edge of shoe top over bottom edge of one leg, right sides upward, overlapping leg by $\frac{1}{2}$in. Baste and topstitch by hand or machine $\frac{1}{8}$in from edge of shoe top (fig. 11). (You may have to stretch the felt slightly.)

Placing right sides together, stitch leg seam and front seam of shoe as one. Trim seam. Clip curve on leg and turn right side out.

Backstitch sole to shoe top $\frac{1}{8}$in from the edge, leaving one side open to enable stuffing to be pushed into the leg from the foot as well as from the top of the leg.

Stuff leg firmly to within 1in of the top. Push stuffing down from the top with a knitting needle if necessary.

Backstitch sole opening; machine-stitch across top of leg, placing seam at center front and stitching $\frac{3}{8}$in from the raw edges.

Machine-stitch two lines along the length of one shoe strap and over-cast to shoe. Sew a button (or felt circle) at outer end of strap.

Make other leg in the same way.

Remove basting from lower edge of body.

Insert legs into body opening so that raw edges are about $\frac{1}{2}$in inside the body.

Baste across lower edge of body, then close permanently with two lines of backstitching, one close to the edge and the other about $\frac{1}{2}$in up from the edge (fig. 12).

Sew center of eye to white (fig. 13).

Arrange eyes and mouth on face and sew in place. Embroider eyebrows and nostrils and then "stars" for cheeks.

Braid the hair if preferred.

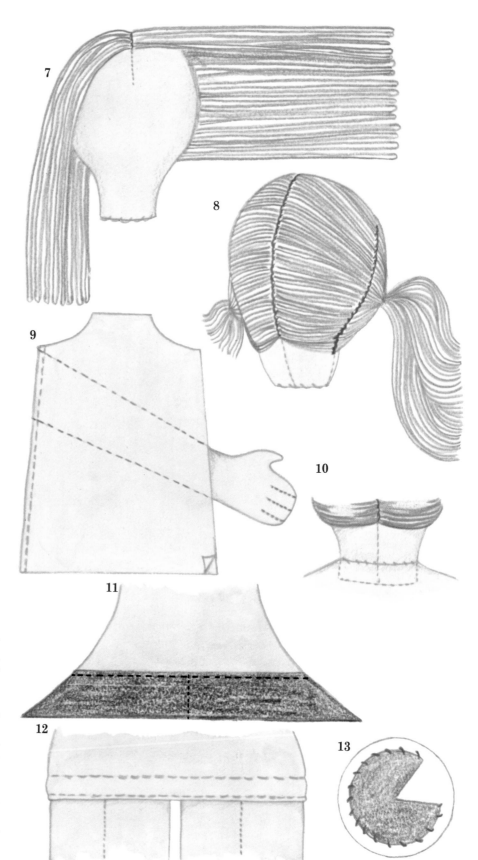

7. *Backstitching for hair starts 1in below seamline.*
8. *Backstitching on side seam.*
9. *Arm stitched in between two body pieces.*
10. *Body overcast firmly to head.*
11. *Shoe top stitched to leg $\frac{1}{8}$in from the edge.*
12. *Legs inserted into body.*
13. *Assembling the eye.*

Rag doll wardrobe

This fetching outfit is designed to fit the rag doll shown on pages 42–46. You can make the dress in several different fabrics, varying the trimmings, to make a whole wardrobe.

Finished size
To fit 24in (height) doll.

Techniques involved
Basic sewing.

Tools required
Basic sewing tools.

Materials
$\frac{5}{8}$yd of 36in-wide printed cotton
  fabric for dress
$\frac{5}{8}$yd of 2in-wide lace for sleeves
8in of $\frac{3}{4}$in-wide lace for neck
3 small buttons or snaps
1yd of $\frac{1}{4}$in-wide elastic for sleeves
  and for waist of petticoat and
  panties
$\frac{1}{2}$yd of 36in-wide white cotton lawn
  for petticoat and panties
1$\frac{1}{4}$yd of 2in-wide eyelet lace
  insertion and edging combined
  (approximately $\frac{5}{8}$in-wide insertion
  and 1$\frac{3}{8}$in-wide edging)
sewing thread
tracing paper and pencil

Dress

Trace the pattern for the bodice and
sleeves.

From printed cotton cut a piece
for the skirt 29in × 10$\frac{1}{2}$in, then cut
out two sleeves, two bodice back
pieces and one bodice front as
instructed.

Placing right sides together, baste
and stitch front and back bodice
together at shoulders.

Run a gathering thread along the
top of each sleeve $\frac{1}{4}$in from the raw
edge. Pin sleeves to bodice armholes
with right sides together and shoulder seams matching center top of
each sleeve. Pull up gathers to fit.
Baste and stitch.

Turn under $\frac{1}{8}$in and then $\frac{5}{8}$in on
bottom of each sleeve. Baste and
stitch close to edge of first fold.

Cut two pieces of 2in-wide lace to
fit the lower edges of sleeves and
topstitch in place along the very
edge of each sleeve.

Cut two pieces of elastic 4$\frac{1}{2}$in long;
thread them through the casings you
have just made and secure the ends.

Placing right sides together and
matching edges at all points, baste
and stitch raw edges of lace, sleeve
seam, and bodice side seam in one
operation (fig. 1). Trim seams to $\frac{1}{4}$in
and finish them together. Repeat
with the other sleeve.

Placing right sides together, stitch

the two short edges of skirt piece
together to within 4in of one long
edge (waist edge). Mark side and
center front of top of skirt with
single tailor's tacks or pins. Run a
gathering thread along top edge of
skirt $\frac{3}{8}$in from the edge. Pin skirt to
bodice with right sides together, pulling up gathers to fit. Baste and
stitch. Press seam toward bodice.
Turn under $\frac{1}{8}$in and then $\frac{1}{4}$in on each
side of back opening. Baste and
stitch close to first fold.

Cut a 1in-wide bias strip in printed
cotton to fit the neck, plus a little
extra for seams. Placing right side of
binding to wrong side of bodice,
baste and stitch the strip to the neck
edge. Trim seam allowances to $\frac{1}{4}$in.

Trim raw ends to $\frac{1}{4}$in and turn to
wrong side of bias strip. Fold binding over right side of neckline. Turn
under $\frac{1}{4}$in, baste, and topstitch close
to lower edge of binding. Slipstitch
the ends. Slipstitch the $\frac{3}{8}$in lace
around the neck on the stitching
line, turning in and finishing the
ends.

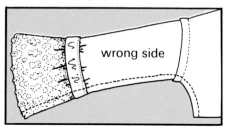

*1. Lace, sleeve seam, and bodice side
seam stitched in one operation.*

Sew buttons to left side of bodice
back and make buttonholes in the
other side to correspond. Or sew on
snaps.

Turn $\frac{1}{8}$in and then $\frac{5}{8}$in on lower
edge of dress, and slipstitch the hem
in place.

Petticoat

Cut a strip of white lawn 29in × 9$\frac{1}{2}$in.

On one long edge turn up $\frac{3}{8}$in onto
the right side; press. This is the
lower edge of the petticoat.

Cut a piece of eyelet lace 29in
long; pin it to the right side of the
bottom of the petticoat. The lower

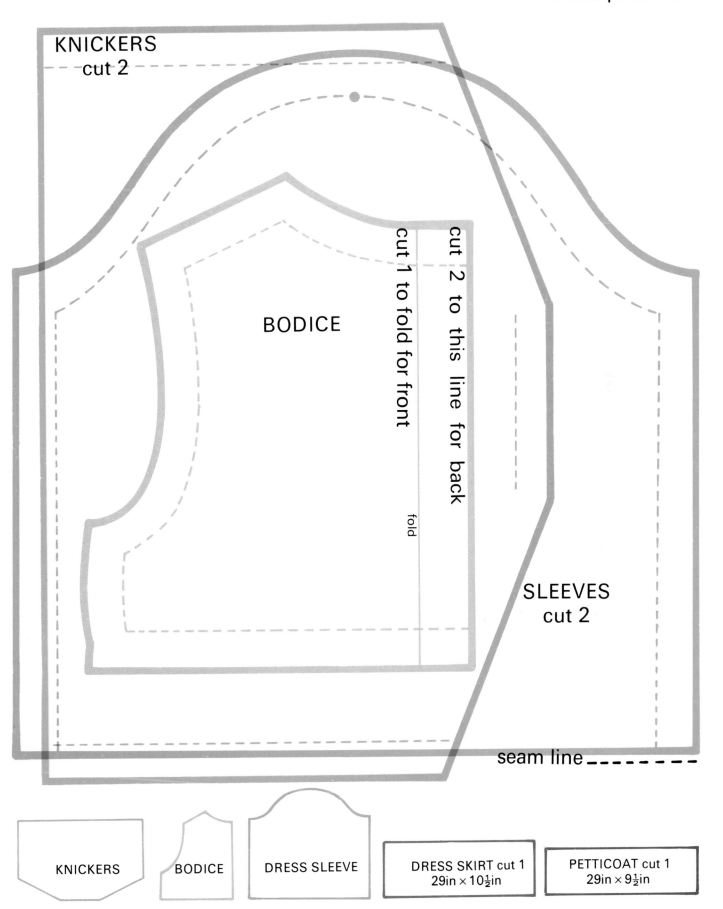

KNICKERS
cut 2

BODICE

cut 1 to fold for front

cut 2 to this line for back

fold

SLEEVES
cut 2

seam line

KNICKERS

BODICE

DRESS SLEEVE

DRESS SKIRT cut 1
29in × 10½in

PETTICOAT cut 1
29in × 9½in

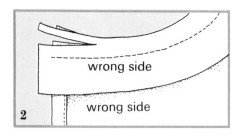

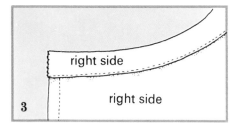

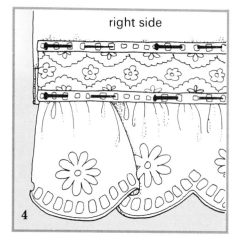

2. *Trimming bias strips and neck edge*
3. *Bias turned to right side of bodice, ¼in turned under and lower edge topstitched.*
4. *Eyelet lace pinned to right side of petticoat bottom*

edge of the insertion should be just above the folded edge of petticoat. Baste and stitch along both edges of the insertion, thus enclosing raw edge of petticoat hem.

Placing right sides together, baste and stitch back seam and eyelet in one operation. Finish the seam.

On the waist edge turn under ⅛in and then ½in. Baste and stitch close to the first fold, leaving a 1in opening for inserting elastic. Cut a piece of elastic to fit the doll's waist, thread it through the casing and overcast the ends together securely. Slipstitch the opening.

Panties

Trace the pattern for the panties and cut two pieces in lawn.

Cut a piece of eyelet lace to fit each leg edge, including seams (four pieces in all).

On one leg edge turn up ¼in onto right side; press. Attach one of the pieces of eyelet lace to cover the raw edge as for the bottom of petticoat. Repeat on other three leg edges.

Placing right sides together, baste and stitch the side seams, stitching short ends of eyelet lace in the same operation. Finish the seams.

Placing right sides together, baste and stitch the crotch seam including ends of eyelet lace. Trim seam to ¼in and finish it.

Make casing and insert elastic at top of panties as for petticoat. Turn finished panties right side out. Press all clothes with a warm iron.

For a crisp country look, make the outfit in gingham check and add a matching sash and ribbon.

Adapting the wardrobe

This rag doll wardrobe can supply you with quite a range of alternative doll's clothes if you adapt the patterns imaginatively. First, different fabrics can give a whole new look. In our illustrations we show a richly colored Victorian type fabric, and a contrasting crisp gingham.

Pattern pieces can also be easily adapted. For example, the bodice and sleeves can be used to make a blouse; the dress skirt-piece can be made into a separate skirt, and if you lengthen the panties to the ankle, you have Victorian knickers.

Topsy turvy doll

Here's a doll to cuddle at sad moments as well as happy ones.
Dressed in pretty, old-fashioned clothes, she's a charmer,
whether tearful or smiling.

Finished size
19in (height).

Techniques involved
Basic sewing; stuffing; embroidery stitches.

Tools required
Basic sewing tools.

Materials
½yd of 36in-wide pale pink cotton fabric for body

⅝yd of 36in-wide floral-printed fabric for one dress

⅝yd of 36in-wide plain fabric for other dress

⅜yd of 45in-wide cream cotton fabric for petticoat and apron

1⅛yd of ⅜in-wide velvet ribbon in two colors harmonizing with dress fabrics

1⅛yd of ⅜in-wide cream satin ribbon

1⅛yd of ⅜in-wide lace edging

2¼yd of 1¼in-wide lace edging

1 ball of reddish-brown bouclé yarn

1 ball of pale brown mohair-type yarn

12in of ⅜in-wide white woven tape

small bunch of pink fabric flowers

stranded embroidery floss in white, black, dusty and dark pink, dark reddish-brown and moss green

3 small pearl buttons

suitable stuffing

sewing threads

tracing paper

dressmaker's carbon paper

Trace the pattern pieces given for the body, hand, and apron (do not trace the features on head or flowers on apron). Using dressmaker's carbon paper, mark these patterns on the wrong side of the appropriate fabrics. Cut out all pieces.

Trace features given alongside head pattern. On one body piece mark the features for the sad face at one end and the features for the happy face at the opposite end. When marking, use the features on head pattern as a guide to position.

Using three strands of embroidery floss, embroider both the faces. Work the lips, tear drops, pupils, and irises in satin stitch. Work edges of cheeks, nostrils, eye lines, and lashes in backstitch. Work eyebrows in split stitch. Use French knots for base of nostrils and eye sparkles. Follow feature patterns for colors. Press embroidery on the wrong side.

1. *Doll body stitched at sides.*
2. *Hand sewn together at wrist.*
3. *Bouclé yarn stitched to tape.*
4. *Hair in position on doll's head.*
5. *Hair tied into bunches.*
6. *Lace stitched to hem of petticoat.*
7. *Petticoat gathered to fit waist.*

Place embroidered body piece on plain body piece, right sides together. Pin, baste, and stitch around body, leaving an opening in one side. Clip into seam allowance all around (fig. 1). Turn body right side out. Stuff body firmly; turn in opening edges and close with slipstitch.

Place hands in pairs with right sides together. Pin, baste, and stitch all around each pair, leaving wrist edges open. Clip into curves all around. Turn each hand right side out. Stuff each hand firmly. Pin, baste, and stitch across each hand at the wrist (fig. 2).

For hair for sad doll, first cut the white tape in half. From reddish-brown yarn cut 18in lengths. Lay the yarn over the tape, with the tape in the middle, leaving $\frac{1}{4}$in of tape free at each end. Pin, baste, and stitch the yarn to the tape, using a zigzag stitch or overcast by hand. Make the yarn thick enough to form a solid covering on the head (fig. 3).

Place the hair on the head with the sad face, with the zigzag stitching forming the center part. Tuck under raw ends of tape to finish. Sew hair to head down center part, using backstitch (fig. 4).

Cut satin ribbon into four equal pieces. Form a bunch of hair at each side of the head. Tie a length of ribbon around each bunch and into a neat bow. Sew bunches to side of head. Sew a few flowers to each bow (fig. 5).

Make and attach hair in the same way for the happy face, using pale brown mohair-type yarn.

For the petticoat, cut out a piece of cream cotton fabric 32in × 12½in.

Turn under a tiny hem along one long edge of petticoat. Pin, baste, and sew in place by hand.

Cut a 50in length of 1¼in-wide lace edging. Run a line of gathering stitches along straight edge of lace edging. Pull up gathering stitches to fit hemmed edge of petticoat. Pin and baste lace to wrong side of petticoat over hem edge. Stitch in place using zigzag stitch or overcast by hand (fig. 6).

Fold petticoat in half crosswise, wrong sides facing and edges matching. Pin, baste, and stitch the side edges together with a French seam.

Run a line of gathering stitches around the top edge of petticoat. Fit the petticoat around the waist edge

of doll with wrong side over happy face and seam at center back. Pull up gathers to fit waist and fasten off (fig. 7).

Make a tiny double hem along side and lower edges of apron. Pin, baste, and hand-hem in place.

Trace flower motif from apron pattern. Using dressmaker's carbon, mark the motif on right-hand side of apron.

Using three strands of pink and green embroidery floss, work the flowers and leaves in chain stitch,

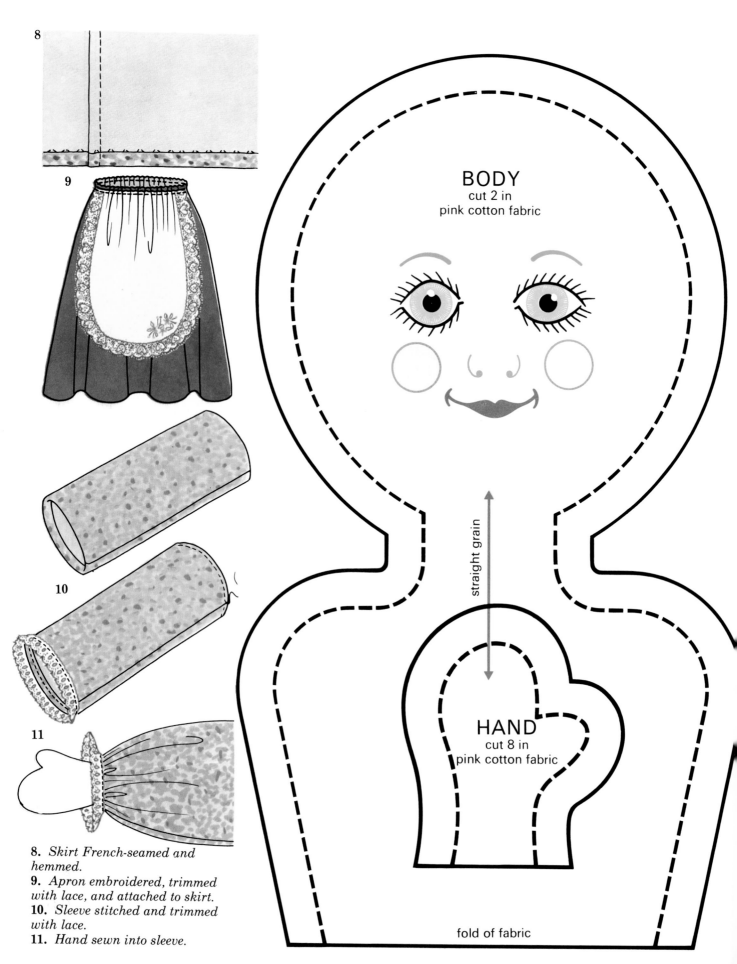

8
9
10
11

BODY
cut 2 in
pink cotton fabric

straight grain

HAND
cut 8 in
pink cotton fabric

fold of fabric

8. Skirt French-seamed and hemmed.
9. Apron embroidered, trimmed with lace, and attached to skirt.
10. Sleeve stitched and trimmed with lace.
11. Hand sewn into sleeve.

Trace patterns

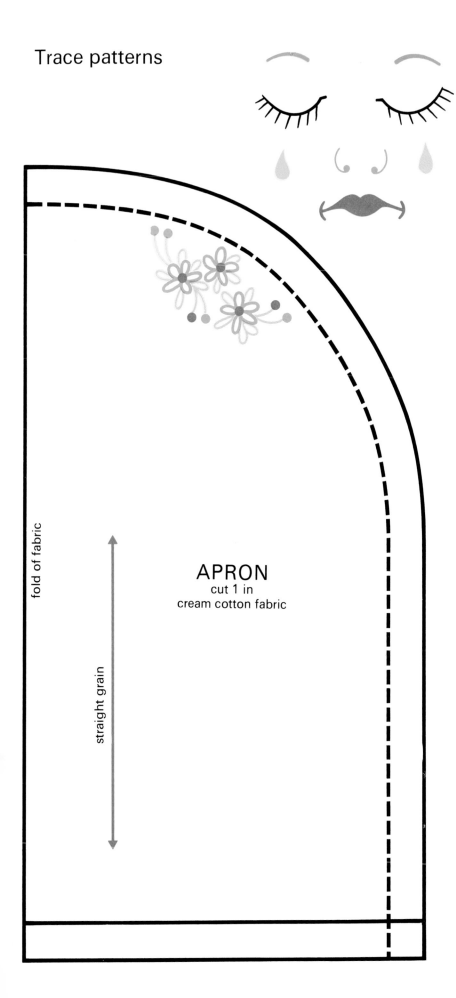

APRON
cut 1 in
cream cotton fabric

fold of fabric

straight grain

backstitch, and French knots.

Gather and attach remaining length of 1¼in lace to apron edge as on petticoat.

For skirt of sad doll cut out one piece of the floral-printed fabric 32in × 11¾in.

Turn under a tiny double hem along one long edge of skirt. Pin, baste, and hem in place by hand.

Fold skirt in half crosswise, with wrong sides together and edges matching. Pin, baste, and stitch together with a French seam (fig. 8).

Run a line of gathering stitches around top edge of skirt. Place skirt on doll with right side up over petticoat and seam at center back, covering head of happy doll. Draw up gathers to fit waist and fasten off threads securely.

Make a skirt for the happy doll in the same way, using plain fabric.

Place apron on center of plain skirt, opposite seam, with top edges matching. Run a line of gathering stitches around top edge of skirt, catching in top edge of apron (fig. 9). Place skirt/apron on doll with right side up, covering head of sad doll. Draw up gathers to fit waist and fasten off securely.

For sleeves for sad doll, cut out two pieces from floral-printed fabric, each 6in square. Fold sleeves in half, right sides together. Pin, baste, and stitch side seams. Turn sleeves right side out.

Turn under ⅜in at one end of each sleeve. Pin, baste, and stitch in place. Cut two 6in lengths of narrow lace edging. Placing right sides together, pin, baste, and stitch each length of lace edging into a ring. Pin and baste lace edging around hem edge of each sleeve, then sew both layers together with running stitch, leaving an end loose for gathering (fig. 10).

Place a hand inside the lace-edged end of each sleeve. Pull up gathering stitches tight around the wrists and secure them (fig. 11).

Make sleeves with hands in the same way for happy doll, using plain fabric.

For bodice for sad doll, cut out a piece of floral-printed fabric measuring 10in × 8in.

Fold bodice in half lengthwise, with wrong sides together and edges matching. Cut a slit along the folded edge for the neck opening, making it

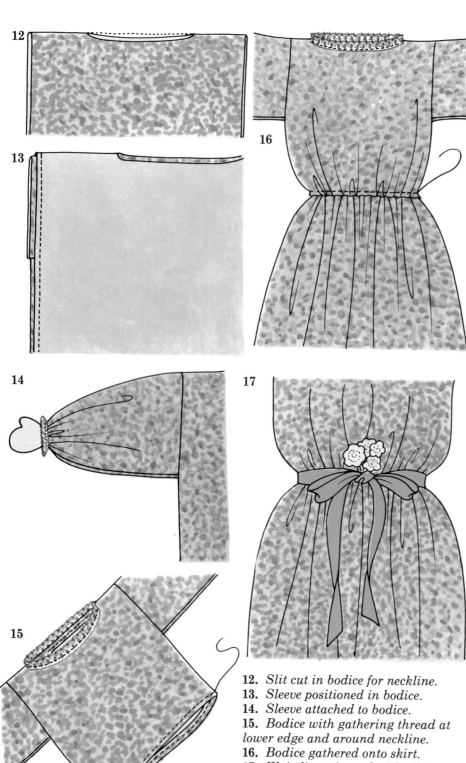

12. *Slit cut in bodice for neckline.*
13. *Sleeve positioned in bodice.*
14. *Sleeve attached to bodice.*
15. *Bodice with gathering thread at lower edge and around neckline.*
16. *Bodice gathered onto skirt.*
17. *Waistline trimmed with ribbon and flowers.*
18. *The finished doll.*

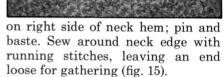

long enough to slip over the head (fig. 12).

Fold bodice with right sides together. Place sleeves inside bodice with tops of sleeves to top of bodice at sides. Pin, baste, and stitch side seams, catching in sleeves (fig. 13). Trim and turn right side out (fig. 14).

Turn under $\frac{3}{8}$in at lower edge. Pin, and baste. Sew hem with running stitches, leaving an end loose for gathering.

Turn under $\frac{3}{8}$in at neck edge of bodice. Cut a length of narrow lace edging to fit neck edge plus seam allowance. Placing the right sides together, pin, baste, and stitch lace edging into a ring. Place lace edging on right side of neck hem; pin and baste. Sew around neck edge with running stitches, leaving an end loose for gathering (fig. 15).

Put bodice on sad doll; draw up gathering stitches to fit the doll's waist, covering the raw upper edge of skirt; fasten off the gathering thread securely (fig. 16). Draw up the gathering thread around the neck to fit and fasten off thread securely.

Make the bodice for the happy doll in the same way, using plain fabric. Sew three buttons to center front of plain bodice, spacing them at equal intervals with the first button $\frac{3}{4}$in down from the neck edge.

Pin, baste, and sew one piece of velvet ribbon around the waist of floral dress and tie in a bow at center front. Slip some flowers into the ribbon at the waist edge (fig. 17).

Pin, baste, and sew the other length of velvet ribbon around waist edge of plain dress and tie in a bow at center front.

Sew a few flowers to the right hand of sad doll.

Boy and girl dolls

These two sweethearts are made from a pair of socks! Their clothes are made from any scraps of fabric you may have on hand, and their old-fashioned charm will delight children and enchant the grown-ups too.

Finished sizes
Both dolls 10in (height).

Techniques involved
Basic sewing; stuffing.

Tools required
Basic sewing tools.

Materials
For Jenny:
a man's plain white cotton sock,
   size 9–11
piece of white cotton fabric
   $10\frac{1}{2}$in × 6in
$8\frac{1}{2}$in of $\frac{1}{4}$in-wide nylon lace
piece of blue and white dotted
   cotton fabric 16in × $11\frac{1}{2}$in
piece of white eyelet lace with
   scalloped edge $8\frac{1}{2}$in × 3in
14in of $\frac{3}{8}$in-wide white woven tape
   for apron strings
piece of white felt $4\frac{1}{4}$in × $\frac{3}{4}$in
piece of red felt $5\frac{1}{2}$in × 2in
one $\frac{3}{8}$in-diameter red button
10in of $\frac{1}{4}$in-wide red ribbon
gold-colored bouclé yarn for hair
small bunch of artificial flowers
6in of $\frac{1}{4}$in-wide purple ribbon
felt-tip markers and crayon for
   features
suitable stuffing
sewing thread
tracing paper
dressmaker's carbon paper
For Johnny:
a man's plain white cotton sock,
   size 9–11
piece of blue and white gingham
   fabric $8\frac{1}{2}$in × 6in
piece of denim fabric $14\frac{1}{4}$in × 6in
piece of yellow felt $5\frac{1}{2}$in × 2in
$5\frac{1}{2}$in square of red and white dotted
   fabric
8in-long $\frac{1}{8}$in-diameter green plant
   stick
four $\frac{3}{8}$in-diameter yellow buttons
brown bouclé yarn for hair
piece of iron-on interfacing 5in × $\frac{3}{4}$in
felt-tip markers and crayon for
   features
tracing paper
dressmaker's carbon paper
suitable stuffing
sewing threads

Jenny
For the body cut off the toe of the
sock across the instep (fig. 1). Fold
the sock so that the back of the heel
is on the top—this will be the face.
Cut up through the middle of the
sock from the ankle for about 4in to

make the legs. Turn the sock wrong
side out. Pin, baste, and stitch
around the slit to form the legs (fig.
2). (Take $\frac{1}{4}$in seams throughout.)
Trim seam and turn the body right
side out.

Stuff the legs. Be careful not to
overstuff them, as the fabric is easily
stretched out of shape. Pin, baste,
and stitch across the tops of the legs,
so they will bend.

Stuff the rest of the body up to the
neck. Wind a length of sewing
thread around the neck and fasten
off (fig. 3).

Stuff the head. Again, be careful
not to overstuff, so that the head will
be the correct shape. Turn in the
open edges of the head and slipstitch
them together to close.

Use the toe part of the sock for the
arms. Cut the toe part in half
lengthwise (fig. 4). Turn each part
wrong side out. Pin, baste, and stitch
around each part to form an arm,
leaving an opening. Turn the arms
right side out.

Stuff each arm as for legs, leaving
the top of each arm flat. Turn in
opening edges and slipstitch together to close (fig. 5).

Stitch an arm to each side of the
body.

Trace pattern pieces for the girl's
clothes, positioning center of dress
on fold of paper. Using dressmaker's
carbon, mark the pattern pieces on
the wrong side of the appropriate
fabrics the number of times specified. Cut out. Cut out shoe soles and
tops in felt.

Finish the lower edges of each
pantaloon leg. Pin, baste, and stitch
a length of narrow lace to these
edges, matching right side of lace to
right side of fabric (fig. 6).

Place pantaloon pieces together
with right sides facing. Pin, baste,
and stitch side and inside leg seams,
catching in lace. Turn pantaloons
right side out.

Make a $\frac{1}{4}$in double hem at waist
edge of pantaloons. Pin, baste, and
run a line of gathering stitches
around the waist hem (fig. 7). Put the
pantaloons on the doll, pull up the
gathers around the waist, and fasten
off securely.

Run a line of gathering stitches
around the edge of each pantaloon
leg. Pull up gathering stitches to fit
each leg and fasten off securely.

Fold the dress in half, right sides

together, at the shoulders. Pin,
baste, and stitch the side and underarm seams (fig. 8).

Make a double $\frac{1}{8}$in hem at each
wrist. Pin, baste, and run a line of
gathering stitches around each wrist
hem. Repeat around the neck edge.

Make a double $\frac{1}{8}$in hem at each
lower edge of dress. Pin, baste, and
stitch in place using zigzag stitch
(fig. 9).

Put the dress on the doll. Pull up
gathers around neck and fasten off
securely. Repeat at wrists.

Place the collar around the neck
over dress with the collar ends meeting at front. Sew in place. Sew
button at the neck (fig. 10).

Run a line of gathering stitches
along the long straight edge of
eyelet lace fabric to make apron.
Pull up gathers to measure $4\frac{1}{4}$in and
fasten off. Turn a $\frac{1}{8}$in double hem at
each side. Pin, baste, and hem by
hand (fig. 11).

Fold the apron waistband in half
lengthwise, edges matching and
wrong side inside. Place it over the
gathered edge of apron. Turn under
edges. Pin, baste, and stitch in place.

Cut white tape in half. Tuck the
ends of the tape into each end of the
waistband. Pin, baste, and stitch in
place to make apron strings (fig. 12).
Tie apron around doll.

Fold one shoe top in half. Pin,
baste, and stitch back seam (fig. 13).
Match shoe sole to lower edge of
shoe top. Blanket stitch the seam.
Make second shoe in the same way.

Push feet into shoes, adding a
little stuffing in the toes of the shoes.
Sew shoes in place.

For the hair, cut enough 9in
lengths of yarn to cover the head.
Place yarn lengths together and
stitch across the center to form a
part (fig. 14).

Place the hair across the head,
slightly in front of the sides, and
hand-sew to the head, along the
center part. Cut red ribbon in half.
Draw the hair into bunches at each
side of the face and fasten with a
length of red ribbon. Tie ribbon into
bows (fig. 15).

Using felt-tip markers, draw features on the doll's face. Use crayon
on the face for rosy cheeks.

Sew the bunch of flowers to one
hand with firm handstitches.

For a final flourish, tie a pretty
ribbon around the flowers.

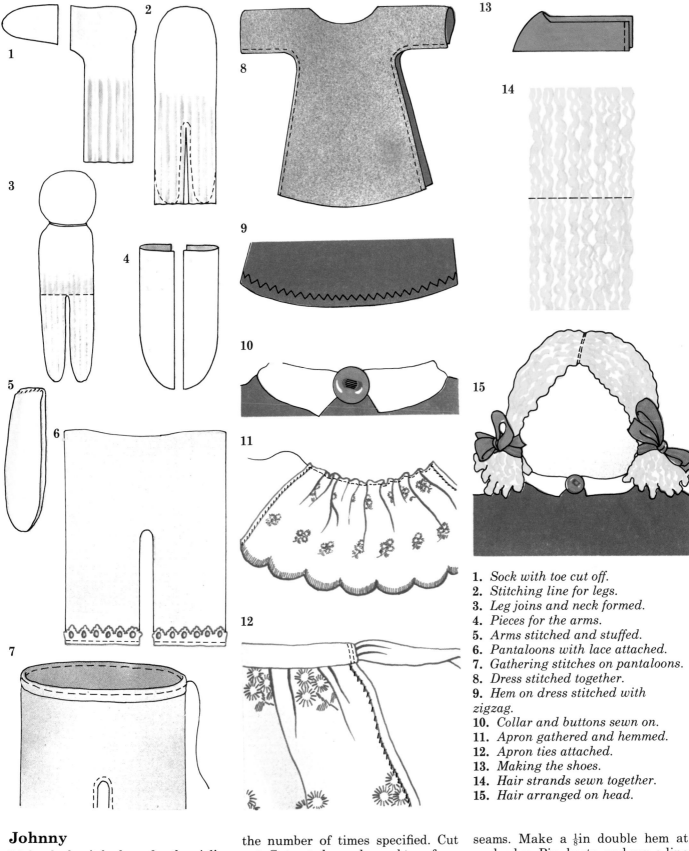

1. Sock with toe cut off.
2. Stitching line for legs.
3. Leg joins and neck formed.
4. Pieces for the arms.
5. Arms stitched and stuffed.
6. Pantaloons with lace attached.
7. Gathering stitches on pantaloons.
8. Dress stitched together.
9. Hem on dress stitched with zigzag.
10. Collar and buttons sewn on.
11. Apron gathered and hemmed.
12. Apron ties attached.
13. Making the shoes.
14. Hair strands sewn together.
15. Hair arranged on head.

Johnny

Make the boy's body as for the girl's.

Trace pattern pieces for the clothes. Using dressmaker's carbon, mark the pattern pieces on the wrong side of the appropriate fabrics the number of times specified. Cut out. Cut out shoe soles and tops from yellow felt.

Fold the shirt in half, right sides together, at the shoulders. Pin, baste, and stitch side and underarm seams. Make a $\frac{1}{8}$in double hem at neck edge. Pin, baste, and run a line of gathering stitches around neck edge (fig. 16).

Make a $\frac{1}{8}$in double hem at the edge of each sleeve. Pin, baste, and stitch

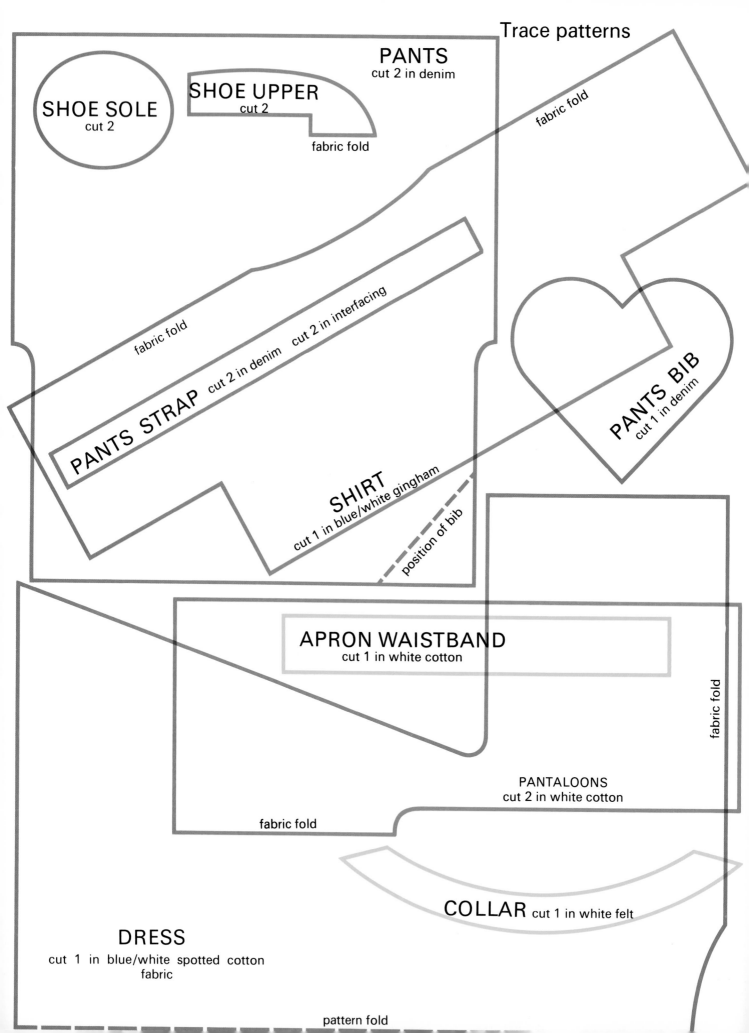

Trace patterns

SHOE SOLE
cut 2

SHOE UPPER
cut 2

PANTS
cut 2 in denim

fabric fold

fabric fold

fabric fold

PANTS STRAP cut 2 in denim   cut 2 in interfacing

PANTS BIB
cut 1 in denim

SHIRT
cut 1 in blue/white gingham

position of bib

APRON WAISTBAND
cut 1 in white cotton

fabric fold

PANTALOONS
cut 2 in white cotton

fabric fold

COLLAR cut 1 in white felt

DRESS
cut 1 in blue/white spotted cotton
fabric

pattern fold

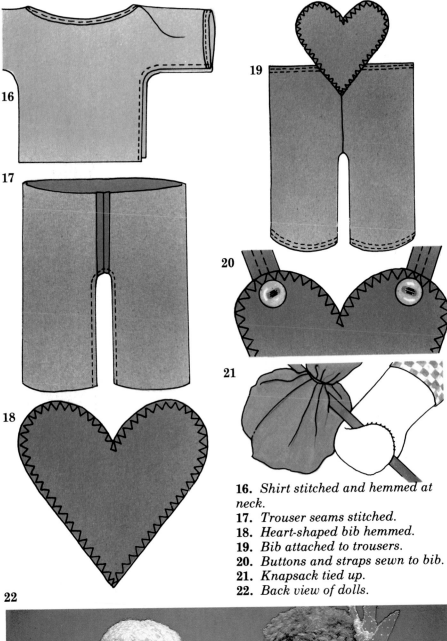

16. *Shirt stitched and hemmed at neck.*
17. *Trouser seams stitched.*
18. *Heart-shaped bib hemmed.*
19. *Bib attached to trousers.*
20. *Buttons and straps sewn to bib.*
21. *Knapsack tied up.*
22. *Back view of dolls.*

in place.

Put shirt on doll. Pull up gathers around neck and fasten off securely.

Place pants pieces together with right sides facing. Pin, baste and stitch back and front seams. Fold pants with seams matching at the center. Pin, baste, and stitch inner leg seams (fig. 17).

Make a $\frac{1}{8}$in double hem at top edge of pants. Pin, baste, and topstitch in place with two rows of stitching, using contrasting sewing thread.

Using contrasting sewing thread, zigzag-stitch all around the outer edge of the heart-shaped bib (fig. 18). Position bib over the top edge of the pants, as marked on pattern. Pin, baste, and stitch in place.

Make a double $\frac{1}{8}$in hem at the lower edge of each pants leg. Pin, baste, and topstitch in place with two rows of stitching, using contrasting sewing thread (fig. 19).

Iron interfacing to wrong side of each pants strap. Then topstitch lengthwise down the center of each strap using contrasting sewing thread.

Tuck one end of each strap under the top edge of the heart-shaped bib and pin in place. Sew two buttons to bib where the straps meet to hold the straps in position (fig. 20). Put the pants on the doll. Take the straps over the shoulders, cross over at the back, and fasten behind the pants with two buttons.

Make shoes and fit them on the boy's feet as for the girl.

For the hair use a single thickness of yarn and a sharp needle. Sew small loops all over the head, knotting the yarn at every stitch, so the hair will not come undone. When the head is covered, cut through all the loops. Trim if necessary.

Make features on boy's face as for girl.

Use the dotted fabric for knapsack. Using pinking shears, pink around the edge of the fabric. Place some stuffing in the center on the wrong side. Bunch the four corners together. Wind a length of matching sewing thread around the sack and fasten off securely.

Cut a small hole through the sack, just underneath the wound threads. Push the green stick through the hole. Sew the sack firmly to one hand, turning the "fingers" around the stick (fig. 21).

Yarn doll

This little doll can be made in an evening from knitting yarn and a child's plastic ball. You can dress her from the basic wardrobe given on pages 65–69.

Finished size
14in (height).

Techniques involved
Basic sewing.

Tools required
Basic sewing tools.

Materials
4oz of knitting worsted in flesh color
2oz of mohair-type brown yarn for hair
hollow plastic ball, about 7in in circumference
scraps of red felt
scraps of non-woven interfacing
fabric glue
10in of ½in-wide ribbon
felt-tip markers in brown and black

Cut two 10in lengths of knitting worsted for binding the arms.

Wind the yarn in a loop to make a skein 16in long (from beginning to end) and 100 strands thick (total). Cut the skein at each end and bind it with a length of yarn about 1in from one end.

Braid the skein to make arms and bind the other end.

Cut five 10in lengths of yarn for binding the body and legs. Make a skein 40in long and 150 strands thick, cut the skein at each end, and bind it firmly in the middle. Lay the arms across the middle of the skein, fold the skein over them, and then bind it firmly just below the arms to hold them in place.

Bind the skein again about 2in farther down to make the hips. From this point, divide the skein in half and braid each half to make the legs. Bind each leg firmly at each end. Trim the ends of the arms and legs into a neat shape.

Cover the plastic ball with fabric glue, leaving a small space at the top and bottom so you can hold it between your thumb and forefinger.

Wind the yarn around and around the ball, taking care that all the strands go in the same direction and cross each other at the top and bottom. The covered ball forms the doll's head. When the ball is completely covered, darn the loose end of the yarn under the strands. Leave the head to dry.

Thread a darning needle with yarn and sew head to body.

Using non-woven interfacing, cut two eye shapes and color them carefully, using felt-tip markers.

Cut the mouth shape from red felt. Glue this and the eyes to the head.

Use felt markers to make the eyebrows, nose and eyelashes.

For hair, cut 80 14in lengths of mohair-type yarn and 20 3in lengths for the bangs.

Sew bangs on first. Taking four strands at a time, fold them in half and sew them to the head. Now sew on the rest of the hair, again working with four strands at a time. Lay them across the head and sew them down to make center part. Sew the grouped strands close together so that the head does not show through.

When all the hair has been sewn, tie it into bunches as shown in the photograph. The back strands will be too long when the bunches are tied. Trim them evenly.

Cut ribbon into two lengths and tie the bunches with bows.

Patterns for dolls' clothes

*Whether you have made a doll or purchased one, she will surely
need a wardrobe. Most of a child's pleasure comes
from dressing a doll to suit the occasion.
Doll clothes can be made from remnants of fabric. Buttons,
beads from a broken necklace, scraps of ribbon and lace can all
be used for trimmings, and small pieces of soft leather from an
odd glove can be used for shoes.*

Drawing patterns

Pattern shapes are based on the
doll's torso, so it is necessary to
draw a template as a guide for
making the pattern pieces. Divide
the torso pattern piece in half
lengthwise and trace around it on a
piece of cardboard. Do not add seam
allowances. Fig. 1 shows the measurements of depth and width to be
taken (half the width of the torso
pattern).

If you are making patterns for a
purchased doll, trace around the
doll's torso and then take the
measurements as before. Many dolls
have plumper figures than the
shapes shown; in this case it is
better to make dresses without fitted
waists, taking a measurement just
below the armholes for a dress without a yoke. With the template completed you can begin your pattern
designing.

Pin a piece of tracing paper over
the template and on it sketch the
shape of the desired garment. Keep
in mind where the pattern can be
placed on a fabric fold and where
seams and facings will be. Remember
to add seam allowances to the pattern
pieces. Also allow a little room for
ease when dressing the doll. Most
dolls have fairly large heads, so
when shaping neck openings allow
for this.

A slip pattern is shown in fig. 2.
This has been drawn over the template. Underwear such as panties
and slips fit more closely than out-
erwear and therefore follow the
shape of the body more distinctly.
Note that the neckline of the slip
falls roughly halfway between the
bottom of the shoulder and the base
of the armhole.

Patterns for smock-type dresses,
jumpers, and dresses with a fitted

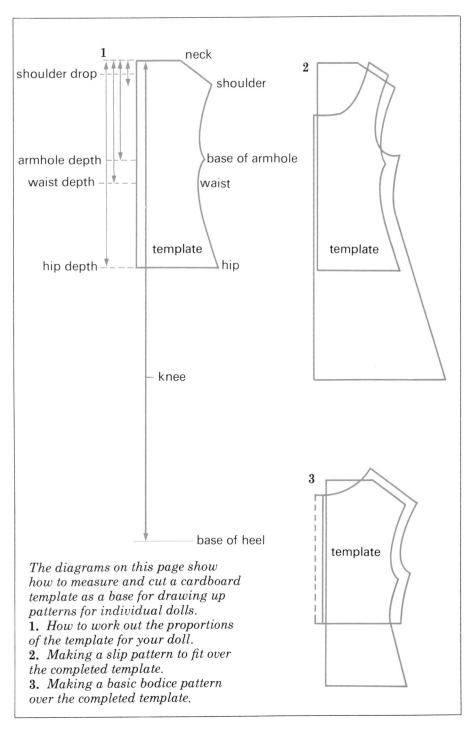

*The diagrams on this page show
how to measure and cut a cardboard
template as a base for drawing up
patterns for individual dolls.*
1. *How to work out the proportions
of the template for your doll.*
2. *Making a slip pattern to fit over
the completed template.*
3. *Making a basic bodice pattern
over the completed template.*

bodice and gathered or pleated skirt are made on the same principle. Figs. 3 and 4 show respectively a bodice pattern and ways of varying the basic shape. Necklines can be round, square, or V-shaped.

To determine fabric requirements for a dress with gathers either at the waistline or at a yoke, double the width measurement to allow for enough fullness. For a pleated skirt the width will be three times the measurement you are fitting.

A gathered skirt can be made using two rectangles of fabric, their size determined by the desired finished length plus hem allowance, and double the waist measurement plus seam allowances. Gather the skirt onto a waistband or stitch a casing for elastic to be threaded through, in which case you must allow for a hem at the waist edge as well as at the bottom. Elastic is probably the better way to finish a waist, as it is simpler than buttons for a small child to manipulate.

Circular skirts are made by drawing a circle with a radius larger than the required finished length of the skirt. Cut out the circle, fold it evenly into four, and trim off a quarter of the total waist measurement at the apex (fig. 5a). Unfold the circle and use it as a pattern. Cut the waist opening on the straight grain and finish it with bias binding and a hook and eye fastening.

The pattern for a gored skirt is made in a similar way, but seam allowances are added to each gore (fig. 5b).

For shoes, use the doll's foot or foot pattern for drawing a template. Allow an extra ¼in all around the sole pattern piece. If you wish to make boots, the width and length of the leg from the knee down must also be taken into consideration. It is best to use felt or soft leather scraps for footwear, as these do not fray and you will not have to worry about hiding seam allowances.

Although it is possible to make a blouse with set-in sleeves, you will probably find this quite a chore. Therefore, try to incorporate the sleeves in the body of the blouse. Fig. 6 gives a shape for a blouse with full sleeves gathered at the wrist.

Don't throw pattern pieces away. Keep them stored with suitable scraps of leftover fabrics.

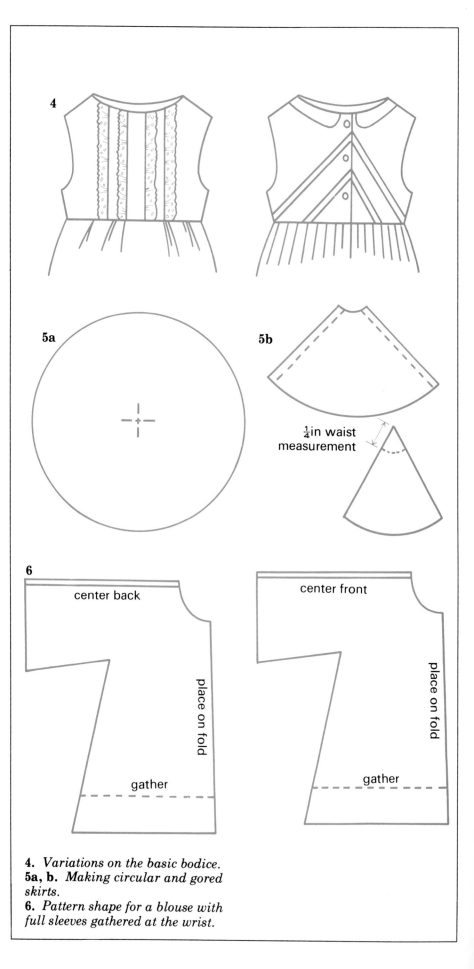

4. *Variations on the basic bodice.*
5a, b. *Making circular and gored skirts.*
6. *Pattern shape for a blouse with full sleeves gathered at the wrist.*

Doll's wardrobe

Everything that the well-dressed doll needs, from dawn to dusk, even including rain boots. You could adapt some or all of these ideas for dolls of different sizes.

Finished size
To fit a 14in (height) doll.

Techniques involved
Enlarging patterns from a graph; changing the size of a pattern; basic sewing.

Tools required
Basic sewing tools.

Materials
For the slip and panties:
graph paper with 1in squares
20in × 12in piece of white cotton fabric
20in of 1¼in-wide gathered eyelet lace
12in of ⅜in-wide lace
white bias binding
4in of ⅜in-wide ribbon
sewing thread
For the skirt and blouse:
graph paper with 1in squares
½yd of 36in-wide cotton fabric
bias binding
hat elastic
sewing thread
For the duffle coat:
graph paper with 1in squares
36in × 12in piece of felt
4 tiny toggles
sewing thread
For the boots:
graph paper with 1in squares
12in × 8in wet-look vinyl
4in square of black felt
cardboard
fabric glue
sewing thread
For the robe:
graph paper with 1in squares
½yd of 36in-wide quilted fabric
3 tiny buttons
3 snaps
sewing thread
For the nightgown:
graph paper with 1in squares
½yd of 36in-wide seersucker
20in of 1in-wide trimming
2 rosebud trims
1 snap
sewing thread

Changing sizes
Before cutting out any of these doll clothes check that each pattern piece fits the doll and make any necessary alterations. If a different size is needed, re-draw the graph patterns and adjust fabric quantities (see Techniques section).

Slip and panties

Using graph paper, draw each pattern piece to scale and cut out.

Stitch all seams with right sides facing unless otherwise indicated; ¼in seam allowances are included.

From white cotton fabric cut out slip front and back, placing pattern on fold of fabric. Cut out panties, placing pattern on fold of fabric.

Turn under ¼in along top edge of each slip piece and trim with narrow gathered eyelet lace. Join side seams and bind armholes with bias binding. Turn under a ¼in hem and stitch wider gathered eyelet lace to edge.

Cut ribbon into two pieces and sew to front and back to form shoulder straps.

Bind legs of panties with bias binding. Join side seams. Make a ⅜in casing along top edge, leaving one end open for elastic. Insert elastic, pull up to fit doll's waist and fasten. Stitch lace around each leg.

1. *A slip and matching panties can be made from fabric scraps with very little effort.*

Skirt and blouse

Using graph paper, draw each pattern piece to scale and cut out.

Stitch all seams with right sides facing unless otherwise indicated; $\frac{1}{4}$in seam allowances are included.

For skirt ruffle cut a $1\frac{1}{2}$in-wide strip from each selvage edge of fabric (using the selvage in this way dispenses with a hem). For skirt cut a rectangle $12\frac{1}{2}$in $\times 4\frac{3}{4}$in. Cut out two blouse fronts and one blouse back, placing pattern on fold. Cut out two blouse sleeves.

Join short edges of skirt piece for center back seam; press. Turn under $\frac{1}{4}$in along top edge to form casing for elastic, leaving an opening for insertion. Join the two ruffle pieces to make a circle. Run a gathering thread along one long edge of ruffle. Pull up the gathers until the ruffle fits lower edge of skirt. Distribute the gathers evenly, pin, and stitch ruffle to skirt. Cover raw edges with bias binding. Insert elastic in waist casing and pull up to fit doll's waist; fasten off securely.

Join the center front seam of blouse as far as notch marked on pattern. Turn in and hem edges above notch for front neck opening. Stitch sleeves between armhole seams of front and back. Clip seam allowances and press.

Run a line of gathering stitches all around neckline. Pull up gathers until neck measures about 7in or to fit neck of doll. Distribute gathers evenly and bind neck with bias binding, leaving 6in at each end for ties. Stitch sleeve and side seams. Turn up and stitch hem of blouse and both wrist edges, making casings for elastic at wrists. Insert the elastic and fasten.

Duffle coat

Using graph paper, draw each pattern piece to scale and cut out.

Stitch all seams with right sides facing unless otherwise indicated; $\frac{1}{4}$in seam allowances are included, but no hems are needed.

From felt cut out two fronts, one back (placing pattern on fold), one hood (placing pattern on fold), two sleeves, two pockets, and two toggle tabs.

2. *Smart separates in printed cotton with contrasting trimming.*
3. *Snug duffle coat and boots.*

Stitch pockets to fronts in positions shown on pattern.

Stitch sleeves to armholes between front and back pieces. Stitch sleeve and underarm seams. Stitch seamline on top of hood, then, matching centers, stitch hood to neckline of coat. Stitch toggle tabs to right front so that half the tab overlaps the coat opening. Make a small slit in the overlap to form buttonhole. Sew on toggles.

Boots

Using graph paper, draw pattern pieces to scale and cut out.

Cut out two boot tops, placing pattern on fold of vinyl. Cut two soles from black felt. Cut two smaller soles from cardboard.

Placing right sides together and taking $\frac{1}{4}$in seam, stitch the seam in each boot top. If you have a wedge-point machine needle, use this; otherwise sew by hand with a leather or darning needle.

Using fabric glue, attach each cardboard sole to felt sole, clearing the seam allowance all around. Allow to dry.

Placing right sides together, stitch soles to tops. Turn right side out.

Robe

Using graph paper, draw each pattern piece to scale and cut out.

Stitch all seams with right sides facing unless otherwise indicated; $\frac{1}{4}$in seam allowances are included.

From quilted fabric cut out two fronts, one back (placing pattern on fold of fabric), two sleeves, and one collar.

Join shoulder seams. Pin and stitch tops of sleeves into armholes.

Turn under and stitch a $\frac{1}{4}$in hem on curved edge of collar. Pin and stitch collar to neck opening, matching center backs and ends of collar to notches on fronts. Overcast seam allowances together so that collar stands up.

Stitch side and sleeve seams.

Turn under front facings and hem in place. Turn up and stitch hems on sleeves and lower edge.

Sew buttons to right side of robe and sew snaps underneath.

Nightgown

Using graph paper, draw each pattern piece to scale and cut out.

Stitch all seams with right sides

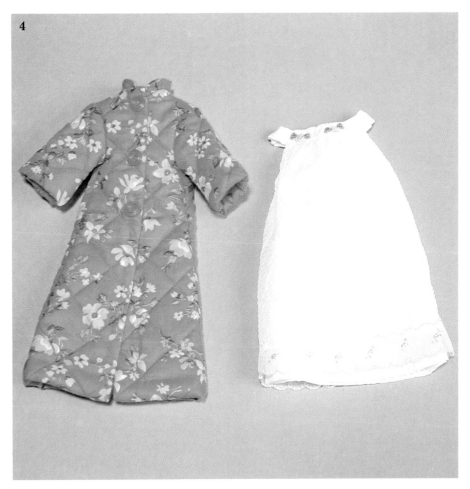

facing; $\frac{1}{4}$in seam allowances are included. Note that the nightgown is made up of two layers.

From seersucker cut out four front and back pieces. Cut four yoke pieces.

Stitch side seams of two front and back pieces. Repeat to make second layer.

Join one shoulder seam of one yoke. Repeat on other yoke.

Slip one layer of gown inside the other, wrong sides facing. Repeat on yoke.

Run a line of gathering stitches along top neck edge of front and back of nightgown. Pull up gathers until they fit between notches on front and back yoke.

Turn in seam allowance all around front and back yoke edges and baste. Sandwich back and front of nightgown in between layers of yoke and slipstitch in place. Slipstitch remaining yoke edges together. Turn in seam allowances on front and back armhole edges and slipstitch together in the same way.

Turn up separate $\frac{3}{8}$in hems on both layers of nightgown and stitch.

4. *Luxurious quilted robe and a pretty nightgown to go with it.*

Stitch trimming to upper layer around hemline. Sew rosebud trims to yoke and fasten shoulders.

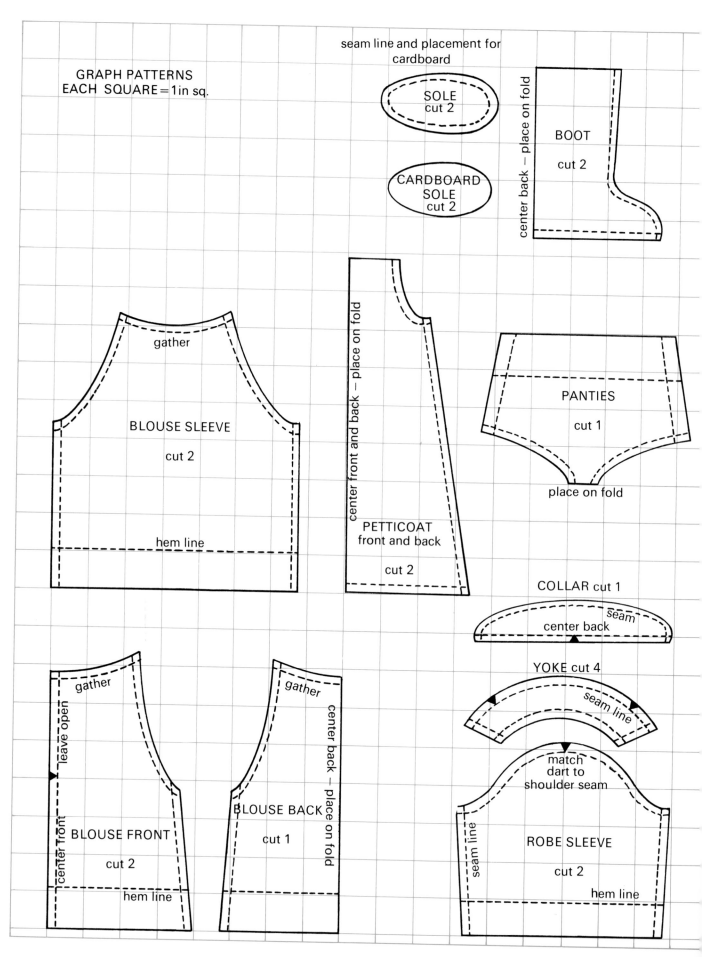

GRAPH PATTERNS
EACH SQUARE = 1 in sq.

seam line and placement for cardboard

SOLE
cut 2

CARDBOARD
SOLE
cut 2

center back – place on fold

BOOT
cut 2

gather

BLOUSE SLEEVE
cut 2

hem line

center front and back – place on fold

PETTICOAT
front and back
cut 2

PANTIES
cut 1

place on fold

COLLAR cut 1
seam
center back

YOKE cut 4
seam line

gather

leave open

center front

BLOUSE FRONT
cut 2

hem line

gather

center back – place on fold

BLOUSE BACK
cut 1

match
dart to
shoulder seam

seam line

ROBE SLEEVE
cut 2

hem line

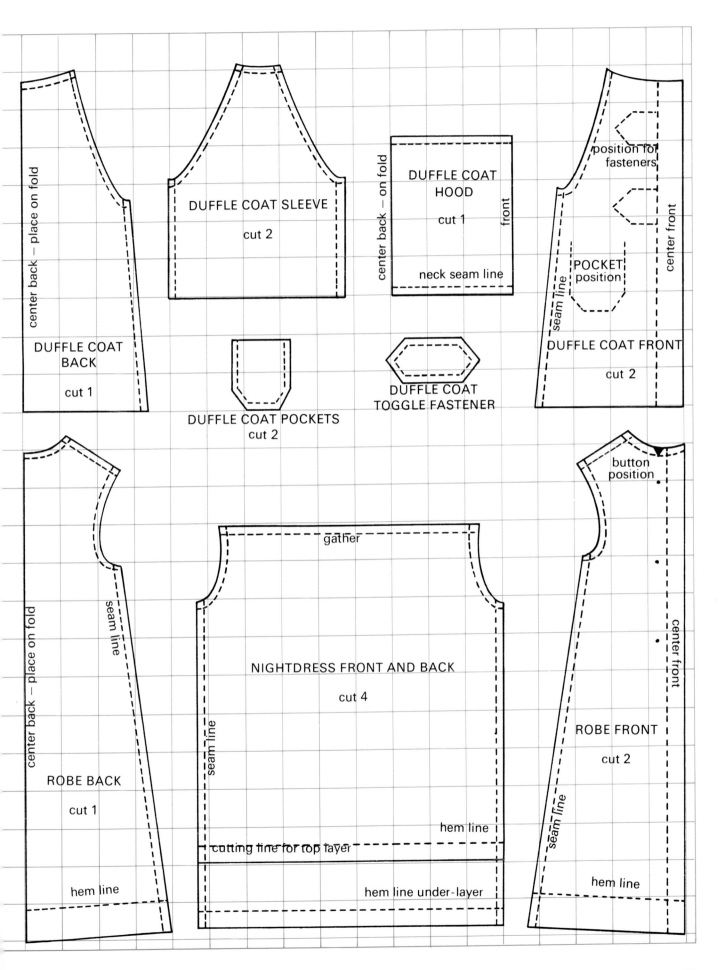

center back – place on fold

DUFFLE COAT
BACK

cut 1

DUFFLE COAT SLEEVE

cut 2

center back – on fold

DUFFLE COAT
HOOD

cut 1

front

neck seam line

position for
fasteners

seam line

POCKET
position

center front

DUFFLE COAT FRONT

cut 2

DUFFLE COAT POCKETS
cut 2

DUFFLE COAT
TOGGLE FASTENER

center back – place on fold

seam line

ROBE BACK

cut 1

hem line

gather

seam line

NIGHTDRESS FRONT AND BACK

cut 4

cutting line for top layer

hem line

hem line under-layer

button
position

center front

ROBE FRONT

cut 2

seam line

hem line

Traditional teddy bear

Every child should have a teddy bear—and many adults have one too! This cuddly companion is made from fur fabric; a "growler" gives him extra personality.

Finished size
23½in (height).

Techniques involved
Basic sewing; stuffing; embroidery stitches.

Tools required
Basic sewing tools; round-nosed pliers.

Materials
tracing paper
1⅛yd of 48in-wide medium-brown fur fabric
piece of leather 13½in × 4in
four 1in joints*
one 1¼in joint*
one pair of ⅝in-diameter brown safety eyes*
one "growler"*
6in square of lightweight fabric to hold growler
black stranded embroidery floss
suitable stuffing
sewing thread
pin
*available from mail order catalog. For address see page 232.

To make the bear
Using tracing paper and a sharp pencil, trace pattern pieces given. (A seam allowance of ⅜in is included.) Cut out each piece.

Cut out all pieces in the appropriate fabrics as instructed, and transfer markings.

Place the head gusset between the two head pieces with right sides together, positioning it between the nose and the back of the neck, matching points A and B. Pin, baste, and stitch both seams (fig. 1). Pin, baste, and stitch head together from point of nose (A) to neck edge (fig. 2).

Run a gathering thread around neck edge (fig. 3). Turn head right side out.

Insert safety eyes into head. Find the most appealing position and fix in place permanently.

Stuff head firmly.

For the neck joint, use the larger joint. Insert one disk with cotter pin and washer inside neck opening of stuffed head (fig. 4). Put second washer of joint to one side. Pack stuffing all around the disk so that the disk cannot be felt from the outside. Pull up the gathering thread around the neck and secure it firmly.

Using all six strands of the black embroidery floss, embroider nose in satin stitch and mouth in backstitch. Position V-shaped nose at point A (fig. 5).

Place two ear pieces together with right sides facing. Pin, baste, and stitch around curved edge, leaving lower edge open (fig. 6). Turn ear right side out.

Turn in lower edges of ear. Pin, baste, and run a line of gathering around lower edge (fig. 7). Pull gathering thread up tight and fasten off. Complete second ear in the same way.

Pin ears on the head in the best position. Baste and stitch firmly in place.

Place two body pieces together with right sides facing. Pin, baste, and stitch around body from one side of neck to the other side of the neck, leaving a 3in opening in the bottom (fig. 8). Turn body right side out.

Turn in neck edge of body. Pin, baste, and run a line of gathering stitches around neck. Pull up gathering thread and fasten off.

Insert cotter pin of head joint through the hole formed by the gathering at the top of the body. Push on the second disk and washer from the inside of the body. Turn the body upside-down and place it on head. Using round-nosed pliers, bend cotter pin so that the head is held securely. Put head and body aside.

Match straight edge of one leather paw to straight edge of one inner arm, right sides together. Pin, baste, and stitch in place (fig. 9).

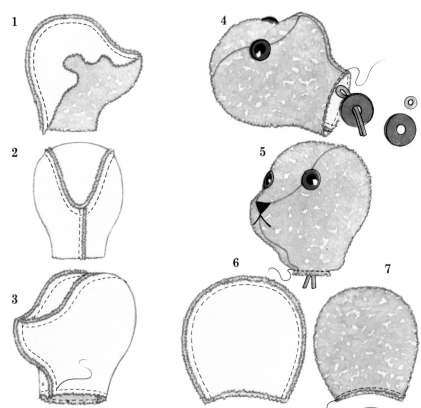

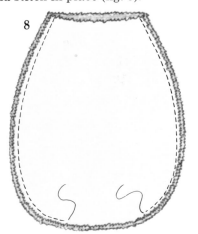

1. *Head gusset stitched to one side of head.*
2. *All head pieces stitched together.*
3. *Gathering stitches around neck.*
4. *Inserting disk and cotter pin in neck.*
5. *Features attached and embroidered on face.*
6. *Ear pieces stitched together.*
7. *Gathering stitches on lower edge of ear.*
8. *Body pieces stitched together.*

71

Match inner arm to outer arm with right sides together. Pin, baste, and stitch all around, leaving a 3in opening at shoulder end (fig. 10). Turn arm right side out. Stuff to within 1¼in of top.

Using one of the smaller joints, push one disk and cotter pin through the inner arm at position marked. Finish stuffing the arm firmly, keeping top part fairly flat. Turn in open edges and slipstitch together to close. Complete second arm in the same way.

Place two leg pieces together with right sides facing. Pin, baste, and stitch around leg from heel to front of toe, leaving a 3in opening in the top and leaving the base of the foot open (fig. 11).

Place a leather sole in base opening of the leg. Pin, baste, and stitch the sole in place (fig. 12). Turn leg right side out. Fill the leg to within 1¼in of top.

Fix half of a joint in leg at position marked. Finish stuffing leg and close opening as for arm. Complete second leg in the same way.

Push the cotter pins of both arms through marked positions on body. Add second disks and washers and secure as for head.

Stuff the upper body firmly, especially around the neck, so that the joint disk in the neck cannot be felt from the outside.

To make a small bag to hold the growler in place inside the body, fold 6in square of lightweight fabric in half. Pin and stitch short edges (fig. 13). Turn right side out. Slip growler inside bag; turn in remaining edges and slipstitch together.

Place the bag containing the growler inside the body, with the holes of the growler against the center back seam. Sew the fabric bag to the center back seam of the bear to anchor the growler. Pack stuffing firmly around the growler, so that it will stay in place.

Fasten the legs to body in the same way as for arms.

Finish stuffing the bear firmly. Turn in opening edges in the base of the bear's body and slipstitch edges together.

Using all six strands of the black embroidery floss, embroider four claws in stem stitch on each of the four paws, stitching the claws at the ends halfway over the edges of the

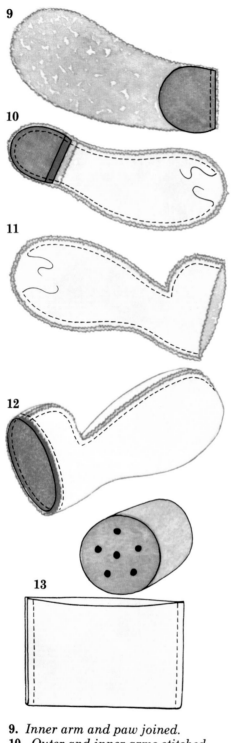

9. Inner arm and paw joined.
10. Outer and inner arms stitched together.
11. Leg pieces stitched together.
12. Sole stitched to leg.
13. Bag for growler.

leather pads (see main photograph).

Using the blunt end of a pin, pull out any fur pile that has been caught when stitching the seams to cover the seamlines. Give the teddy a good brushing to raise pile, and tie a ribbon around his neck.

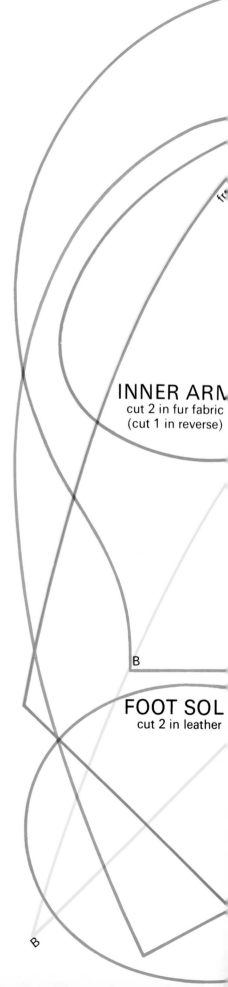

INNER ARM
cut 2 in fur fabric
(cut 1 in reverse)

B

FOOT SOL
cut 2 in leather

B

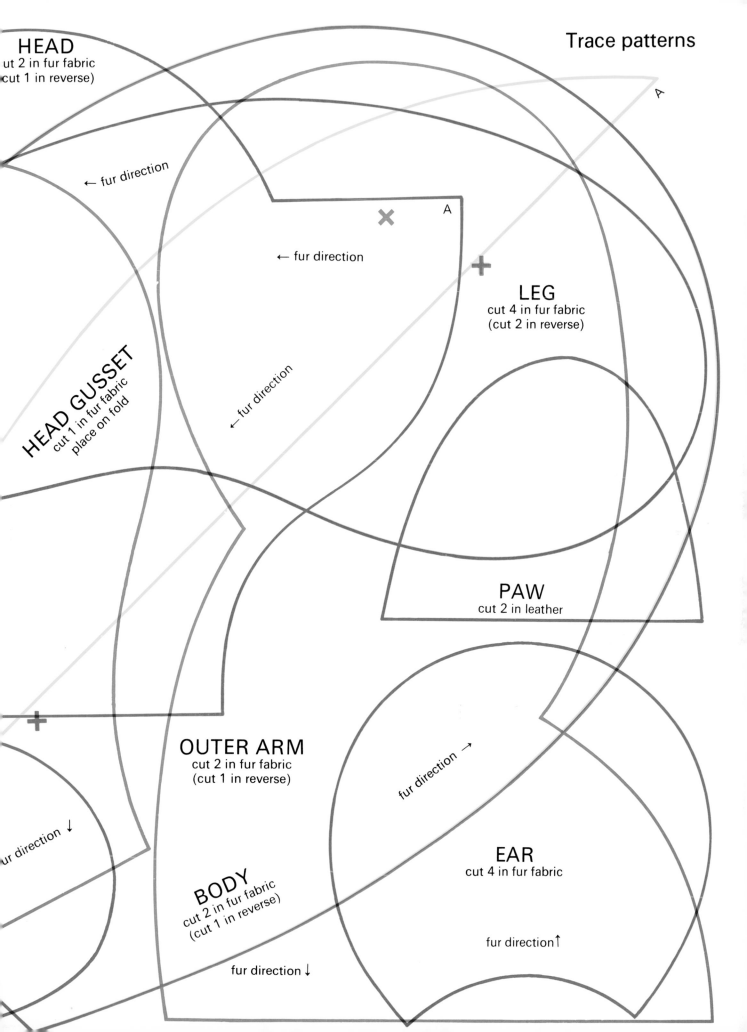

Trace patterns

HEAD
cut 2 in fur fabric
(cut 1 in reverse)

← fur direction

← fur direction

✗

A

← fur direction

LEG
cut 4 in fur fabric
(cut 2 in reverse)

+

HEAD GUSSET
cut 1 in fur fabric
place on fold

A

PAW
cut 2 in leather

+

OUTER ARM
cut 2 in fur fabric
(cut 1 in reverse)

fur direction →

EAR
cut 4 in fur fabric

ur direction ↓

BODY
cut 2 in fur fabric
(cut 1 in reverse)

fur direction ↑

fur direction ↓

Patchwork animals

These delightful patchwork toys can be made for next to nothing from scraps of fabric. Whether they are sewn by hand or by machine, they are quick and simple to run up. Instructions are given for a dog, cat, horse, and doll.

Finished sizes
Dog: 39½in (height); cat: 36in (height); horse: 44in (length); doll: 44in (height).

Techniques involved
Basic sewing; enlarging patterns from a graph; hand- or machine-sewn patchwork fabric made up as described in the know-how section; stuffing; embroidery stitches.

Tools required
Basic sewing tools.

Materials
graph paper with 1in squares
scraps of assorted plain and patterned, brightly colored fabrics of equal weight
synthetic stuffing
sewing thread
embroidery thread
knitting yarn for horse's mane and doll's hair
scraps of colored felt for doll's hands and boots
scraps of colored felt for features
fabric glue

Making the patterns
Draw enlarged paper patterns for the toys from the graph patterns given. A seam allowance of ⅜in is included.

The dog
Using the paper patterns and following the graph pattern given, cut two head pieces from plain fabric. Cut two pieces each for cheeks, eyes, irises, and tail, using patterned fabric.

Cut eight foot pieces and four ear pieces from patterned fabric.

For the body, make up two pieces of patchwork in squares and rectangles to measure $27\frac{1}{2}in \times 10\frac{3}{4}in$ plus ⅜in seam allowance all around.

Place each head piece at the short end of each patchwork body piece, right sides facing, and sew together along the edge.

Place one completed head and body section over the other, right sides facing, and stitch around the edges, leaving the tail end open for stuffing.

Turn right side out and stuff head and body firmly.

Turn in seam allowance of opening and slipstitch edges together.

Stitch the two tail pieces together, right sides facing, leaving the body end of the tail open. Turn right side out and stuff.

Stitch the foot pieces together in pairs, right sides facing, leaving the top ends open. Turn each foot piece right side out and stuff.

Turning in the seam allowance as you work, overcast tail and feet to body in positions shown in fig. 1.

Stitch each pair of ears together, right sides facing, leaving an opening for turning.

Turn right side out. Fold in the raw edges at the opening. Topstitch around the edges and hand-sew ears to body (fig. 1).

Sew or glue eye pieces and cheeks to face.

Embroider mouth and eyelashes.

The cat
Using the paper patterns and following the graph pattern given, cut two head pieces from plain fabric.

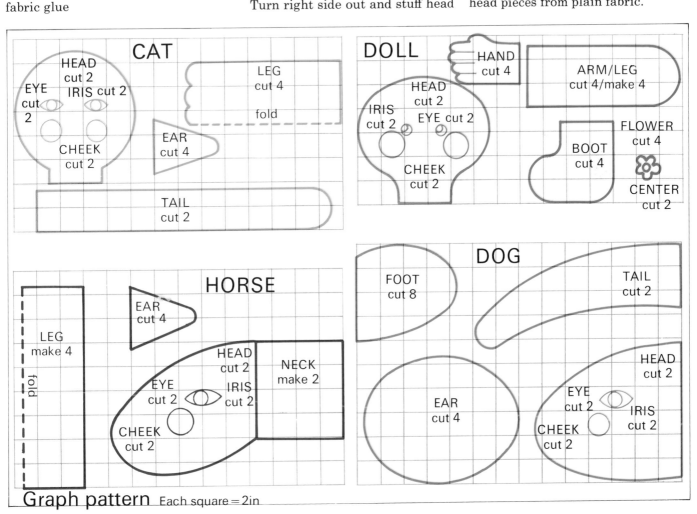

Graph pattern Each square = 2in

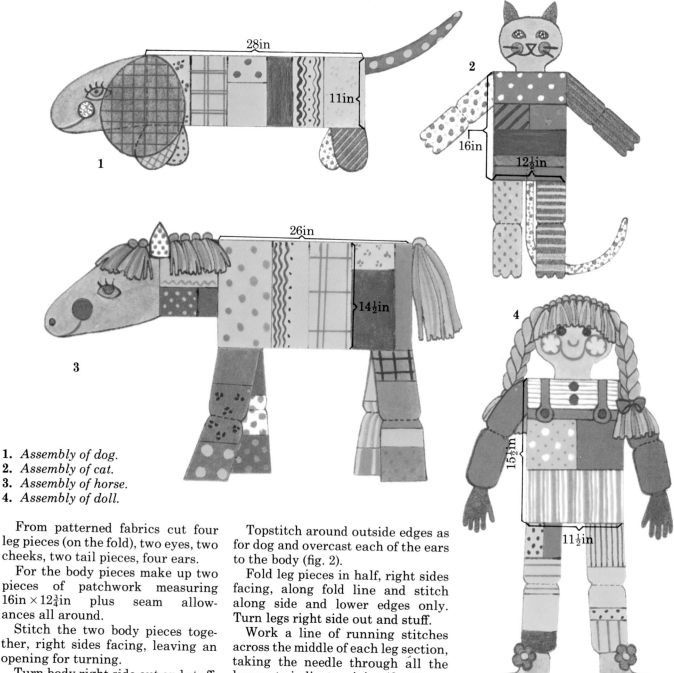

28in

11in

1

2

16in

12½in

26in

14½in

3

15½in

11½in

4

1. *Assembly of dog.*
2. *Assembly of cat.*
3. *Assembly of horse.*
4. *Assembly of doll.*

From patterned fabrics cut four leg pieces (on the fold), two eyes, two cheeks, two tail pieces, four ears.

For the body pieces make up two pieces of patchwork measuring 16in × 12¾in plus seam allowances all around.

Stitch the two body pieces together, right sides facing, leaving an opening for turning.

Turn body right side out and stuff.

Turn in raw edges and slipstitch opening.

Stitch tail pieces together, right sides facing, leaving an opening for turning. Turn tail right side out and stuff.

Folding in raw edges as you work, sew tail to back body piece in position shown in fig. 2.

Stitch the two head pieces together, right sides facing, leaving the neck edge open. Turn head right side out and stuff.

Stitch each pair of ears together, right sides facing, leaving the base edges open. Turn ears right side out.

Topstitch around outside edges as for dog and overcast each of the ears to the body (fig. 2).

Fold leg pieces in half, right sides facing, along fold line and stitch along side and lower edges only. Turn legs right side out and stuff.

Work a line of running stitches across the middle of each leg section, taking the needle through all the layers, to indicate a joint (fig. 2).

Folding in raw edges as you work, overcast legs to body in positions shown in fig. 2.

Sew or glue the eye pieces and cheeks to the face.

Embroider nose and mouth.

Sew or glue narrow strips of fabric to the face to suggest whiskers.

The horse

Using the paper patterns and following the graph pattern, cut two head pieces from plain fabric. Cut four ear pieces from patterned fabric.

Cut two eyes, two irises, and two cheeks from felt.

For the body, make up two pieces of patchwork 26in × 14½in plus seam allowance.

Following the appropriate pattern pieces, make up four leg pieces and two neck pieces from patchwork.

Join each head piece to one neck piece, right sides facing; similarly join the base of each neck piece to one body piece.

Sew the two complete head and body sections together, right sides facing, leaving an opening for turning.

Turn right side out, stuff, and

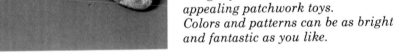

Delight your children with these appealing patchwork toys. Colors and patterns can be as bright and fantastic as you like.

slipstitch opening, folding in raw edges.

Fold each leg piece in half along fold line, right sides facing, and stitch around the edges, leaving top edges open.

Turn legs right side out and stuff.

Work a line of running stitches across middle of legs as for cat.

Turning in the seam allowance, overcast each leg to body in position shown in fig. 3.

Sew each pair of ears together, right sides facing, leaving base edges open. Turn right side out.

Topstitch around edges (folding in seam allowance at opening) and overcast to body.

Make six bundles of 10in lengths of yarn for mane and knot each one in the middle.

Sew mane to horse's head and neck along seam in positions shown in fig. 3.

Make another bundle of yarn, using 28in lengths, for the tail. Knot in the center and sew to body.

Sew or glue the felt eye pieces and cheeks to the face.

Embroider mouth, nostrils, and eyelashes.

The doll

Using the paper patterns and following the graph pattern, cut two head pieces and four arm pieces from plain fabric. Cut four hand pieces, four boot pieces, two eyes, two irises, and two cheeks, four flowers, and two flower centers from felt.

For the body, make up two patchwork rectangles $15\frac{1}{4}$in $\times$ $11\frac{1}{2}$in plus seam allowance. Scraps of fabric can be used ingeniously to represent buttons and suspenders as illustrated.

Following the appropriate pattern pieces, make up four leg pieces in patchwork.

Sew the two body pieces together, right sides facing, leaving an opening for turning. Turn right side out and stuff.

Fold in seam allowance and slipstitch the opening edges together.

Sew or glue features to one head piece and decorate the cheeks with two felt flowers.

Embroider mouth and nose. Make a happy expression by following the design shown (fig. 4).

Stitch the two head pieces together, right sides facing, leaving the neck edge open. Turn right side out and stuff.

Folding in seam allowance, overcast head to body.

Sew the arm pieces together in pairs, right sides facing, leaving the hand edges open.

Turn right side out. Make a line of gathering stitches around each hand edge. Stuff the arms.

Sew the hand sections together, right sides facing. Turn right side out and stuff lightly.

Draw up gathers on arms and sew the hands over them.

Make joints in arm pieces as for cat.

Make the legs as you did the arms, using patchwork leg pieces and felt boots.

Decorate the boots with felt flowers and flower centers.

Sew the arms and legs to the body as shown in fig. 4.

Cut 36in lengths of yarn for the hair and lay them together in a bundle. Sew the center of the bundle to the center back of head. Braid hair and tie with ribbons.

Make bangs, using 10 small bundles of yarn as for horse's mane.

Owl and pussycat

*"... went to sea in a beautiful pea-green boat." These jolly
traveling companions would make a marvelous present for a
child or an adult.*

Finished size
About 12in (height).

Techniques involved
Basic sewing; stuffing; embroidery stitches.

Tools required
Basic sewing tools.

Materials
For owl:
¾yd of 36in-wide brown wide-wale corduroy
piece of brown felt 12in × 16in
piece of white felt 10in × 12in
piece of orange felt 10in × 12in
4in square of black felt
sewing thread
¾yd of 1½in-wide blue checked ribbon
stuffing
tracing paper
dressmaker's carbon paper

For cat:
¾yd of 36in-wide black wide-wale corduroy
piece of white felt 10in × 12in
piece of pink felt 10in × 12in
4in square of green felt
scraps of black felt
sewing thread
one skein of white stranded embroidery floss
¾yd of 1½in-wide green checked ribbon
fine string, 63in long, for whiskers
starch stiffening for whiskers
stuffing
large-eyed needle
tracing paper
dressmaker's carbon paper

Owl

Trace all the pattern pieces and transfer them onto the appropriate fabrics using dressmaker's carbon paper.

Place the body feathers on one body piece. On top of this place the white bib and eye rim pieces. Pin, baste, and stitch around the bib and the eye rims, keeping close to the edge, securing feathering in place at the same time (fig. 1).

Center black eye circles on brown circles; pin and stitch in place. Stitch white cross in place (fig. 2a). Pin eyes to rim section and topstitch close to edge of eyes (fig. 2b). During stitching, pad the eyes to give a slightly raised effect.

Pin and stitch the darts on the two beak pieces, tapering the stitching toward the points to form a ridge on the outside of the beak (fig. 3a). Pin the two beak pieces together and stitch close to edge along sides (fig. 3b). Stuff beak. Pin in position on the face and hand-sew securely.

Place feather strip along lower curved edge of wing on right side of fabric. Pin and baste in place, then place wing pieces together, right sides facing. Stitch along curved edges along seamline (fig. 4a). Turn right side out and topstitch close to seamline (fig. 4b). Stuff and stitch across open end to hold stuffing in place.

Fold two claw pieces in half with right sides outside. Stitch a narrow line along fold, tapering toward the point of the central claw (fig. 5a). Placing wrong sides together, pin these upper claw pieces to the lower pieces. Stitch close to edge around claws, leaving straight edge open. Stuff and stitch along open edge to hold stuffing in place (fig. 5b).

Pin and baste wings in correct position on seamlines as indicated on pattern of front body (fig. 6). Placing right sides together, pin, baste, and stitch the body seamlines together, making sure they meet neatly and accurately at top of body. Similarly, pin and baste the feet in position on the base seamline of the front body piece. Placing right sides together and matching the "corners" of the base with the body seamlines, pin, baste and stitch the base, remembering to leave an opening for turning (fig. 7). Turn right side out and stuff firmly, making sure all the curves, particularly along seams, are well packed and shaped. Hand-sew opening edges together.

Tie a bow, using the checked ribbon, and securely hand-sew it to the bib.

If the corduroy has become flattened, brush up the pile.

1. *Bib and eye rims stitched in place.*
2a. *White cross stitched to black circle.*
2b. *Eyes stitched to eye rims.*
3a. *Darts stitched on beak.*
3b. *Beak pieces stitched together.*
4a. *Feathers basted to wing and wing pieces stitched together.*
4b. *Topstitching around wing.*

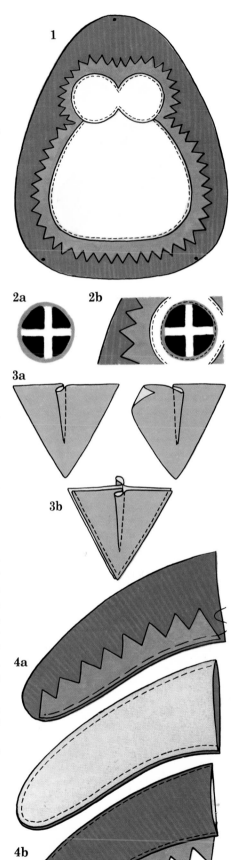

Trace patterns (Owl)

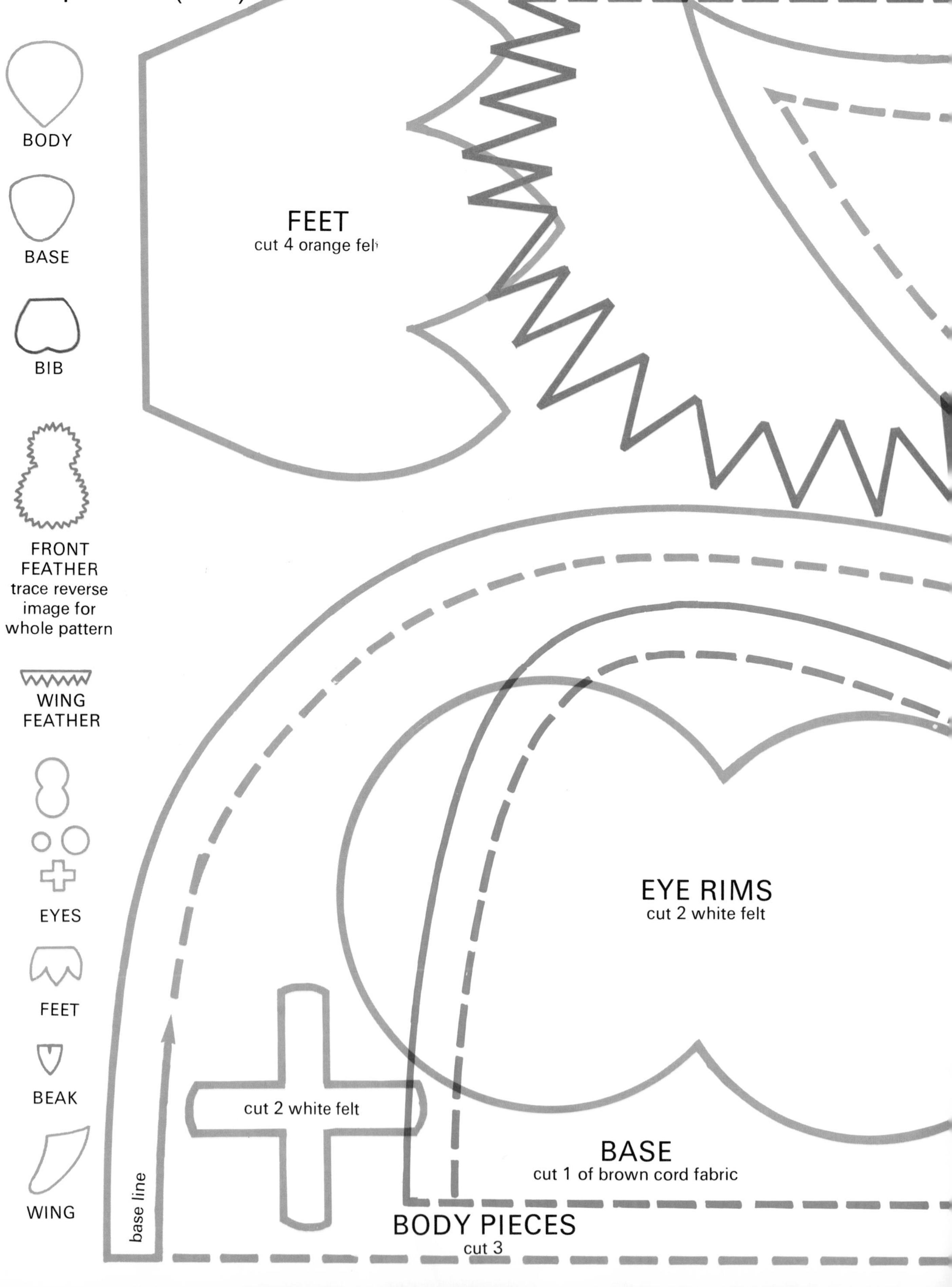

BODY

BASE

BIB

FRONT
FEATHER
trace reverse
image for
whole pattern

WING
FEATHER

EYES

FEET

BEAK

WING

base line

FEET
cut 4 orange felt

EYE RIMS
cut 2 white felt

cut 2 white felt

BASE
cut 1 of brown cord fabric

BODY PIECES
cut 3

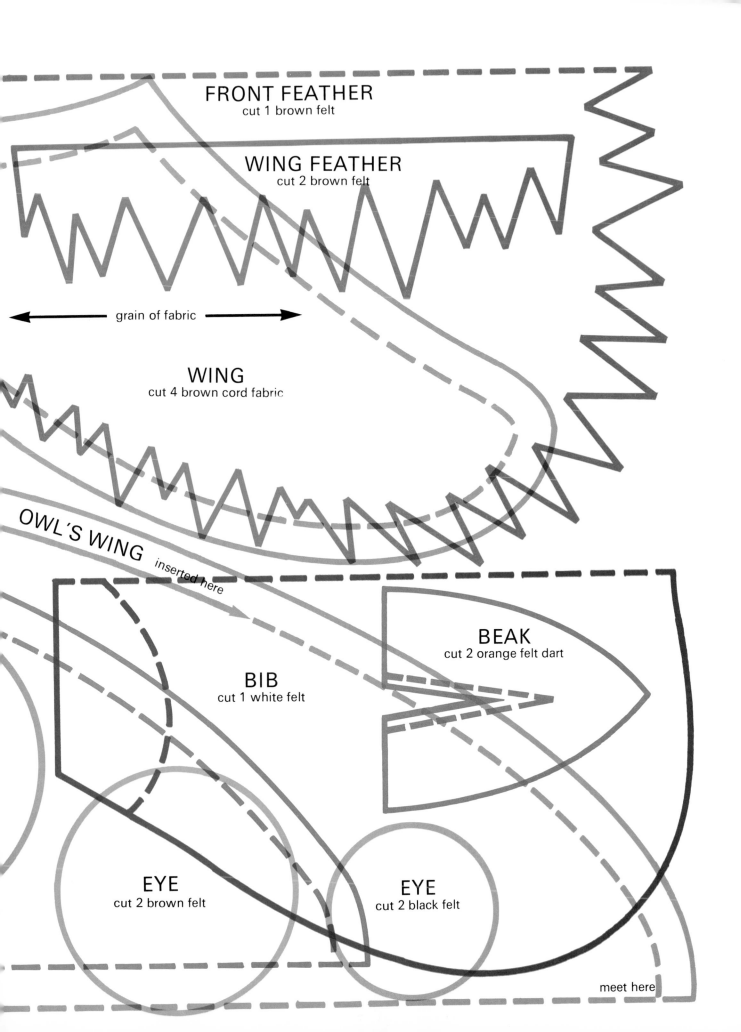

FRONT FEATHER
cut 1 brown felt

WING FEATHER
cut 2 brown felt

← grain of fabric →

WING
cut 4 brown cord fabric

OWL'S WING inserted here

BIB
cut 1 white felt

BEAK
cut 2 orange felt dart

EYE
cut 2 brown felt

EYE
cut 2 black felt

meet here

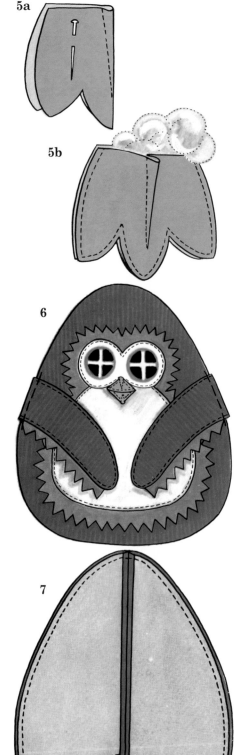

5a. *Dart stitched on claw.*
5b. *Stuffing the joined claw pieces.*
6. *Wings basted to front body piece.*
7. *Base being stitched to body sections.*

Pussycat

Trace all the pattern pieces and transfer them onto the appropriate fabrics using dressmaker's carbon.

Pin and topstitch the white bib in place. Topstitch the two tongue pieces together, keeping close to the edge. Pin this in place on the body as shown (fig. 8). Place the cheeks over the upper edge of the tongue and pad with a bit of stuffing while stitching them in place.

Topstitch the green eye pieces onto the white, and then the black pupils onto the green, placing them in the center. Using white embroidery floss and making four straight stitches, hand-embroider a "twinkle" on the pupil of each eye (fig. 9). Pin and stitch eyes to the body piece.

Placing right sides together, pin and baste one felt and one corduroy ear piece together. Stitch along seamlines, leaving straight edge open. Turn right side out and topstitch along edge, using matching thread. Fold over one edge of each ear and baste along seamline to give shape to ear (fig. 10). Remember to make a right and a left ear.

Placing right sides together, pin and stitch foot pieces together along seamlines, leaving straight edge open (fig. 11a). Turn right side out and stuff. Stitch along opening to hold stuffing in place. With white stranded floss, hand-embroider four straight stitches on each foot to suggest claws (fig. 11b).

Placing right sides together, pin and stitch the straight edge of the white tail tip to the black corduroy strip. Press seam open. Fold tail in half lengthwise and stitch along seamline. Leave short, straight end

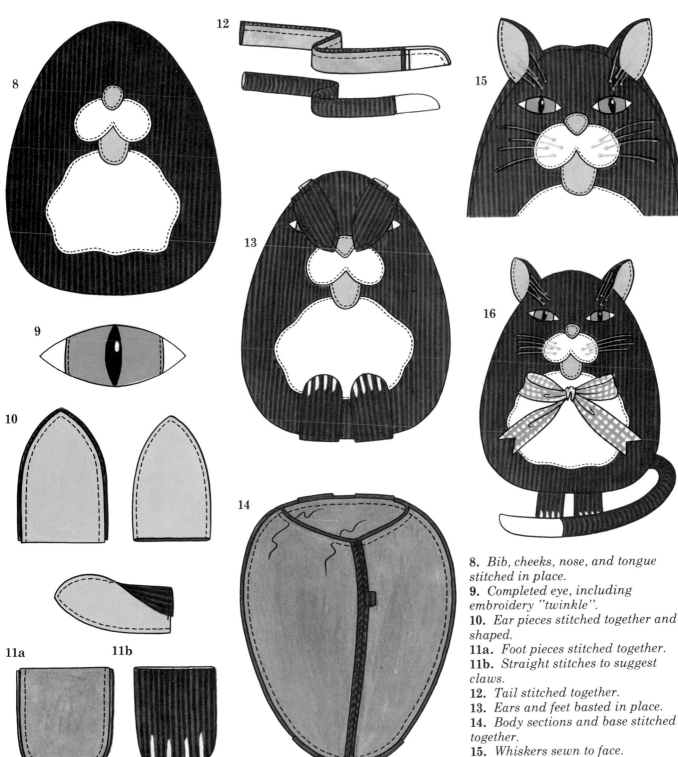

8. Bib, cheeks, nose, and tongue stitched in place.

9. Completed eye, including embroidery "twinkle".

10. Ear pieces stitched together and shaped.

11a. Foot pieces stitched together.

11b. Straight stitches to suggest claws.

12. Tail stitched together.

13. Ears and feet basted in place.

14. Body sections and base stitched together.

15. Whiskers sewn to face.

16. The completed pussycat.

open. Turn right side out and stuff. Stitch across open end to hold stuffing in place (fig. 12).

Pin and baste ears in place on body front. Pin and baste feet in place along base seamline of body front (fig. 13). Placing right sides together, join side seams and back seams, inserting tail at base of back seam. Placing right sides together

and matching the "corners" of the base with the body seamlines, pin, baste, and stitch the base to the body section. Remember to leave an opening (fig. 14). Turn body right side out.

Coat the string several times with starch until it is reasonably rigid. Cut eight lengths approximately 4in long and eight lengths 8in long. Thread four 4in lengths through

each cheek and four 8in lengths above each eye, using a large-eyed needle. Tie a knot on each side of the fabric to hold the string whiskers in place (fig. 15).

Stuff body firmly and hand-sew opening edges together.

Tie a bow in the checked ribbon and hand-sew it securely in place (fig. 16).

Trace patterns (Cat)

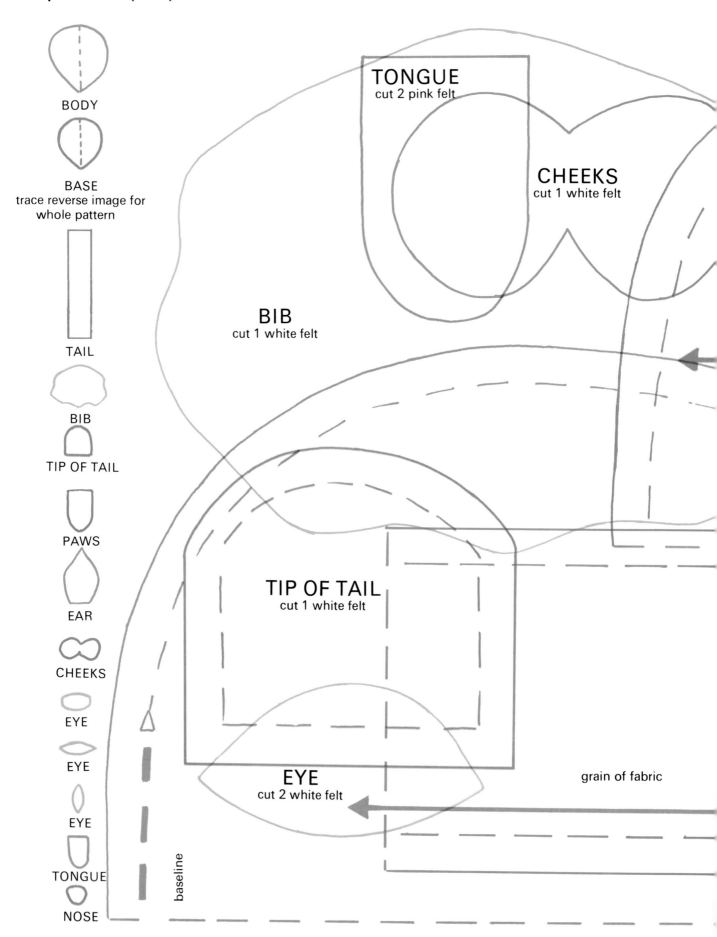

BODY

BASE
trace reverse image for
whole pattern

TAIL

BIB

TIP OF TAIL

PAWS

EAR

CHEEKS

EYE

EYE

EYE

TONGUE

NOSE

baseline

TONGUE
cut 2 pink felt

CHEEKS
cut 1 white felt

BIB
cut 1 white felt

TIP OF TAIL
cut 1 white felt

EYE
cut 2 white felt

grain of fabric

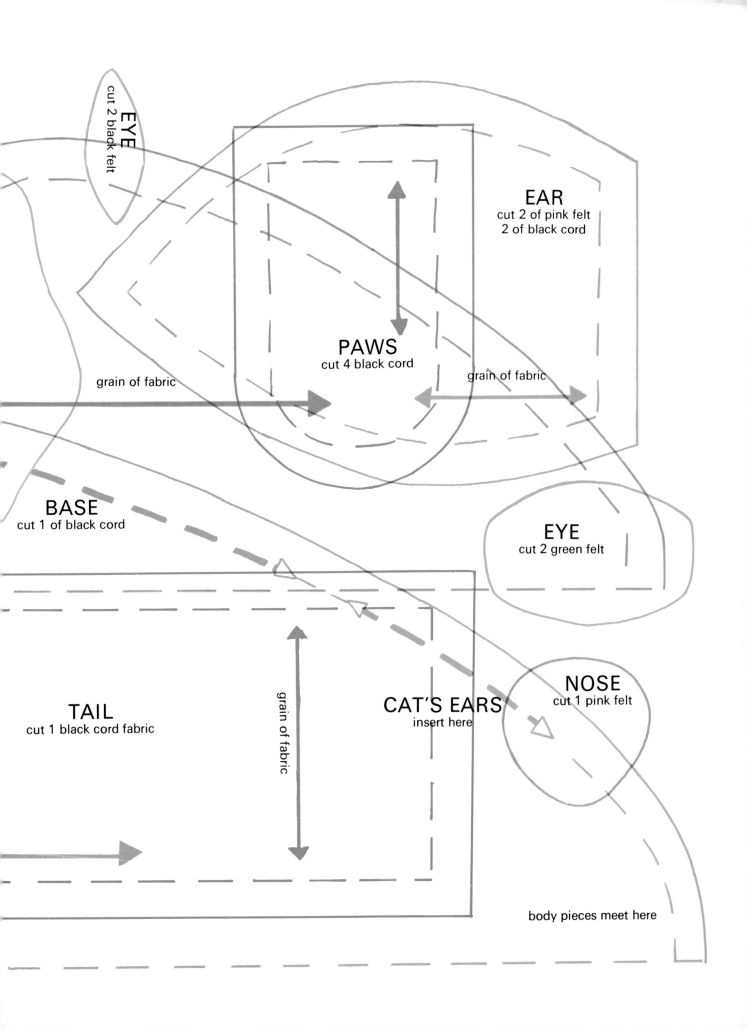

EYE
cut 2 black felt

EAR
cut 2 of pink felt
2 of black cord

PAWS
cut 4 black cord

grain of fabric

grain of fabric

BASE
cut 1 of black cord

EYE
cut 2 green felt

NOSE
cut 1 pink felt

TAIL
cut 1 black cord fabric

grain of fabric

CAT'S EARS
insert here

body pieces meet here

Fabric book

Learning to dress yourself is child's play with the help of this appealing rag book. A bright red felt shoe and a jaunty frog will help your child master zippers and shoe laces; a button-down pocket and snap-on flower petals will also teach and amuse at the same time. Some children take longer than others to learn the skills required for dressing and undressing themselves. This is an excellent and unstressful way of letting them experiment in their own time and at their own pace, free from pressure.

Finished size
Approximately 13¾in × 11¾in.

Techniques involved
Basic sewing.

Tools required
Basic sewing equipment.

Materials
¾yd medium muslin, 36in wide
4in each of 4 contrasting printed
    cotton fabrics, 36in wide
felt—orange, turquoise, pink, red,
    dark green—each 4in square;
    light grass green—11¾in square;
scraps of white and black felt
white sewing thread
black and white stranded cotton
    embroidery thread
6in white zipper
3 medium-sized snap fasteners
1 green button, 1in in diameter
1 white shoelace, 18in long
8 white eyelets and punch
tracing paper
dressmaker's carbon paper

To make the book
First wash the muslin, as this fabric will probably shrink quite a lot. Iron it while it is still damp.

Trace all pattern pieces on the tracing paper. Cut out each piece on the appropriate fabric according to its type. Large, simple shapes can be pinned to the fabric and cut around. Smaller pieces and those with intricate shapes should be drawn on the fabric using dressmaker's carbon paper. Place the carbon between the fabric and the tracing paper, carbon side toward fabric and firmly trace the outline. Cut out the shapes.

Cut the muslin into 6 pieces, each of them measuring approximately 13¾in × 11¾in. In the center of each piece of muslin measure and draw a rectangle 11¼in × 8⅝in, which represents the finished size of each page (fig. 1). Baste along this outline.

Cover page
Place the letters, flower pieces, and leaf stem in position within the basted lines on one of the muslin pages. When you are satisfied that the lettering is well spaced and straight, pin and baste all the pieces in place (fig. 2). Set your sewing machine to a narrow zigzag stitch, and—using white thread—work around the edge of all the letters and leaves.

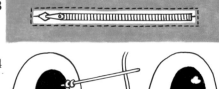

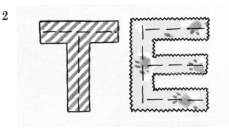

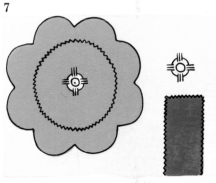

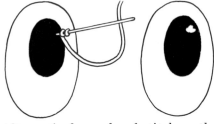

Alternatively, hand-stitch the shapes to the page, using blanket stitch. Make sure the raw edges are covered by the line of stitching, as this not only attaches the pieces to the muslin but also keeps the appliqués from fraying.

Draw all loose ends through to the wrong side and tie securely. Remove all basting threads. Do not, however, remove the basting lines around the pages at this stage.

Page 1—frog and zipper
Pin, baste, and zigzag-stitch the grass in position on a muslin page. Pin and baste the zipper in position under the frog's mouth slit (fig. 3). Using the zipper foot and a straight stitch, carefully machine-stitch all around mouth, close to edges, to secure the zipper in place.

Using six strands of black em-

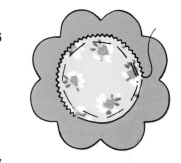

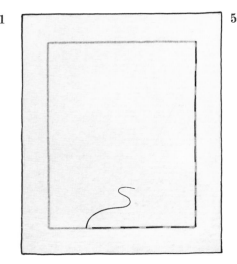

1. *Baste around rectangle.*
2. *Baste letters in place.*
3. *Baste zipper in position.*
4. *Work French knots in eyes.*
5. *Frog positioned on page.*
6. *Stitching centers on flowers.*
7. *Sew on ball part of snap.*

broidery cotton, work two French knots to form the nostrils. Hand stitch the black pupils to the white eye pieces, and then work two French knots in white stranded embroidery cotton to make a "twinkle" in each eye (fig. 4). Pin and baste the eyes in position.

Pin and baste the frog in position on the muslin page and zigzag-stitch around all raw edges. Also stitch around the eyes and around the body shape, using the dashed line on the pattern as a guide. Remove basting threads and tie loose ends (fig. 5).

LETTERS FLOWER PETALS FLOWER CENTER LEAF STEM EYE PUPIL GRASS

FROG

Trace patterns

EYE
cut 2 white felt

PUPIL
cut 2 black felt

FROG
cut 1 light green felt

cut 1 printed cotton

cut 2 printed cotton

cut slit for zipper mouth

cut 1 light green felt

cut 1
printed cotton

line of stitching

FLOWER
PETALS
cut 1 cotton

cut 1
printed cotton

cut 1
printed
cotton

FLOWER
CENTER

cut 1 cotton

GRASS
cut 1 dark green felt

LEAF STEM
cut 1 dark green felt

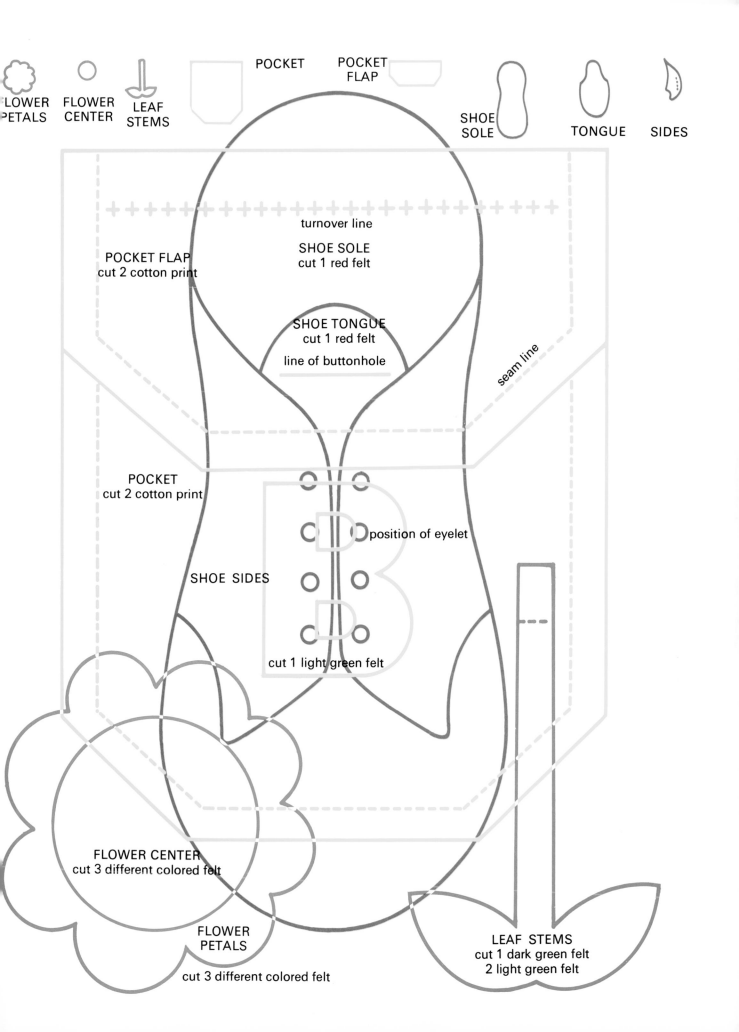

FLOWER PETALS

FLOWER CENTER

LEAF STEMS

POCKET

POCKET FLAP

SHOE SOLE

TONGUE

SIDES

turnover line

POCKET FLAP
cut 2 cotton print

SHOE SOLE
cut 1 red felt

SHOE TONGUE
cut 1 red felt

line of buttonhole

seam line

POCKET
cut 2 cotton print

position of eyelet

SHOE SIDES

cut 1 light green felt

FLOWER CENTER
cut 3 different colored felt

FLOWER
PETALS

cut 3 different colored felt

LEAF STEMS
cut 1 dark green felt
2 light green felt

Page 2—flowers and snap fasteners

Pin and baste the centers of the flowers in place on the felt shapes. Zigzag stitch around the raw edges of centers and tie ends off (fig. 6).

In the center of the wrong side of each flower, hand-sew ball part of a snap (fig. 7); make sure you do not stitch through to the right side of the flower centers. Arrange the flower heads above each stalk, and lightly mark on the muslin the position of the snaps. Sew the socket parts of the snaps in place. Remove basting threads and tie off loose ends.

Place the leaf stems in position on muslin page as shown (fig. 8). Pin and baste. Zigzag-stitch in place.

Page 3—pocket and button

Pin and baste the two pocket pieces together, right sides facing (fig. 9); repeat for the pocket flap pieces. Machine-stitch along seamlines of pocket and flap, leaving 2in along top edges. Turn both sections right side out through opening.

Press both sections of the pocket with a hot iron. Baste around all the edges, including the 2in gap that was left unstitched.

On the pocket piece pin and baste the letter "B"; zigzag-stitch along edges. On the flap, work a buttonhole—either by machine or by hand—to fit the green button (fig. 10). Straight-stitch around lower and side edges of flap, close to the edge. Add a second line of stitching about $\frac{1}{4}$in inside the first line. Repeat on upper edge of pocket.

Center the pocket on a muslin page; pin and baste. Using straight stitch, machine-sew the pocket in place with two lines of stitching along the sides and base. Place the pocket flap slightly above the pocket and straight-stitch along top of flap with two lines of stitching. Hand-sew the button onto pocket, positioning it directly underneath the buttonhole on the flap (fig. 11).

Page 4—shoe and laces

Straight-stitch around the edge of shoe side pieces, except for outer edges. Also stitch around the upper edge of the tongue, working two lines of stitching close to each other.

If you have an eyelet punch, use it to make four eyelets on each of the side pieces (fig. 12).

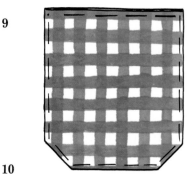

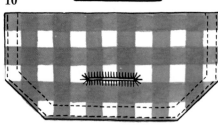

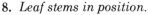

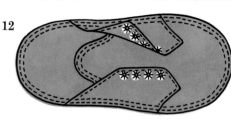

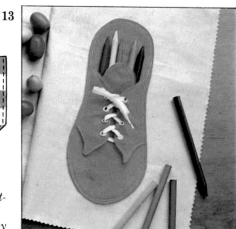

8. *Leaf stems in position.*
9. *Pin and baste pocket pieces together, right sides facing.*
10. *Work a buttonhole on the flap by hand or machine.*
11. *Sew the button onto the pocket directly under the buttonhole.*
12. *Make four eyelet holes along both sides of the side pieces.*
13. *Thread the shoelace through the eyelets and tie a bow.*
14. *When pages are assembled trim the completed book with pinking shears.*

Pin pieces of shoe to sole, then position shoe on muslin page; pin, baste, and straight-stitch a double line around the shoe edge. Thread shoelace through eyelets (fig. 13).

Press each page on the wrong side. Pin and baste the cover page and page 1 together. Similarly, join pages 2 and 3, page 4 and the blank page. Remember to match up the original basted lines; these rep-resent the page edges. Straight-stitch inside the new basting lines, $\frac{1}{4}$in from the original basting line around each page. Trim away excess muslin using pinking shears (fig. 14).

Put the basted pages on top of one another in the correct order. Pin them along the left side and then straight-stitch close to the edge several times in the same place to hold the pages together securely. Remove all basting threads.

Hobby horse

All kinds of adventures are possible with a dashing hobby horse. You can make one for your child with only a few inexpensive materials and simple techniques.

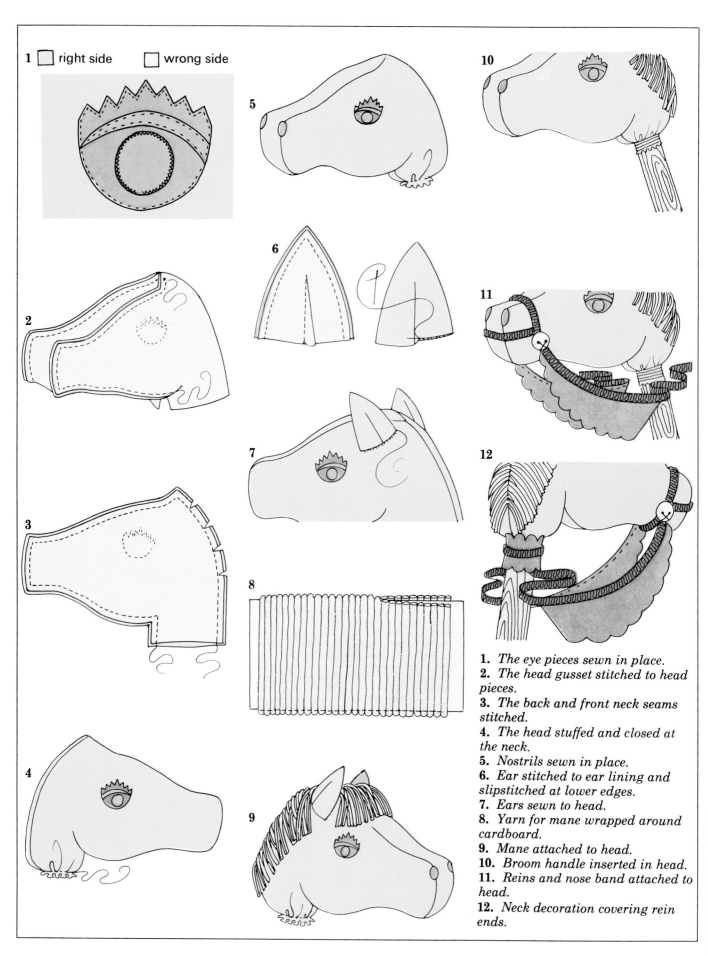

1. right side / wrong side

1. *The eye pieces sewn in place.*
2. *The head gusset stitched to head pieces.*
3. *The back and front neck seams stitched.*
4. *The head stuffed and closed at the neck.*
5. *Nostrils sewn in place.*
6. *Ear stitched to ear lining and slipstitched at lower edges.*
7. *Ears sewn to head.*
8. *Yarn for mane wrapped around cardboard.*
9. *Mane attached to head.*
10. *Broom handle inserted in head.*
11. *Reins and nose band attached to head.*
12. *Neck decoration covering rein ends.*

Finished size
Approximately 4½ft (length).

Techniques involved
Basic sewing; enlarging a design; stuffing.

Tools required
Basic sewing tools.

Materials
¾yd of 36in-wide fabric
graph paper with 1in squares
sewing thread
1oz of knitting worsted for mane
6in square of yellow felt
two 10in squares of brown felt
2yd of decorative braid for reins
2 small jingle bells
1lb of synthetic stuffing
broom handle 1in in diameter
strong all-purpose glue
piece of cardboard 4in × 8in
yarn needle

Head

Using graph paper, enlarge the ear, head, gusset, rein decoration, and neck decoration pieces from the patterns given. A ⅝in seam allowance is included.

Mark dots, lines, and positions for eyes. Trace the pattern for the eye, eyelid, pupil, and nostril (from pupil). Cut out pattern pieces.

Fold the fabric in half with the selvages together and pin the three main pattern pieces to it, placing gusset on fold and making sure all grain lines follow the straight grain of the fabric. Cut out the pieces.

From yellow felt cut out the ear piece twice and the eyelid and pupil twice. From brown felt cut out the neck decoration once, the rein decoration twice, the nostril piece twice, and the eye piece twice.

Transfer all markings from the pattern pieces to the fabric.

Baste and topstitch the yellow eyelid to the brown eye piece where indicated. Using a small zigzag stitch or close blanket stitch, sew the yellow pupil to the brown eye piece where marked. Catch-stitch eyes to head pieces in the positions indicated (fig. 1).

Placing right sides together and matching dots, baste and stitch the gusset to the head pieces, easing carefully on curves (fig. 2).

Baste and stitch the back neck seam and the front neck seam from the point of gusset to the neck edge (fig. 3). Fasten off securely. Trim seams, clip curves, and turn right side out. Run a gathering thread around neck ¼in from the edge.

Stuff head carefully, making sure it is firmly and evenly packed. Pull up gathers around neck and secure to prevent stuffing from escaping (fig. 4).

Catch-stitch nostrils to the front of nose, positioning them on upper curve (fig. 5).

Placing right sides together, baste and stitch the darts on outer ear and yellow felt ear linings. Press darts to one side. Placing right sides together, baste and stitch ears to ear linings on the seamline. Make a small hem on the bottom edge of each ear, turn right side out and slipstitch folded edges together (fig. 6).

Place an ear on each side of the head close to the gusset seam. Sew firmly in place, making sure that the ears are upright (fig. 7).

Wind the yarn evenly around the cardboard. Using matching thread, backstitch through yarn at one edge of cardboard to hold the strands together. Cut through the loops on the other edge (fig. 8). Place the mane over the back neck seam, starting from behind the ears. Using a length of same yarn, sew mane in place, covering the backstitches.

Cut 1in off cardboard to make it 3in wide and make a short mane in the same way. Sew it to the head between the ears, just where the long mane ends. Fold the mane forward between the ears (fig. 9).

Carefully open the neck gathers and push the broom handle as far as possible into the head. Pack stuffing around the broom handle and pull up the gathering thread. Glue the neck seam allowance to the broom handle with strong glue and bind the head to the handle by winding it with several strands of thread—preferably heavy-duty or button thread (fig. 10).

Cut the braid into three lengths: one piece for neck decoration, 4in long; one piece for the nose band, 16½in long; and the remainder for the reins.

Find the center of the long piece of braid and mark a point 5½in to each side of this point. Starting at these points, baste the braid over the rein decorations, along the straight edge. Topstitch in place.

Pin braid for nose band over horse's nose and join the ends under the chin. Pin reins to head with center of rein in center of mouth. Sew the reins to the nose band where they cross and attach bells (fig. 11).

Baste and stitch braid to the neck decoration. Glue the ends of the reins to the neck and cover these by gluing the neck decoration over all raw edges. Neatly sew the two ends together (fig. 12).

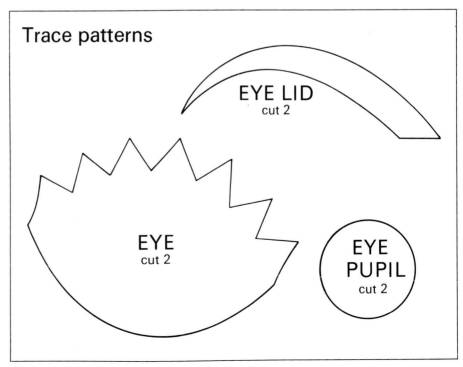

Trace patterns

EYE LID
cut 2

EYE
cut 2

EYE
PUPIL
cut 2

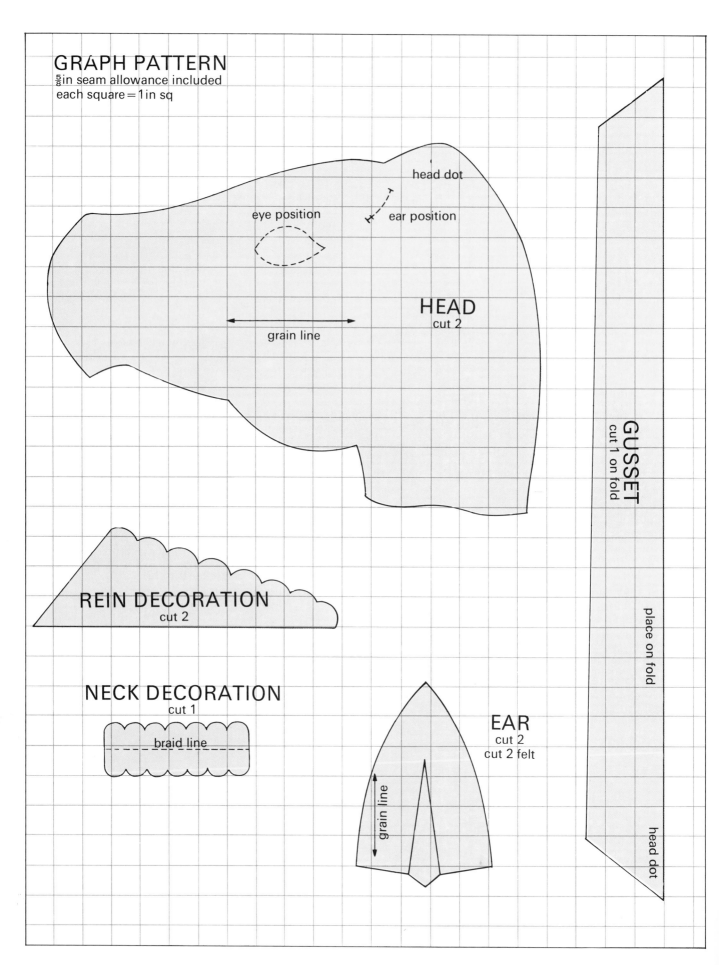

GRAPH PATTERN
5/8 in seam allowance included
each square = 1 in sq

head dot

eye position

ear position

HEAD
cut 2

grain line

GUSSET
cut 1 on fold

place on fold

head dot

REIN DECORATION
cut 2

NECK DECORATION
cut 1

braid line

EAR
cut 2
cut 2 felt

grain line

Tepee

The tepee was the home of the Plains Indians—well-suited to their nomadic way of life. It was made from the skins of the buffalo, on which they depended for food and clothing also. The tepee shown here can be made of canvas, sailcloth, or other strong fabric and makes an authentic-looking setting for games of cowboys and Indians.

Finished size
Approximately 5ft (height).

Techniques involved
Basic sewing.

Tools required
Basic sewing tools; yardstick;
hammer.

Materials
11yd of 54in-wide sturdy cotton
   fabric; or 13yd of 48in fabric
7yd of woven tape for binding edges
5yd of 1in-wide masking tape
strong sewing thread
felt-tip marker or tailor's chalk
33 large grommets as used for tents
   (optional)
strong cord
string, chalk, and thumbtack
2 12in wooden stakes
11 bamboo poles 10ft long
1 bamboo pole 2½ft long
7 wooden pins 12in long, made from
   ¼in dowelling
25 tent pegs

Making the tepee cover

Cut and stitch the fabric together to
form a piece 14ft long and 8½ft wide.
It does not matter where the seams
lie, but it is important to use flat fell
seams in order to make them strong
and neat.

Divide the fabric crosswise into
three 56in sections, marking them
off with tailor's chalk or marking
pen. Cut a 16in slit at one end of both
dividing lines (fig. 1). Bind the outer
raw edges of the slits (fig. 2).

On the outer pieces turn up a
double hem, 8in deep, on the right
side, and machine-stitch along both
edges close to the folds.

Keeping your material on a flat
surface, and working on the wrong
side, fix a thumbtack at point A—the
center point of the length of the
fabric even with the lower edge of
the two outer panels (fig. 3). Tie a
length of string to the tack and tie
the string around a piece of chalk, so
that string between chalk and tack
measures 84in. Then draw a semicircle beginning and ending at the
hemmed corners of the outer sections (fig. 3).

Fix the tack 20in from the outside
edge in line with A, adjust the length
of the string to 12in, and draw another semicircle. Repeat the process
on the other side. These two semi-

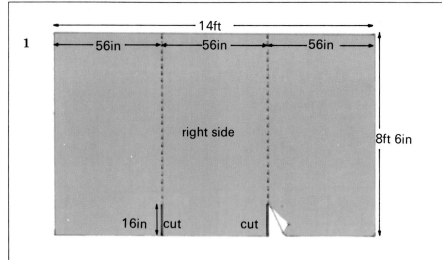

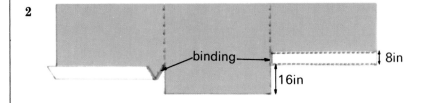

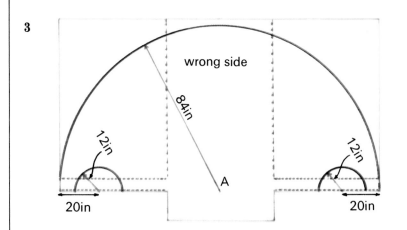

1. *Fabric divided into three sections
and cut partway along dividing
lines.*
2. *Outer edges of slits bound and*
panels hemmed on right side.
3. *Drawing semicircles for lower
edge and front opening using a tack,
string and marking chalk.*

circles will form the front opening.

Turn up a ¾in double hem all along
the curved edge of the tepee and
machine-stitch. Stitch 3in-long loops
of strong tape around this edge at
about 11in intervals (fig. 4a).

On the front hem mark two parallel rows of holes for the wooden pins
that will close the tepee, placing
them about 4in apart. Be careful to
match up holes on each side and to
keep them within lines of stitching.

To make the "wings" at the top of

the tepee, follow the measurements
and draw a freehand shape on the
wrong side of the fabric as shown in
fig. 4. You will find it easier to obtain
a symmetrical shape for the wings if
you fold the fabric in half, right sides
facing, with the center point A lying
along the fold, and cut through both
layers of fabric. The "wings" let in
light but can be closed to keep out
rain. (On real Indian tepees they
also let out smoke.)

Next, mark the holes for the tent

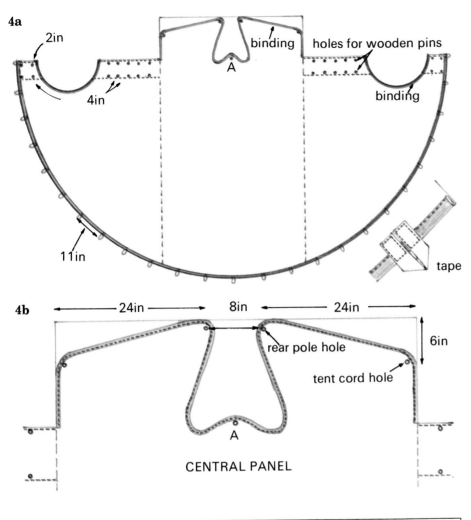

4a

2in

binding · holes for wooden pins

A

binding

4in

11in

binding

tape

4b

← 24in → · 8in · ← 24in →

rear pole hole

6in

tent cord hole

A

CENTRAL PANEL

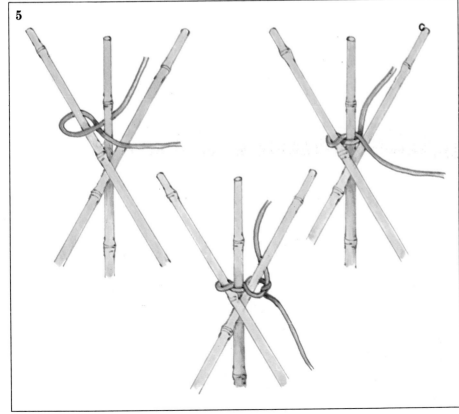

5

cords and rear poles on the center panel, following measurements given in fig. 4b. Having marked all the holes, cut out small diamond shapes with sharp scissors. If you are using grommets, make sure the holes are smaller than the grommets so that they can be pushed through firmly. Grommets are available from most good outdoor-gear suppliers and are sold with instructions for fitting. If, however, you are unable to find them, you can simply round off the holes and overcast the edges with strong thread.

Bind the edges of the front opening and the wings. If you have any extra fabric you can use it instead of binding tape. It is advisable to cut it on the bias, so that it eases around the curved edges. Turn in the edges to prevent fraying.

Assembling the tepee

The tepee is quite easy to assemble. Put up the frame by tying three bamboo poles together to form a tripod, making sure that you loop the string firmly in a chain around all three poles (fig. 5). Set up the tripod on the ground (you will need a stepladder for this), and tie in six more poles securely to form a circular frame.

Attach the tepee to the frame by drawing a string through the center hole of the wings and tying it to the top of the poles underneath their intersection so that the lower edge of the tepee is level with the ground. Drape the tent around all the poles, and close the front opening with wooden pins so that the double rows of holes overlap and each pin goes through four holes, as shown in the photograph.

Peg the bottom edge down with tent pegs through the loops. Tie the top of the wings to two poles and prop up the poles behind the tepee so that they cross diagonally (fig. 6). Tie a cord to each of the bottom holes of the wings and attach each

4a. *Finished tepee cover, raw edges bound or hemmed, showing position of loops for tent pegs and holes and line of wing shape.*
4b. *Detail of wing shapes, showing positions of holes for cords and rear pole holes.*
5. *Tying three poles together to form a tripod.*

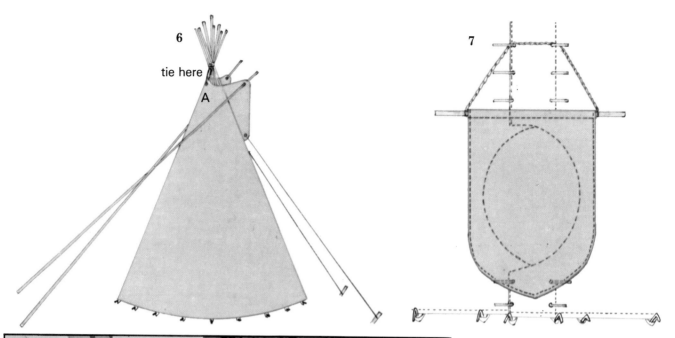

6. *Wings held open by combination of rear poles and front cords.*

7. *Positioning of door flap over front opening.*

8. *The front of the tepee is easily closed by inserting 12in long wooden pins into the holes made by the grommets.*

cord to a stake hammered into the ground at the front of the tepee; the cords should be taut. The combination of the two rear poles and the front cords will open out the wings (fig. 6).

It is easier to measure and make the flap after the tepee cover has been placed over the frame. Measure the width and length of the door opening. Draw a shield-shaped piece of fabric for the door flap about 12in wider and 11in longer than this opening. Draw this shape freehand, fold fabric in half, and cut double to obtain a symmetrical shape. Hem the edge of the door flap.

Turn under the straight edge of the top and machine-stitch it down, leaving enough room for the small bamboo pole. Tie an end of a piece of string to each end of the pole and hang it from one of the wooden pins (fig. 7). You can add finishing touches to the door with embroidery or macramé knotting.

It is a good idea to waterproof the finished tepee with waterproofing liquid, available from camping suppliers. If the tepee gets wet, make sure it is dry before storing it away; dampness will rot the material.

Playhouse

A colorful playhouse made to look like a rustic cottage is a perfect hideaway for a child.

Finished size
Variable according to table, but approximately 50in × 30in × 30in.

Techniques involved
Basic sewing; enlarging a design; embroidery stitches.

Tools required
Basic sewing tools.

Materials
sturdy white or cream-colored cotton fabric, such as sailcloth or unbleached muslin, amount calculated as follows:
  side walls, height of table + 2in × width of table + 2in
  back wall height of table + 2in × length of table + 11in for underwrap at door;
  front wall height of table + 2in × length of table + 7in
red sailcloth for door to fit height of table + 2in × width of table + 8in
two pieces of red sailcloth for shutters 14in × 7½in
lace curtain fabric 15in × 14in
two pieces of gingham 16½in × 9½in
2yd of ⅝in-wide black grosgrain ribbon
blue cotton fabric for roof, to fit width of table + 2in × length of table + 2in
sewing thread
postcard for brick template
8in square of black felt for door hardware
two pieces of green felt 20in × 9in and 12in × 7in for shrubs
two pieces of brown felt 7in × 5½in and 3½in × 2in for shrub tubs
7in square of navy felt for bird-house
scraps of red and blue felt for birds
scraps of red and black felt for ladybugs
3yd of 1in-wide brown grosgrain ribbon for apple tree
1¾yd of ⅝in-wide brown grosgrain ribbon for apple tree
large quantity of scrap felt in two shades of green for leaves and flower stems and in red for apples
felt in various colors for flowers
graph paper with 1in squares

Choosing a table
It is best to use a very simple table—basically a slab of wood with a leg at each corner. A table with braces near the floor is unsuitable as it would make play very difficult. The

table should be big enough to let at least two children be inside at a time. If you are using a table of very different proportions from the one illustrated, you will need to alter the shapes of both door and window accordingly, and you may have to change the position of the decorations slightly. It may be helpful to make a scale drawing first, showing the proportions of each item and your intended color scheme.

To make the house
Calculate the measurements of the walls, door, and roof according to the size of the table. Cut the pieces from the appropriate fabrics.

Enlarge the graph patterns to the

These four pictures show the front, back, and sides of the playhouse with suggested decorations. You can vary the decorations to suit the children.

correct size and then cut out the appliqué decorations from fabrics in suitable colors.

Cut about 16–17 apples and plenty of leaves. Cut flower shapes and flower centers in several colors, also a few plain large circles for different flowers. Cut flower stems of varying height, about 1in wide.

Indicate the corner folds in the long back and front walls with lines of basting (see diagram on page 101). Pin, baste, and stitch the side wall to

| door overlap | corner fold | BACK WALL | SIDE WALL | FRONT WALL | corner fold | DOOR |

Above: *This diagram shows you how to assemble and sew the pieces of the playhouse together.*

the back and front walls, making flat fell seams for a strong neat finish and taking a 1in seam. Stitch one side edge of the door to the front wall, leaving the other edge of the door free.

Turn under a 1in hem on the side edge of the door, on the side edge of the back wall, and all around the bottom of the house.

Stitch the roof to the walls and door, overlapping the open side of the door with the back wall for about 3in.

Stitch the black felt knocker, mail slot, and doorknob in place on the door as illustrated.

Using a postcard as a template, draw around the four sides on the walls with a felt marker to suggest bricks. Place bricks at random on the walls, round off the corners. Machine-stitch three times around each shape, making the lines a bit irregular for a softer effect.

Draw the shape of the window (14in tall × 15in wide) in pencil on the right side of the fabric. Stay-stitch the corners to strengthen them. Cut out the center area of the window to within $\frac{3}{8}$in of the pencil

line. Slash the corner up to the stay-stitching. Fold the seam allowance to the right side along the pencil line. Lay the house flat on a large table with the right side upward. Place the lace curtain fabric over the hole; pin and baste it firmly in place.

For the window frame, make the center cross first, using grosgrain ribbon. Pin and stitch the ribbon in place along its edges. Then apply ribbon to the top and bottom edges, covering all raw edges.

Turn under the edges of the shutter pieces, then pin, baste, and stitch in place.

Turn under and stitch a hem on all four edges of the curtain pieces. Stitch upper edge of each curtain to the top of the window inside the house.

Lay the back wall face up on a flat surface, so that the whole area can be seen at once, and attach the apple tree. Begin by pinning on the most important branches, using the wider brown grosgrain ribbon, making neat folds at the corners and folding under the ends of the branches. Fill in the gaps with

smaller branches, using the narrower ribbon, tucking the lower ends under the main branches. When stitching the branches, begin with the ones whose ends will be hidden under other branches. The ribbon that forms the trunk should be sewn down last of all.

Pin and sew leaves and apples in place on branches.

Pin and stitch flower stems, and leaves, at intervals around house. Sew flower heads and centers in place, using embroidery stitches. Blanket stitch, herringbone stitch, French knots, and stem stitch are simple and pretty.

Machine-stitch the birdhouse in place. A length of black grosgrain ribbon forms the post.

The birds are decorated and sewn to the birdhouse with embroidery stitches. Work blanket stitch around the bodies, stem stitch around the heads, and lazy daisy stitch around the necks and wings.

Stitch the shrubs and their tubs in place.

Stitch the ladybug pieces together, placing red wings over black body and black spots (hand-sewn) on top.

Other ideas for playhouses

Fabric houses can be designed to suit all kinds of games and require only simple materials and a little imagination. A pair of old blue sheets decorated with clouds, birds, a bright yellow sun, and a rainbow would make a delightful house in the sky. Or cover yellow sheets with pretty shells, fish, a mermaid or two and attach green ribbon for a seaweed door curtain to make an underwater house. A jungle house with animals would also be fun.

101

Graph pattern
Each square = 1 in

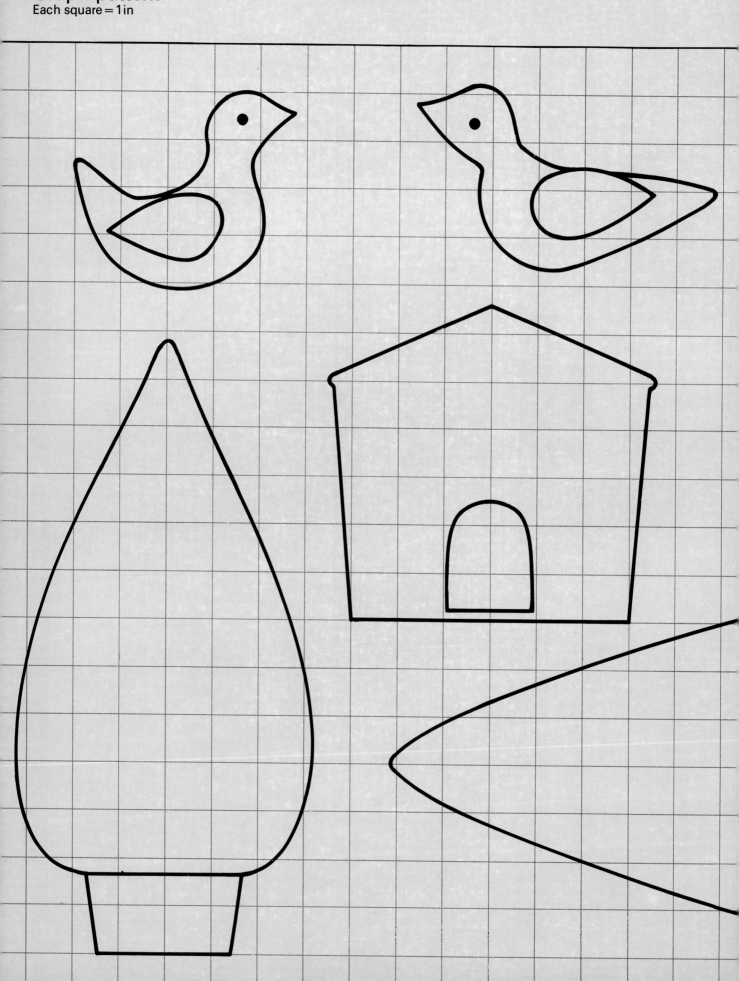

Knitted doll

With her mischievous expression and red hair, this saucy doll is full of personality.

Finished size
Approximately 24in (height).

Techniques involved
Simple knitting; simple crochet; embroidery stitches.

Tools required
No. 3 knitting needles; medium-sized crochet hook; basic sewing tools.

Materials
9oz of washable sport yarn in green
5oz of flesh color
4oz of white
1oz of black
1oz of rust
suitable stuffing
1⅛yd of 1in-wide ribbon
scraps of colored felt for features
1¾yd of hat elastic
3 buttons
piece of cardboard

Gauge
24sts and 32 rows to 4in over stockinette st worked on No. 3 needles.

Body and head
Using No. 3 needles and B, cast on 33sts. Beg with a K row, cont in stockinette st inc one st at beg of next 4 rows. 37sts.

Work 58 rows without shaping. Bind off 6sts at beg of next 2 rows. 25sts.

Dec one st at each end of next row. 23sts. Inc one st at each end of next 3 rows. 29sts. Inc one st at beg of next 8 rows. 37sts. Work 38 rows without shaping. Dec one st at each end of next 9 rows. 19sts. Bind off.

Make another identical piece.

Arms (make two)
Using No. 3 needles and flesh, cast on 11sts. Beg with a K row, cont in stockinette st inc one st at beg of next 6 rows. 17sts. Work 6 rows without shaping. Dec one st at beg of next 4 rows. 13sts. Work 1 row, so ending with a K row. Cut off yarn and leave sts on a spare needle. Make another piece in the same way, but do not cut off yarn.

Next row P to end, then onto same needle P the sts of first piece. 26sts. Work 8 rows.

Next row K1, pM1k, K to last st, pM1k, K1. 28sts.

Work 9 rows.

Next row K1, pM1k, K to last st, pM1k, K1. 30sts.

Work 40 rows without shaping. Dec one st at each end of next 14 rows. Cut off yarn, leaving a long end. Thread end through rem sts, draw up tightly, and secure.

Legs (make two)
Using No. 3 needles and flesh, cast on 18sts. Beg with a K row, cont in stockinette st inc one st at beg of next 4 rows. 22sts. Work 4 rows. Dec one st at beg of next row and at this same edge on foll 7 rows. 14sts. Work 1 row, so ending with a K row. Cut off yarn and leave sts on a holder.

Using No. 3 needles and flesh, cast on 18sts. Beg with a K row, cont in stockinette st inc one st at beg of next 4 rows. 22sts. Work 4 rows. Dec one st at end of next row and at this same edge on foll 7 rows. 14sts. Work 1 row, so ending with a K row.

Next row P to end, then onto same needle P the sts of first piece. 28sts.

Work 8 rows.

Next row K1, pM1k, K to last st, pM1k, K1. 30sts.

Work 9 rows.

Next row K1, pM1k, K to last st, pM1k, K1. 32sts.

Work 60 rows. Bind off.

To finish
With RS of both pieces of body tog, sew around outer edge, leaving an opening for stuffing. Turn right side out. Stuff body, then slipstitch the opening. Join seams of arms and legs, leaving top edge open. Stuff arms and legs, then slipstitch the opening. Work 4 lines of backstitch along each hand to indicate fingers. Sew arms and legs in place.

Cut features from felt, then sew to face. Make hair in rust as follows: cut a piece of cardboard three times the length of braid desired and as wide as the distance from upper hairline down to nape of neck. Wind yarn lengthwise over cardboard, covering it completely. Backstitch strands tog at one edge, cut along other edge. Place hair on head, centering stitching line, and sew in place. Braid hair at sides. Tie ribbon into a bow around each end of braid.

Dress
Using No. 3 needles and green, cast on 149sts. K 3 rows. With green K 1 row and P 1 row. Join on white.

Commence patt.

1st row K2 green, 1 white, (3 green, 1 white) to last 2 sts, 2 green.
2nd row P with green.
3rd row K with green.
4th row P1 white, (3 green, 1 white) to end.
5th row K with green.
6th row P with green.

These 6 rows form patt. Rep them 8 times more, then work the 1st row again.

Dec row P2, (P2 tog, P1) 49 times. 100sts.

Cut off yarn.

Divide for yoke
With RS of work facing, place first 25sts on a holder, rejoin yarn to next st. K49 for front, turn and leave rem 25sts on a holder.

Beg with a 4th row, patt 17 rows.

Cast on 22sts at beg of next 2 rows for sleeves. 93sts. Working 22sts of each sleeve in green only, cont in patt on center 49sts, work 30 rows. Bind off. With RS of work facing, rejoin yarn to first set of 25sts and K to end of row. Cont in green only, work 18 rows.

Cast on 22sts at beg of next row for sleeve. 47sts. Work 30 rows. Bind off.

With RS of work facing, rejoin yarn to rem sts and work as first side, but work 17 rows before casting on sts for sleeve.

Pocket
Using No. 3 needles and white, cast on 8sts.

Work 1 row, then inc one st at beg of next 4 rows. 12sts. Work 8 rows. Bind off.

To finish
Join back seam of skirt to beg of yoke. Join underarm seams and yoke and shoulder seams to fit neck of doll. Using crochet hook and green, work a row of single crochet evenly along back opening and edge of each sleeve. Work three button loops on right side of back opening.

Collar
Using No. 3 needles and white, cast on 30sts. K 8 rows. Bind off.

Make another piece in the same way. Sew on buttons. Sew on collar and pocket as shown.

Bloomers
Using No. 3 needles and white, cast on 58sts. K 2 rows.

Cut off white, join on green.

Beg with a P row, work 48 rows

stockinette st, so ending with a K row. Cut off yarn and leave sts on a spare needle.

Work another piece in the same way, but do not cut off yarn.

Next row P to end, then onto same needle P the sts of first piece. 116sts. Work 34 rows stockinette st, then work 3 rows K1, P1 rib. Bind off in rib.

Join center back seam and inner leg seam. Thread elastic through WS of knitting, 7 rows from cast-on edge, to gather.

Cap

Using No. 3 needles and green, cast on 150sts for brim. K 2 rows.

Cut off green, join on white.
K 6 rows.

Dec row (K1, K2 tog) to end. 100sts. Work 5 rows stockinette st. Cut off yarn and leave sts on a spare needle.

Using No. 3 needles and white, cast on 22sts for crown. Beg with a K row, cont in stockinette st inc one st at each end of next 14 rows. 50sts. Now inc one st at beg of next 22 rows. 72sts. Work 15 rows without shaping. Dec one st at beg of next 22 rows. 50sts. Now dec one st at each end of next 14 rows. Bind off.

With RS of work facing, using No. 3 needles and white, pick up and K 100sts evenly around outer edge of crown. With RS of brim and crown tog, K 1 row, working into sts on crown and corresponding sts on brim. Bind off.

Thread elastic through back of sts

The above illustration shows the back view of the completed doll with detail of the dress fastening.

around join, draw up tightly to fit head. Join row ends of brim.

Shoes (make two)

Using No. 3 needles and black, cast on 22sts. Beg with a K row, cont in stockinette st inc one st at beg of next 4 rows. 26 sts. Work 6 rows. Dec one st at beg of next row and at this same edge on foll 7 rows. 18sts. Bind off.

Make another piece, reversing shaping.

Join back and toe seam.

Make a button loop to simulate fastening.

Knitted rabbit

A jaunty bow tie puts the finishing touch to this amusing rabbit, who's equally at home on a picnic in the woods or lounging on the bed in a college dorm.

Finished size
Approximately 30in (height).

Techniques involved
Simple knitting; embroidery stitches.

Tools required
No. 3 knitting needles; medium-size crochet hook; basic sewing tools.

Materials
7oz of washable sport yarn in white
5oz in blue
1oz in red
piece of gray felt 12in × 18in
piece of pink felt 9in × 12in
scraps of black, blue and white felt
sewing thread
two blue buttons
suitable stuffing

Gauge
24sts and 32 rows to 4in over stockinette stitch on No. 3 needles.

Back

1st leg
Using No. 3 needles and white, cast on 36sts for sole of foot.

Working in stockinette st throughout, inc one st at beg of next 8 rows. 44sts.

Work 11 rows without shaping. Dec one st at beg of next row and at this same edge on foll 9 rows. 34sts. Now dec two sts at beg of next row and at this same edge on foll 3 rows. 26sts.

Work 1 row.

Cut off white.

Join on blue.

Inc one st at end of every alt row until there are 38sts, ending with a P row.

Cut off yarn and leave sts on a spare needle.

2nd leg
As 1st leg, reversing shaping; do not cut off yarn.

Next row K to end, then onto same needle K the sts of 1st leg. 76sts.

Work 3 rows. Inc one st at each end of next and foll 4th row. 80sts.

Work 24 rows without shaping. Now dec one st at each end of next and every foll 6th row until 72sts rem. Work 5 rows. Cut off blue. Join on white.

Work 4 rows. Dec one st at each end of next and foll 4th row. 68sts. Work 4 rows.

Cast on 20sts at beg of next 2 rows

for arms. 108sts. Inc one st at beg of next 8 rows. 116sts. Work 14 rows without shaping. Dec one st at beg of next 8 rows. 108sts. Bind off 28sts at beg of next 2 rows. 52sts.

This completes the arms.

Dec one st at each end of next 4 rows. 44sts. Work 1 row. Inc one st at each end of next 12 rows. 68sts. Work 15 rows without shaping. Dec one st at each end of next and every foll 3rd row until 50sts rem, then at beg of every row until 40sts rem. Work 8 rows. Dec one st at each end of next 9 rows. 22sts.

Bind off.

Front
Work as given for back.

Suspenders (make two)
Using No. 3 needles and blue, cast on 12sts.

Work in stockinette st for 47cm. Bind off.

Bow tie
Using No. 3 needles and red, cast on 12sts. Work in stockinette st for 8½in.

Bind off.

Using crochet hook and red, make a ch 22in long.

Fasten off.

To finish
With RS of both pieces facing, sew around outer edge, leaving an opening for stuffing. Turn right side out. Stuff firmly, then slipstitch the opening. Sew suspenders in place on back, cross them at back, then fasten at front with buttons. Join short ends of bow tie, then fold in half. Tie crochet chain around center of tie to gather, then tie chain around neck.

Using trace pattern, cut cheeks and outer ears from gray felt. Cut inner ears from pink felt. Cut eyelids and nose from black felt. Cut pupils from blue felt. Sew pupils, eyelids, and nose to cheeks. Embroider features on face as indicated, working French knots, backstitch, and long straight stitches.

Place felt on face, then, using matching thread, sew all around outer edge, inserting stuffing in

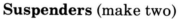

The illustration above shows the back view of the finished rabbit, with his crossed suspender straps and bob tail attached.

The diagrams opposite are the trace patterns for the rabbit's ears and features. These are cut and padded to produce the characteristic full-cheeked bunny expression.

Adults as well as children will take to this white rabbit.

cheeks. Sew inner ears to outer ears, then sew ears in place. Using white, make a pompon for tail. Sew tail to back.

Knitted pirate

Here's a jolly buccaneer to share whatever adventures a small boy can devise. Made of washable yarn and stuffing, he'll survive many battles.

Finished size
Approximately 17in (height).

Techniques involved
Simple knitting.

Tools required
No. 4 and No. 5 knitting needles; basic sewing tools.

Materials
2oz of washable sport yarn in main color A
1oz each of contrasting colors B, C, D, and E
a small brass buckle
two large brass rings
scraps of black felt
small piece of cardboard
aluminum foil
8in length of narrow elastic
suitable stuffing

Gauge
24sts and 32 rows to 4in over stockinette st worked on No. 4 needles.

Doll

Shape feet
*Using No. 4 needles and A, cast on 48sts.
1st row K to end.
2nd row P to end.
3rd row K22, K2 tog, K2 tog tbl, K22.
4th row P21, P2 tog tbl, P2 tog, P21.
5th row K20, K2 tog, K2 tog tbl, K20.
6th row P19, P2 tog tbl, P2 tog, P19.
  Cont to dec in this way until 28sts rem.

Work legs
Beg with a K row, work 30 rows in stockinette st. * Break off yarn and leave sts on holder.
  Make another foot and leg by working from * to * once more. Break off yarn.

Join legs
**With RS of leg facing, sl first 7sts onto safety pin and fold to back of work, rejoin A to next st and inc by working twice into it, K12, inc in next st, sl rem 7sts onto another

safety pin and fold to back of work.
** Cont across next leg on st holder by working from ** to ** once more still using same needle, turn. 32sts.
Note The legs are seamed at back but remainder of doll is seamed at sides.

Body front

***Beg with a P row, work 27 rows in stockinette st on these 32sts.
Shape arms
Cast on 30sts at beg of next 2 rows. 92sts.
Next row Inc in first st, K28, inc in each of next 2sts, K30, inc in each of next 2sts, K28, inc in last st.
Next row P to end.
Next row Inc in first st, K30, inc in each of next 2sts, K32, inc in each of next 2sts, K30, inc in last st. 104sts.
Next row P to end.
Next row K to end.
  Dec 1st at both ends of next row and foll alt row. 100sts.
Shape shoulders
Bind off 17sts at beg of next 4 rows. 32sts. Bind off 8sts at beg of next 2 rows. 16sts.
Shape neck
Beg with a K row, work 4 rows in stockinette st.
Shape head
Inc 1st at both ends of next row and every foll row until there are 32sts on needle.
  Work 10 rows in stockinette st. Break off A. Join on B.
  Beg with a K row, work 2 rows in stockinette st.
  Dec 1st at both ends of each of foll 8 rows. 16sts. Bind off. ***.

Body back

Return to sts left on safety pins at top of legs. With WS of body facing but right side of folded back sts facing, place 4 lots of 7sts on left-hand needle so that the RS rows are facing and ready to form back body. 28sts. Join on A.
Next row Inc in first st, K12, inc in each of next 2sts, K12, inc in last st. 32sts.

Now work on these sts as given for front body from *** to ***.

Clothes
Sweater
Using No. 5 needles and B, cast on 32sts.
  Beg with a K row, work in stockinette st in striped patt of 2 rows B, 2 rows C, until 22 rows have been completed.
Shape sleeves
Cast on 26sts at beg of next 2 rows. 84sts. Keeping striped patt correct, work 12 more rows in stockinette st.
Next row K26, rib 32, turn, bind off 32sts in rib, turn, cast on 32sts, K26 to end.
Next row P26, rib 32, P26. Beg with a K row, work 12 rows in striped stockinette st.
  Bind off 26sts at beg of next 2 rows. 32sts. Cont on these sts in striped stockinette st for 22 rows. Bind off.

Headband
Using No. 5 needles and B, cast on 1st.
1st row P1, K1, P1 into same st. 3sts.
2nd row Inc in first st, K1, inc in last st. 5sts.
3rd row Inc in first st, K3, inc in last st. 7sts.
  K 100 rows.
  Dec 1st at both ends of next 2 rows. 3sts. K3 tog and fasten off.
Belt
Using No. 5 needles and D, cast on 9sts and work in garter st for 13in, then dec 1st at each end of every row until 3sts rem. K3 tog and fasten off.
Pants
Using No. 5 needles and E, cast on 40sts. Beg with a K row, work in stockinette st for 3 rows.
Next row K to mark hemline.
  Beg with a K row, work 18 rows in stockinette st.
Shape leg
Work 10 rows in stockinette st. (Note on other leg this should be 4 rows only.)
Next row K6, K2 tog, turn, P to end.
  Cont in stockinette st, dec 1st at

end of every K row until 2sts rem. P1 row. K2 tog and fasten off. Rejoin yarn to remaining 28sts, K2 tog, K8, K2 tog, turn, P to end.

Next row K2 tog, K6, K2 tog.

Next row P to end.

Cont to dec each end of every K row until 2sts rem.

P1 row.

K2 tog and fasten off.

Rejoin yarn to rem 16sts, K8, turn and P back.

Next row K2 tog, K4, K2 tog.

Next row P to end.

Cont to dec both ends of each K row until 2sts rem.

P 1 row.

K2 tog and fasten off.

Rejoin yarn to remaining 8sts, K2 tog, K6.

Next row P to end.

Cont in stockinette st, dec 1st at beg of every row until 2sts rem.

P 1 row.

K2 tog and fasten off.

Work another piece in the same way, noting that the number of rows worked for leg should be reduced as given in note to make pants uneven length.

To finish

Join seams of doll, stuffing each section firmly as you work.

Sew headband around head over color change, crossing ends over and leaving approximately 1in free at one side of head. Join side and sleeve seams of sweater and put on doll. Join center front and back seams of pants. Join leg seams. Sew elastic tog to form circle. Turn waistband over circle of elastic to form hem and sl st to WS of trousers. Put pants on doll. Sew ragged ends to legs. Sew buckle to unshaped end of belt and fasten around waist of doll.

Cut curved dagger out of cardboard. Wind thread or yarn around handle section and cover blade section with foil. Cut features and patch out of felt and glue or sew to face.

This colorful sea dog comes complete with "silver" dagger made from cardboard and aluminum foil. Add glittering brass rings to his ears for an authentic "swashbuckling" look.

111

Knitted doctor and nurse

These professional characters, complete with make-believe equipment, will give an authoritative air to games of playing doctor and nurse. They are both dressed in a delightfully old fashioned style, reminiscent of medical uniforms of the turn of-the century. The medical accessories are easily purchased from toy departments—don't forget to add a realistic looking watch for the nurse. These dolls are very useful for reassuring those children who are nervous or shy about visiting the doctor.

Finished size
Approximately 21in (height).

Techniques involved
Simple knitting; grafting; simple crochet; embroidery stitches.

Tools required
No. 1 knitting needles; size C crochet hook; basic sewing tools.

Materials
For doctor:
4oz of fine crochet cotton in pink
4oz in white
1oz in brown
3 buttons
3 snaps
waist length of elastic
suitable stuffing
pair of safety eyes, or felt
scrap of fabric for cravat
toy spectacles
toy medical accessories
For nurse:
4oz of fine crochet cotton in pink
4oz in white
2oz in black
1oz in ginger
4oz in blue
short length of red yarn
8 snaps
length of narrow ribbon for dress
suitable stuffing
pair of safety eyes, or felt
toy spectacles
toy medical accessories

Gauge
32sts and 40 rows to 4in over stockinette st worked on No. 1 needles.

Doctor
Body
Using No. 1 needles and pink crochet cotton, cast on 112sts. Beg with a K row, work in stockinette st for 7½in. Bind off.
Head
Using No. 1 needles and pink, cast on 46sts. Beg with a K row, work 10 rows stockinette st.
Shape head
Next row K1, (pick up loop lying between needles and K tbl—called inc 1—, K14, inc 1, K1) 3 times. 52sts.
Next row P to end.
Next row K1, (inc 1, K16, inc 1, K1) 3 times. 58sts.
Cont inc 6sts in this way on every alt row until there are 88sts. Cont without shaping until the work measures 4¼in from beg, ending with

a P row.
Shape crown
Next row K1, (K2 tog, K1) to end. 59sts.
Work 3 rows stockinette st.
Next row K2 tog, (K1, K2 tog) to end. 39sts.
Work 3 rows stockinette st.
Next row K1, (K2 tog) to end. 20sts.
Work 1 row stockinette st.
Next row (K2 tog) to end. 10sts.
Break off yarn, thread through rem sts, draw up.
Fasten off.
Legs (make two)
Using No. 1 needles and pink, cast on 48sts.
Beg with a K row, work 14 rows stockinette st.
Shape leg
Dec one st at each end of next and every foll 8th row until 32sts rem. Cont without shaping until work measures 7¾in from beg, ending with a P row.
Break off pink. Join on black and work 2 rows stockinette st.
Shape shoe
1st row K20, turn.
2nd row P8, turn.
Cont on these 8sts in stockinette st for 1½in, ending with a P row. Break off yarn.
With RS of work facing, rejoin yarn at inner edge of 12sts that were left, pick up and K 10sts along side of foot, K across 8 instep sts, pick up and K 10sts along other side of foot, then K rem 12sts. K9 rows garter st. Bind off 22sts at beg of next 2 rows. Cont on rem 8sts in garter st until this piece is long enough to fit along bottom of shoe to heel.
Bind off.

Arms (make two)
Using No. 1 needles and pink, cast on 32sts. Beg with a K row, work 4½in stockinette st, ending with a P row.
Next row K1, (K2 tog, K2) to last 3sts, K2 tog, K1. 24sts.
Work 3 rows stockinette st.
Shape hand
1st row K11, inc 1, K2, inc 1, K11.
2nd row P11, pick up loop lying between sts and P tbl—called inc 1—, P4, inc 1, P11.
3rd row K11, inc 1, K6, inc 1, K11.
4th row P11, inc 1, P8, inc 1, P11.
5th row K21, turn.
6th row P10, turn.
7th row K2 tog, (K2, K2 tog) twice. 7sts.

8th row P1, (P2 tog, P1) twice. 5sts.
Bind off rem 5sts and join thumb seam.
With RS of work facing, rejoin yarn to rem sts, pick up and K 2sts from base of thumb, K to end. 24sts.
Beg with a P row, work 7 rows stockinette st.
Next row (K2 tog, K8, sl 1, K1, psso) twice.
Next row (P2 tog tbl, P6, P2 tog) twice.
Next row (K2 tog, K4, sl 1, K1, psso) twice.
Next row (P2 tog tbl, P2, P2 tog) twice.
Fold work in half and graft rem sts tog.

Nose
Using No. 1 needles and pink, cast on 2sts. Beg with a K row, cont in stockinette st, inc one st at each end of 2nd and every foll row until there are 12sts. Work 5 rows stockinette st. Dec one st at each end of every row until 2sts rem. Bind off.

Pants
Using No. 1 needles and black, cast on 48sts. Beg with a K row, cont in stockinette st, inc one st at each end of 21st and every foll 20th row until there are 56sts. Cont without shaping until work measures 8¾in from beg, ending with a P row. Cast on 3sts at beg of next 2 rows. 62sts. Mark each end of last row for crotch. Work 2 rows without shaping. Dec one st at each end of next and every foll 10th row until 56sts rem. Cont without shaping until the work measures 5in from markers. Bind off.
Make another leg in same way.

Coat back
Using No. 1 needles and white, cast on 56sts. Beg with a K row, work 7¾in stotckinette st, ending with a P row.
Shape armholes
Bind off 2sts at beg of next 2 rows. Dec one st at each end of next and foll 3 alt rows. 44sts. Cont without shaping until armholes measure 3in from beg, ending with a P row.
Shape shoulders
Bind off 5sts at beg of next 4 rows. Bind off rem 24sts.

Right front
Using No. 1 needles and white, cast on 26sts. Beg with a K row, work 7 rows stockinette st. With separate

length of contrasting yarn cast on 13sts and leave.

Next row P to end, then P across 13sts.

Next row K6, sl 1, K to end.

Next row P to end.

Rep last 2 rows until work measures same as back to underarm, ending with a P row.

Shape armhole and front edge
Next row Inc in first st, K3, K2 tog, sl 1, K2 tog, K to end.

Next row Bind off 2sts, P to end.

Next row Inc 1, K3, K2 tog, sl 1, K2 tog, K to last 2sts, K2 tog.

Cont dec at armhole edge on alt rows 3 times more, *at the same time* cont to shape front edge on every alt row until 17sts rem.

Cont without shaping until armhole measures same as back to shoulder, ending at armhole edge.

Shape shoulder
Bind off at beg of next and foll alt row 5sts twice.

Cont on rem 7sts for 1½in. Bind off.

Left front
Work as given for right front, reversing all shaping.

Sleeves
Using No. 1 needles and white, cast on 40 sts. Beg with a K row, cont in stockinette st, inc one st at each end of 15th and every foll 10th row until there are 46sts. Cont without shaping until work measures 5¾in from beg, ending with a P row.

Shape top
Bind off 2 sts at beg of next 2 rows. Dec one st at each end of next and foll 4 alt rows. 32sts.

Bind off at beg of next and every foll row 2sts 4 times, 3sts 4 times and 12sts once.

Large pockets (make two)
Using No. 1 needles and B, cast on 14sts. K 24 rows garter st.

Bind off.

Small pocket
Using No. 1 needles and white, cast on 8sts. K 12 rows garter st.

Bind off.

To finish
Press or block each piece according to yarn used.

Body Join back and lower seam. Join top seam for 1¾in from each side, leaving center open for neck.

Join head seam. Stuff body and head firmly and sew tog. Join arm seams, stuff, and sew to sides of body so that thumb comes to front of each arm. Join leg seams, stuff, and sew to bottom of body so that seams go to back. Run thread around outer edge of nose, draw up, stuff, and sew to face. Sew on eyes. Make cravat and tie around neck.

Hair Using size C hook and brown, make ch 40.

1st row Into 3rd ch from hook work 1sc, 1sc into each ch to end. 39sc.

2nd row 1ch, *insert hook into next sc, take yarn around 2 fingers of left hand and draw a loop through, yo and draw through one loop on hook, yo and draw through 2 rem loops on hook, rep from * to last st. 1sc into turning ch.

Rep these 2 rows 6 times more. Fasten off and sew around head.

Moustache Cut brown yarn into 2in lengths. Using 3 strands tog, knot fringe under nose.

Pants Join back and front seams to markers. Join leg seams. Turn ¾in hems at waist and legs to WS and sl st down. Thread elastic through waist.

Coat Join shoulder, side, and sleeve seams. Set in sleeves. Take out contrasting yarn from fronts, fold in half at sl st line and graft sts. Turn front edges to WS and sl st down. Join ends of neck facing and sew to back neck. Turn up ¾in hems at lower edge and cuffs to WS and sl st down. Sew on pockets. Sew on 3 snaps and sew buttons on top.

Nurse
Make head, arms, and nose as given for doctor.

Using the black yarn throughout, make legs as given for doctor. Using the pink yarn, cast on 100sts and make the body as for doctor.

Dress
**Using No. 1 needles and blue, cast on 157sts and work in one piece. Beg with a K row, work 8½in stockinette st, ending with a P row.

Next row K1, (K2 tog, K1) to end. 105sts. **

Cast on 3sts at beg of next 2 rows, then cont in stockinette st for a further 24 rows, ending with a K row.

Divide for armholes
Next row P28, bind off 4sts, P47, bind off 4sts, P28.

Complete left back first. Cont in stockinette st, dec one st at armhole edge on next and foll 2 alt rows, then cont without shaping until 47 rows have been completed from beg of armhole shaping, ending with a K row.

Shape shoulder
Bind off at beg of next and every alt row 5sts twice and 15sts once.

With RS of work facing, rejoin yarn to 47 front sts. Cont in stockinette st, dec one st at each end of next and foll 2 alt rows, then cont without shaping until 43 rows have been completed from beg of armhole shaping.

Shape neck and shoulder
Next row P16, bind off 9sts, P16.

Complete this side first.

Next row K to end.

Next row Bind off 2sts, P to end.

Rep last 2 rows once more. Bind off at beg of next and every foll row 5sts once, 2sts once and 5sts once.

With RS of work facing, rejoin yarn to rem sts and complete to match first side.

With RS of work facing, rejoin yarn to rem sts and complete right back to match left back, reversing shaping.

Sleeves
Using No. 1 needles and blue, cast on 40sts. Beg with a K row, cont in stockinette st, inc one st at each end of 5th and every foll 10th row until there are 46sts. Cont without shaping until work measures 4½in from beg, ending with a P row.

Shape top
Work as given for doctor's jacket sleeve.

Apron
Using white, work as given for dress from ** to **, working 6¼in before dec row.

Next row K to end to form ridge.

Beg with a K row, work 9 rows stockinette st.

Next row Bind off 35sts K-wise to form ridge, K35, bind off 35sts K-wise. Break off yarn.

With RS of work facing, rejoin yarn to center 35sts.

Next row K to end.

Next row K5, P25, K5.

Rep last 2 rows 13 times more, then first row again. K4 rows garter st.

Next row K5, bind off 25, K5.

Cont on each set of 5sts in garter st for approx 7in.

Bind off.

Pockets (make two)

Using No. 1 needles and white, cast on 10sts. K 17 rows garter st. Bind off.

Cap

Using No. 1 needles and white, cast on 101sts. P 1 row. Beg with a P row, work 9 rows stockinette st. P 1 row to reverse work. Beg with a K row, work 10 rows stockinette st.

Next row K2, *K twice into next st, K4, rep from * to last 4sts, K twice into next st, K3. 121sts. Beg with a P row, work 11 rows stockinette st.

Shape top

Next row *K8, K2 tog, rep from * to last st, K1.

Next row P to end.

Next row *K7, K2 tog, rep from * to last st, K1.

Next row P to end.

Cont dec in this way on next and every alt row until 25sts rem, ending with a P row.

Next row *K2 tog, rep from * to last st, K1.

Break off yarn, thread through rem sts, draw up.

Fasten off.

To finish

Body as given for doctor.

Hair Cut brown yarn into 30in lengths. Lay across top of head evenly and sew securely along center. Catch ends tog at nape of neck. Braid ends tog, then form into a bun and sew in place.

Dress Join shoulder and sleeve seams. Set in sleeves. Join skirt seam to 1¼in below waist. Turn in 3sts at both sides of center back and sl st down. Make collar and cuffs from ribbon and sew in place. Sew 4 snaps at center back.

Turn 8 rows for hem at lower edge to WS and sl st down.

Apron Using red yarn, embroider red cross on front as given in chart. Sew on pockets. Sew 2 snaps to back waist and one to end of each strap to fasten at back. Turn up hem as given for dress.

Cap Using red yarn, embroider red cross on band as given in chart. Join center back seam.

Turn headband to RS and catch-stitch in place.

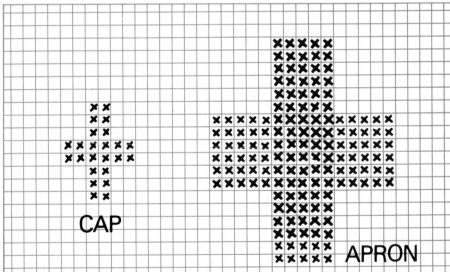

The nurse wears the traditional uniform of European nurses; the doctor wears the familiar white coat.

115

Crochet airplanes

These gallant little ancestors of the 747 make amusing toys. To get them "flying", string them up as a mobile.

Finished size
Approximately 10in (length).

Techniques involved
Simple crochet; simple woodworking.

Tools required
Size E crochet hook; basic sewing tools.

Materials
For each plane:
2oz of washable crêpe knitting worsted in main color A
2oz of contrasting color B
small amount of contrasting color C
cardboard for wings
balsa wood
wood glue
chenille pipecleaners for propeller
suitable stuffing

Gauge
20sc and 24 rows to 4in worked on size E hook.

Monoplane
Body
Using size E hook and A, ch 21.
Base row 2sc into 2nd ch from hook, 1sc into each of next 4 sc, *2sc into next sc, 1sc into each of next 4sc, rep from * to end. Turn.
1st-5th rows 1 ch, 1sc into each sc to end. Turn.
6th row 1ch, work next 2sc tog, 1sc into each sc to within last 2sc, work last 2sc tog. Turn.
7th-9th rows 1ch, 1sc into each sc to end. Turn.
Rep last 4 rows 6 times more. 10sc.
Next row 1ch, 1sc into each sc to end. Turn.
Next row 1ch, *work next 2sc tog, rep from * once more, 1 sc into each of next 6sc. Turn. 8sc.
Next row 1ch, 1sc into each sc to end. Turn.
Next row 1ch, work next 2sc tog, 1sc into next sc, work next 2sc tog, 1sc into each of next 3sc. Fasten off.
Using size E hook and A, ch 4, sl st into first ch to form a circle.
1st round 1ch, work 7sc into circle, sl st into first sc.
2nd round 1ch, 1sc into sl st, *2sc into next sc, 1sc into next sc, rep from * twice more, 2sc into last sc, sl st into first sc. 12sc.
3rd round As 2nd. 18sc. Fasten off.

Wing
Using size E hook and B, ch 45.

Base row 1sc into 2nd ch from hook, 1sc into each ch to end. Turn.
1st row 1ch, 1sc into each sc to end. Turn.
2nd row 1ch, 2sc into next sc, 1sc into each sc to within last sc, 2sc into last sc. Turn. 46sc.
3rd and 4th rows As 1st.
5th row As 2nd. 48sc.
6th-9th rows As 1st.
Fasten off.
Make another piece in the same way.

Tail
Using size E hook and B, ch 11.
Base row 1sc into 2nd ch from hook, 1sc into each ch to end. Turn.
1st row 1ch, 2sc into next sc, 1sc into each sc to within last sc, 2sc into last sc. Turn.
2nd and 3rd rows 1ch, 1sc into each sc to end. Turn. 12sc.
4th row 1ch, 2sc into next sc, 1sc into each of next 5sc. Turn.
5th row 1ch, work next 2sc tog, 1sc into each of next 5sc. Turn.
6th row 1ch, 1sc into each sc to within last 2sc, work last 2sc tog. Fasten off. Rejoin yarn to center of rem 6sc and work 1sc into each sc to end. Turn. Work 4th-6th rows once. Fasten off.
Make another piece in the same way.

Rudder
Using size E hook and B, ch 6.
Base row 1ch, 1sc into each sc to end. Turn.
1st row 1ch, 1sc into each of next 4sc, 2sc into last sc. Turn.
2nd-4th rows 1ch, 1sc into each sc to end. Turn.
5th row 1ch, 2sc into next sc, 1sc into each sc to end. Turn.
6th row 1ch, work next 2sc tog, 1sc into each of next 3sc, work next 2sc tog. Turn.
7th row 1ch, work next 2sc tog, 1sc into next sc, work next 2sc tog.
Fasten off.
Make another piece in the same way.

Wheels (make two)
Using size E hook and C, ch 4, sl st into first ch to form a circle.
1st round 1ch, work 7sc into circle, sl st into first sc.
2nd round 1ch, 1sc into sl st, *2sc into next sc, 1sc into next sc, rep from * to last sc, 2sc into last sc, sl st

into first sc. 12sc.
3rd round As 2nd. 18sc. Fasten off.
Make another piece in the same way.

To finish
Using wing, tail, rudder, and wheel as pattern, cut cardboard to shape. Join long seam of body section, stuff firmly, then sew circle in place. Join wing, tail, rudder, and wheel sections together over cardboard. Fold a set of chenille pipecleaners in half to form propellers. Sew to body. Attach wing to body, then, using balsa wood, form struts and undercarriage as shown in picture (we painted the wood to match the propellers). Attach wheels to undercarriage. Sew rudder to tail, then sew tail to body.

Biplane
Work as given for monoplane, but make two wings and join wings together with balsa wood as shown in picture.

Triplane
Work as given for monoplane, but make three wings and join wings together with balsa wood as shown in picture.

Crochet snail and alligator

*You don't have to like real snails or alligators to enjoy the
company of these colorful specimens.*

Finished size
Snail: 18in (length) 12in (height).
Alligator: 29in (length).

Techniques involved
Simple crochet.

Tools required
Size F crochet hook; basic sewing tools.

Materials
For snail:
3oz of washable sport yarn in color A for body
2oz of contrasting color B for shell
suitable stuffing
two long bugle beads and two small round beads
For alligator:
2oz of washable flecked sport yarn in color A for body
4oz of contrasting color B for legs and eyes
scraps of white felt for eyes
2 glass safety eyes
$\frac{3}{8}$yd of rickrack

Gauge
19sc and 24 rows to 4in worked on size F hook; 19hdc and 16 rows to 4in worked on size F hook.

Snail
Body
Using size F hook and A, ch 41.
Base row 1sc into 3rd ch from hook, 1sc into each ch to end. Turn. 40sc.
Patt row 1sc into each sc to end. Turn.
Rep the patt row until work measures 18in from beg. Fasten off.

Shell
Using size F hook and B, ch 44.
Base row 1hdc into 3rd ch from hook, 1hdc into each ch to end. Turn. 43hdc.
Patt row 2ch to count as first hdc, 1hdc into each hdc to end. Turn.
Rep the patt row until work measures 29in from beg. Fasten off.

To finish
Join long seam of body. Gather one end, stuff firmly, gather other end.
Join long seam of shell. Gather one end, stuff firmly, then roll and sew shell and sew to body.
Make antennae from beads and sew to body.
If making snail for a very ·small child, leave off antennae.

Alligator
Body
Using size F hook and A, ch 41.
Base row 1hdc into 3rd ch from hook, 1hdc into each ch to end. Turn.
Patt row 2ch to count as first hdc, 1hdc into each hdc to end. Turn.
Rep the patt row until work measures 14in from beg.
Cut off A, join on B.
Cont in sc for head until work measures 29in from beg. Fasten off.

Legs (make two)
Using size F hook and B, ch 41.
Base row 1sc into 2nd ch from hook, 1sc into each ch to end. Turn.
Patt row 1sc into each sc to end. Turn.
Rep the patt row for 6in. Fasten off.

Eyes (make two)
Using size F hook and B, ch 27. Work base row as given for legs, then rep the patt row until work measures 2in from beg. Fasten off.

To finish
Join long seam of body. Fold body in half, placing seam at center, and join one short end. Stuff firmly, then gather other end.
Join long seam of each leg. Gather one end, stuff firmly, then gather other end. Sew legs to body, sewing through center to form two legs each side. Join short ends of eyes. Gather one end.
Cut two circles of felt each 1$\frac{1}{4}$in in diameter. Sew felt to eyes, then place glass eyes in position. Attach eyes, stuff firmly, then gather other end. Sew rickrack around head section.

Use fanciful colors for these droll creatures. Rickrack gives the alligator a characteristically jagged smile. Omit the snail's antennae for a very young child.

Crochet clown

With his flopsy body sprawled over a shelf, this happy-go-lucky
clown brings a bit of circus atmosphere to the playroom.

Finished size

Approximately 13in (height). Each circle 2½in (diameter).

Techniques involved

Simple crochet; embroidery stitches.

Tools required

Size C and size F crochet hooks; basic sewing tools.

Materials

4oz of washable knitting worsted in main color A
2oz each of contrasting colors B, C, D, E, and F
69 small beads to match colors of yarn
4 larger orange beads
suitable stuffing
6yd of strong cotton thread

Gauge

24sc and 26 rounds to 4in worked on size C hook.

Circle

Using size F hook and A, ch 3 and join with sl st to form a ring.
1st round 1ch to count as first sc, 7sc into ring, sl st into first ch. 8sts.
2nd round 1ch, *1sc into next sc, rep from * to end, sl st into first 1ch.
3rd round 1ch, 1sc into same place, *2sc into next sc, rep from * to end, sl st into first 1ch.
16sts.
4th round As 2nd.
5th round As 3rd.
32sts.
6th and 7th rounds As 2nd.
8th round Sl st into each sc all around, sl st into first sl st.
Fasten off.
Make 12 circles in A, 12B, 13C, 12D, 12E, 14F.

Collar

Using D, work 6 rounds as given for circle.
7th round As 3rd.
64sts.
8th and 9th rounds As 2nd.
10th round *Sl st into next sc, rep from * to end, sl st into first sl st.
Fasten off.
Using E, make a second piece in the same way.

Make this jolly clown from bits of leftover yarn. He is made from lots of colorful crochet disks threaded over tiny beads.

Head

Using size C hook and A, ch 3 and join with sl st to form a ring.
1st round 5sc into ring, do not join end of round.
*1sc into each of next 2sc, 2sc into next sc, rep from *, working in rounds without joining until there are 44sc in the round.
Mark this point.
Continue in rounds of sc without joining or further shaping until 10 more rounds have been worked from the marker.
**1sc into each of next 2sc, insert hook into next st and draw up a loop, insert hook into next st and draw up a loop, yo and draw through all 3 loops on hook—called 2sc tog—, rep from ** until 24sc rem in the round.
Stuff head firmly, then continue with 1sc into next sc, 2sc tog, until only 3sts rem; stuff the remainder of head as work progresses.
Break off yarn, thread it through rem sts, and draw up tight.
Fasten off.
Embroider eyes and nose in stem stitch as illustrated.

Hat

Using size C hook and B, ch 3.
1st round 6ch into first of 3ch, join with sl st to form a ring.
2nd round 1ch, 1sc into same place, *2sc into next sc, rep from * to end, sl st into 1ch.
12sts.
3rd round 1ch, *1sc into next sc, rep from * to end, sl st into 1ch.
4th round As 2nd.
24 sts.
5th round *Sl st into next sc, rep from * to end, sl st into first sl st.
Break off B and join on F.
6th round 1ch, *1sc into next sl st, rep from * to end, sl st into 1ch.
7th and 8th rounds Work in sc without further shaping.
9th round 1ch, 1sc into same place, 1sc into each of next 3sc, *2sc into next sc, 1sc into each of next 3sc, rep from * to end, sl st into 1ch. 30sts.
Break off F and join on E.
10th round 1ch, *1sc into next sc, rep from * to end, sl st into 1ch.
11th and 12th rounds As 7th and 8th.
13th round 1ch, 1sc into same place, 1sc into each of next 4sc, *2sc into next sc, 1sc into each of next 4sc, rep from * to end, sl st into 1ch. 36 sts.
Break off E and join on D.

14th round As 10th.
15th and 16th rounds As 7th and 8th.
17th round 1ch, 1sc into same place, 1sc into each of next 5sc, *2sc into next sc, 1sc into each of next 5sc, rep from * to end, sl st into 1ch. 42sts.
Break off D and join on B.
Work 9 rounds without shaping.
Turn work inside out and continue in B for 5 rounds more.
Fasten off.
Turn work right side out, fold up brim at turning line.

To finish

Thread a fairly large tapestry needle with a double strand of strong cotton thread.
Beginning with one arm, thread the needle through one circle in F, leaving a tail of about 10in; thread on a small bead, then continue, placing one bead between the circles, with 3 circles in A, 3 in B, 3E, 3D, 3C. Thread on one larger orange bead for hand, then take the thread back through all these circles and beads to the beginning.
Continue threading one circle in F without a bead, then 8 circles in F with one bead between, then one more without a bead for the body.
Continue with one leg, working as given for the arm with one larger orange bead for foot, then thread back through the leg.
Assemble the second leg in the same way, bringing the thread back to the top of the leg and then through the circles of the body.
Make a second arm in the same way as the first, then bring the thread back to the beginning of the arm as before.
Take the needle thread, together with the thread that was left at the beginning of the first arm, and thread all four thicknesses through one circle in C, the E collar circle and then the D collar circle (without beads). Then thread on the last beads and tie the ends firmly but do not trim. Continue with the same four threads through the head to the top and fasten off securely.
Catch-stitch hat in place on head.

Crochet lion

Not a cowardly lion, but certainly a cuddly one, Lester will appeal to anyone who has a soft spot for cats.

Finished size

13in (height).

Techniques involved

Simple crochet; embroidery stitches.

Tools required

Size F and size H crochet hooks; basic sewing tools.

Materials

4oz of washable knitting worsted in gold
small amounts of contrasting colors: orange, black, camel, rust, and brown
suitable stuffing
scraps of black and pink felt for eyes and tongue
cardboard for base

Gauge

16sc and 20 rows to 4in worked on size F hook.

Body and head (make two)

Using size F hook and gold, ch 25.
Base row Into 2nd ch from hook work 1sc, 1sc into each ch to end. Turn. 24sc.
1st row (sc row) 2ch to count as first sc, skip first sc, 1sc into each sc to end, working last sc into turning ch. Cont in sc until work measures 4in from beg, ending with a WS row.
Next row 2ch, (insert hook into next st, draw loop through) twice, yo and draw through 3 loops on hook—called dec 1—, 1sc into each sc to last 3sts, dec 1, 1sc into turning ch.

Work 3 rows sc without shaping. Rep last 4 rows 3 times more. 16sts. Dec in same way at each end of next and every alt row until 10sts rem, ending with a WS row.

Shape head

Work 2 rows without shaping. Inc 1st by working 2sc into 1sc at each end of every row until there are 18sts. Work 8 rows without shaping. Dec 1st at each end of every row until 10sts rem. Work 2 rows without shaping. Fasten off.

Legs

**Using size F hook and gold, ch 6.
Work base row as given for body. 5sc. Work 1 row sc. Inc 1st at each end of next row. Work 1 row without shaping. **. Inc 1st at beg of next row. Dec 1st at beg of next row, (7sc), work 2ch at end of row. Fasten off.

Work another piece in same way

from ** to **. Inc 1st at end of next row. Dec 1st at end of next row, (7sc).
Next row 2ch, miss first sc, (insert hook into next sc, draw loop through) 3 times, yo and draw through 4 loops on hook—called dec 2—, 1sc into each sc to end, work 1sc into each of 2ch of other foot, 1sc into each sc to last 4sts, dec 2, 1sc into turning ch. 12sc.

Shape legs

Work 11 rows without shaping. Inc 1st at each end of next and every foll 4th row 3 times. 18sc. Work 5 rows without shaping. Dec 1st at each end of next and every alt row until 12sc rem. Work 1 row. Fasten off.

Base

Using size F hook and gold, ch 13. Work base row as given for body. 12sc. Work 1 row sc. Inc 1st at each end of every row until there are 24sc. Work 4 rows without shaping. Dec 1st at each end of every row until 12sc rem. Work 2 rows without shaping. Fasten off.

Tail

Using size F hook and gold, ch 11. Work base row as given for body. 10sc. Cont in sc until work measures 12in from beg, ending with a WS row. Fasten off.

Using rust, make a tassel and sew to inside of one end of tail. Fold tail in half and join seam, padding out slightly as you sew. Leave end open.

Ears (make two)

Using size F hook and gold, ch 11. Work base row as given for body. 4sc. Work 1 row sc. ***Inc 1st at each end of next 2 rows. 8sc. Work 2 rows without shaping. Dec 1st at each end of next 2 rows. 4sc. ***. Work 4 rows without shaping. Rep from *** to ***. Work 2 rows without shaping. Fasten off.

Fold each ear in half and sew shaped edges tog, leaving straight edge open. Pad out slightly.

Muzzle

Using size F hook and camel, ch 4. Work base row as given for body. 3sc. Inc 1st at end of next row, work 2ch at end. Fasten off.

Make another piece in same way, inc 1st at beg of next row.
Next row Ch 2, inc 1, 1sc into each sc to end, 1sc into each of 2ch of other piece, 1sc into each sc to last

2sc, inc 1, 1sc into turning ch. 12sc. Work 3 rows without shaping. Dec 1st at each end of next 2 rows. 8sc. Work 1 row without shaping. Fasten off.

Using black, work small French knots or cross sts on each side of muzzle as shown.

Nose

Using size F hook and black, ch 7. Work base row as given for body. 6sc. Work 2 rows without shaping. Dec 1st at each end of next row. Work 1 row.
Next row Ch 2, skip first sc, dec 1, 1sc into turning ch. 3sc.
  Work 1 row.
  Fasten off.

Mane

Using size F hook and brown, ch 57 loosely. Work base row as given for body. 56sc.
Next row (loop row) Ch 2, miss first sc, *insert hook into next sc, wind yarn around two fingers of left hand and draw a loop through, yo and draw through 1 loop on hook, yo and draw through 2 loops on hook—called L1—, rep from * into each sc to last sc, 1sc into turning ch.

Change to size H hook. Cont working 1 row sc and 1 row L1 in each of rust, orange, and gold. Fasten off.

Work another piece in same way. Join short ends and gold loop edges tog.
  Press seam.

To finish

Press or block each piece according to yarn used. Join back and front parts of body and head tog, leaving lower edge open. Stuff firmly. Cut piece of cardboard to fit base, place inside and sew base to lower edge of body.

Place legs on front of body as shown and sew in place, leaving one side of legs and foot open. Stuff top part and legs and foot firmly. Sew other side of legs and foot to body.

Sew muzzle to head as shown, stuffing firmly. Sew nose in place, padding out slightly. Sew ears in place. Cut lengths of black yarn for whiskers and sew in place as shown. Cut felt shapes for eyes and tongue and sew in place. Pad out mane slightly and sew in place around head as shown. Sew tail to lower edge of back.

Crochet lamb

Loop stitch gives a realistically wooly texture to this appealing toy lamb. And he's just the right size for tiny hands.

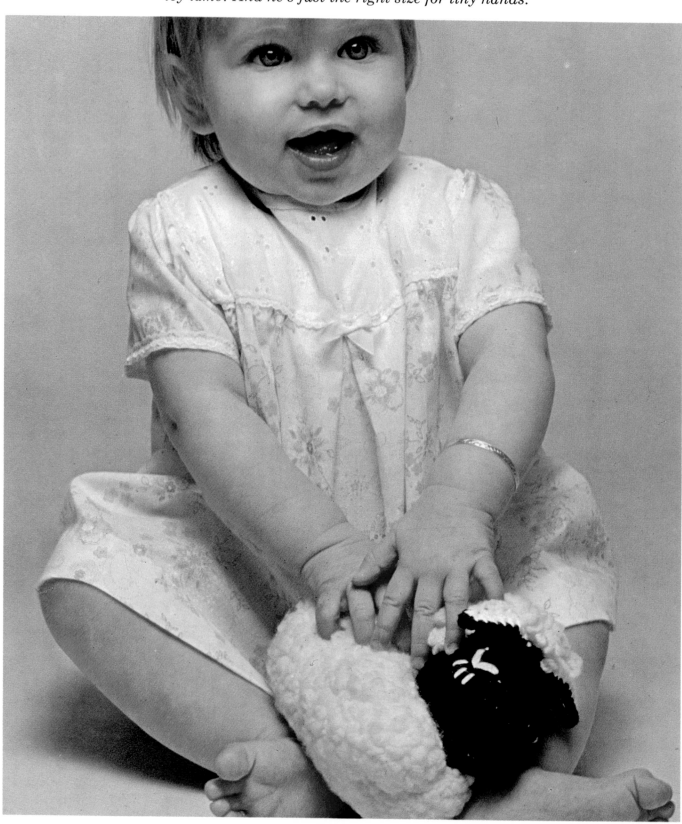

Finished size
7in (length); 5in (height).

Techniques involved
Simple crochet; embroidery stitches.

Tools required
Size F crochet hook; basic sewing tools.

Materials
3oz of washable sport yarn in white
1oz in black
suitable stuffing

Gauge
24sts and 22 rows to 4in worked on size F hook.

Head
Using size F hook and black, ch 4, join with sl st to form ring.

1st round Work 6sc into ring.

2nd round *1sc into next sc, 2sc into next sc, rep from * all around.

3rd and 4th rounds *1sc into each of next 2sc, 2sc into next sc, rep from * all around.

5th round *1sc into each of next 3sc, 2sc into next sc, rep from * all around. 20sc. Continue inc 4sts evenly on each round in this way (working one more st between inc) until there are 40sc.

Continue without inc until work measures 3¼in from beg.

Next round *1sc into each of next 6sc, keeping last loop of each st on hook work 1sc into each of next 2sc, yo and pull through all loops—called dec 1—, rep from * all around. 35sc.

Next round *1sc into each of next 5sc, dec 1, rep from * all round. 30sc.

Continue dec 4sts evenly on each round (working one st less between dec) until 10sc rem.

Fasten off.

Body
Using size F hook and white, ch 5, join with sl st to form a ring.

1st round Work 10sc into ring.

2nd round Insert hook into first st, yo hook and over index finger of left hand twice, yo and draw through 3 loops, yo and draw through 2 loops—called loop st—, 1 loop st into same st, *2 loop sts into next sc, rep from * all around.

3rd round *1 loop st into next st, 2 loop sts into next st, rep from * all around. 30 loop sts.

4th-17th rounds *1 loop st in next st, rep from * all around.

18th round 1 loop st into each of the next 8sts, (2 loop sts into next st, 1 loop st into next st) 7 times, 1 loop st into each of next 8sts.

19th round As 4th.

20th round 1 loop st into each of next 11sts, (2 loop sts into next st, 1 loop st into each of next 2sts) 5 times, 1 loop st into each of next 11sts.

21st-26th rounds As 4th.

27th round 1 loop st into each of next 12sts, (skip next st, 1 loop st into each of next 2sts) 6 times, 1 loop st into each of next 12sts.

28th round As 4th.

29th round 1 loop st into each of next 9sts, (skip next st, 1 loop st into each of next 2sts) 6 times, 1 loop st into each of next 9sts.

30th round As 4th.

Continue dec in this way, working 3sts less at beg and end of each dec round until 18sts rem.

Next round (Skip next st, 1 loop st into each of next 2 sts) 6 times.

Next round *Skip next st, 1 loop st into next st, rep from * all around.

Fasten off.

Topknot
Work as given for first 3 rounds of body.

Fasten off.

Back head piece
Using size F hook and white, ch 11.

1st row 1sc into 2nd ch from hook, 1sc into each of the next 8ch, 3sc into last ch, turn and work along other side of foundation ch, 1sc into each of 9ch, turn.

Next row 1 loop st into each of next 10sts, 3 loops sts into next st, 1 loop st into each st to end, 2ch, do not turn but continue around other side of work.

Next row 1 loop st into each of next 11sts, 3 loop sts into next st, 1 loop st into each st to end. Fasten off.

Ears
Using size F hook and white, chain 7.

1st row 1sc into 2nd ch from hook, 1sc into each of next 4ch, 3sc into last ch, turn and work along other side of foundation ch, 1sc into each of 5ch, turn.

Next row 1ch, 1sc into each of next 6sc, 3sc into next sc. 1sc into each of next 6sc, turn.

Next row 1ch, 1sc into each of next 7sc, 3sc into next sc, 1sc into each of next 7sc.

Fasten off.

Join on B, 1ch, 1sc into each of next 8sc, 3sc into next sc, 1sc into each of next 8sc.

Fasten off.

Make a second ear in the same way.

To finish
Stuff body and head and close up openings.

Sew ears to head and position topknot over them; catch-stitch ears to fold in half. Sew head to body. Work backstitches in white down center front of body to suggest a division.

Embroider white eyes and lashes and a black nose. Attach back head piece to back of head.

Crochet rabbits

These frolicsome rabbits are sure to amuse. And you'll enjoy making them too.

Finished sizes
10in, 13in, 16in (height).

Techniques involved
Simple crochet; embroidery stitches.

Tools required
Size C crochet hook; basic sewing tools.

Materials
Note: figures in brackets [] refer to the medium and large sizes.
3[3:4]oz of washable knitting worsted in main color A
small amounts of contrasting yarn for ears and embroidery
suitable stuffing

Gauge
22sc and 26 rows to 4in worked on size C hook.

Back
Using size C hook and A, ch 16 [19:21] and beg at foot.
Base row Into 2nd ch from hook work 1sc, 1sc into each ch to end. Turn.
Work 3 rows sc. **.
Next row Dec 1, work in sc to end.
Dec 1st at same edge on next 2[3:3] rows. Work 7[8:12] rows without shaping. Inc 1st at straight inside edge on next and foll alt row. Work 1 row. Fasten off.
Make another piece in same way to **.
Next row Work in sc to the last 2sts, dec 1.
Dec 1 at same edge on next 2[3:3] rows. Work 7[8:12] rows without shaping. Inc 1st at straight inside edge on next and foll alt row. Work 2 rows to end at inner edge.
Now cont working in sc across other piece to end.
30[34:38]sc.
Next row *** Dec 1, work in sc to last 2sts, dec 1.
Work 3 rows without shaping.
Rep last 4 rows until 26[28:30]sc rem. Cont without shaping until 11[13:17] rows have been worked from ***.
Next row Inc 1, work to the last sc, inc 1.
Fasten off. 28[30:32]sts.
Shape arms
Using size C hook and A, ch 13

This toothy trio will keep the children entertained.

[15:17], now work in sc across main part, turn and ch 14[16:18].
Next row Into 3rd ch from hook, work 1sc, 1sc into each ch, work in sc across main part inc 1sc in first and last st, 1sc into each ch to end.
Next row Skip 1sc, work in sc to last sc, turn.
Work 1[1:3] rows sc.
Next row 1ch, work in sc across 5 [5:6]sc, sl st into next sc, turn, skip sl st, work in sc to end. Fasten off.
Rejoin yarn to inner edge of other arm, 1ch, work in sc across 5[6:6]sc, sl st into next sc, turn, skip sl st, work in sc to end. Turn.
Work 4[6:6] rows across all sc. Fasten off.
Rejoin yarn to center 30[32:34]sc for neck and head. Work 1 row sc.
Next row Sl st across 4sc, work to last 4sc, turn.
Next row Sl st across 3sc, work to last 3sc, turn.
Next row Inc 1, 1sc into each sc to last sc, inc 1.
Inc 1sc at each end of next 3 rows. Work 1 row sc.
Next row Inc 1, 1sc into each sc to last sc, inc 1.
2nd and 3rd sizes only
Rep last 2 rows 1[2] times more.
All sizes
Work 3 rows sc. Inc 1sc at each end of next row. Work 3 rows sc. Dec 1 at each end of next row. Rep last 4 rows once more. Work 1 row sc. Dec 1sc at each end of next and every alt row 2[3:4] times in all. Dec 1st at each end of next 3 rows. Fasten off.

Front
Work as given for back.

Ears (make two)
Using size C hook and A, ch 14[16:18]. Work base row as given for back. Work 10[12:14] rows sc. Dec 1st at each end of next row. Work 3 rows sc. Dec 1st at each end of next and every alt row until 2sts rem. Fasten off.
Using size C hook and contrasting yarn, work 2 inner ears in the same way.

Tail
Using size C hook and A, ch 3. Join with a sl st to first ch to form circle.
Next round Work 6sc into circle. Join with a sl st to first sc.
Next round Work 2sc into each sc. 12sc. Join with a sl st to first sc.

Next round *1sc into next sc, 2sc into next sc, rep from * to end. Join with a sl st to first sc.
2nd and 3rd sizes only
Next round *1sc into each of next 2sc, 2sc into next sc, rep from * to end. Join with a sl st to first sc.
3rd size only
Next round *1sc into each of next 3sc, 2sc into next sc, rep from * to end. Join with a sl st to first sc.
All sizes
Work 5[6:6] rounds sc. Break off yarn, thread through last round of sc, insert stuffing, draw up tightly and fasten off.

To finish
Press or block pieces according to yarn used. With RS facing and leaving opening at top of head, join body pieces tog. Turn right side out and stuff very firmly, joining rem part of head. With RS of ear and inner ear tog, join long sides. Turn right side out and press if appropriate. Sew ears to head. Sew tail in place. Embroider face.

Crochet Dutch doll

With her crisp white cap and apron, this appealing doll has plenty of Old World charm.

Finished size
Approximately 16in (height).

Techniques involved
Simple crochet; embroidery stitches.

Tools required
Size C and size G crochet hooks; basic sewing tools.

Materials
3oz of washable knitting worsted in main color A
3oz each of contrasting colors B and C
1oz each of contrasting colors D and E
suitable stuffing

Gauge
24sc and 26 rounds to 4in worked on size C crochet hook.

Legs

Using size C hook and A, ch 3.
1st round 10sc into first of 3ch, do not join end of round.
2nd round *1sc into next sc, 2sc into next sc, rep from * to end.
15sts.
3rd round 2sc into first sc, *1sc into next sc, rep from * to end.
Rep 3rd round twice more.
18 sts.
6th round 2sc into first sc, 1sc into each of next 8sc, miss 1sc, 1sc into each of next 8sc.
18sts.
7th round As 3rd.
19sts.
8th round 2sc into first sc, 1sc into each of next 8sc, miss 1sc, 1sc into each of next 9sc.
19sts.
Rep 3rd round 3 times more. 22sts.
Mark this point, then continue in rounds of sc without joining at ends for 10 rounds more.
Break off A and join on B. Continue in sc for 8 rounds more.
Fasten off.
Make a second leg in the same way.
Place the two legs together and

mark the center 3sts on the inside of each leg.
Gusset
Using size C hook and B, ch 6.
1st row 1sc into 3rd ch from hook, 1sc into each of next 3ch. 5sts.
2nd row 1ch, *1sc into next sc, rep from * to end.
Rep 2nd row 3 times more.
Join gusset to legs
Continue working with yarn from gusset and beg with left leg: skip 3 marked sts, 1sc into each of rem 19sts, 1sc into each of foundation ch of gusset (5sts), continue with right leg: skip 3 marked sts, 1sc into each of rem 19sts, sl st to first st of gusset.
48sts.

Body

Continue in sc for 17 rounds in B, 15 rounds D, 2 rounds E.
Break off yarn.

Arms

Using size C hook and A, ch 3.
1st round 5sc into first of 3ch, do not join end of round.
2nd round *2sc into next sc, rep from * to end.
10sts.
3rd round *1sc into next sc, 2sc into next sc, rep from * to end.
15sts.
4th round *1sc into next sc, rep from * to end.
5th round *1sc into each of next 2sc, 2sc into next sc, rep from * to end.
20sts.
Mark this point.
Work 20 rounds more in sc. Break off A.
Join arms to body
Mark 4sts at each side of body for the underarms, making them slightly to the front (i.e. 3sts to the front and one st to the back on each side of body).
Beg at back of body, skip first st after right underarm, join B to next st, 1ch to count as first sc, 1sc into each of next 18sc, insert hook into next sc and draw up a loop, insert hook into 1sc of left arm and draw up

a loop, yo and draw through all three loops on hook, 1sc into each of next 14sc around left arm, insert hook into next st and draw up a loop, skip the 4sts marked for left underarm on body, insert hook into next st and draw up a loop, yo and draw through all 3 loops on hook, 1sc into each of next 17sc across front of body, join next st to one st of right arm as before, 1sc into each of next 14sc around arm, join next st of arm to rem st beyond the 4 marked sts of right underarm.
68sts.
Next round *1sc into each of next 15sc, insert hook into next st and draw up a loop, insert hook into next st and draw up a loop, yo and draw through all 3 loops on hook—called 2sc tog—, rep from * to end.
64 sts.
Work 2 rounds sc without shaping.
Do not break off yarn.
Stuff arms, legs, and body, joining the openings at underarms and between legs and gusset.
Next round Continue with B, *1sc into each of next 6sc, 2sc tog, rep from * to end.
56sts.
Work 1 round without shaping.
Next round *1sc into each of next 5sc, 2sc tog, rep from * to end.
48sts.
Work 1 round without shaping.
Next round *1sc into each of next 2sc, 2sc tog, rep from * to end.
36sts.
Work 1 round without shaping.
Next round *1sc into each of next tog, rep from * to end.
24sts.
Break off B and join on E.
Next round Sl st into next sc, rep from * to end.
Next round *1sc into next sl st, rep from * to end.
Next round *1sc into next sc, rep from * to end.
Next round *Sl st into next sc, rep from * to end.
Break off E.
Stuff remainder of body firmly.

Head

Using size C hook, join A to back of neck, *1sc into next sl st, rep from * to end.

24sts.

Next round *1sc into each of next 2sc, 2sc into next sc, rep from * to end.

32sts.

Next round *1sc into next sc, 2sc into next sc, rep from * to end.

48sts.

Work 14 rounds without shaping.

Next round *1sc into each of next 4sc, 2sc tog, rep from * to end.

40sts.

Work 2 rounds without shaping.

Next round *1sc into each of next 3sc, 2sc tog, rep from * to end.

32sts.

Work 1 round without shaping.

Stuff head to here.

Next round *1sc into each of next 2sc, 2sc tog, rep from * to end.

24sts.

Work 1 round.

Next round *1 sc into next sc, 2sc tog, rep from * until only 5sts rem and stuff the remainder of head as work progresses.

Break off yarn, thread through rem sts and draw up tight.

Fasten off.

Embroider eyes and nose in stem stitch as illustrated.

Dress

Left sleeve

Using size G hook and C, ch 23.

1st row 1sc into 3rd ch from hook, *1sc into next ch, rep from * to end. 22sts.

2nd row Join in E, 1ch, *1sc into next sc, rep from * to end.

3rd row Using E, as 2nd. Break off E.

Using C, work 9 rows more.

Left bodice

Using a separate length of C, ch 6 and join to beg of last row.

Next row ch7, 1sc into 3rd ch from hook, 1sc into each of next 4ch, *1sc into next sc, rep from * to end, 1sc into each of 6ch.

34sts.

Continue for 8 rows more.

Next row 1ch, 1sc into each of next 14sc, turn and continue on these sts.

Back

Work 6 rows more. Break off yarn.

Right bodice

Using size G hook and C, ch 20.

Next row 1sc into 3rd ch from hook,

1sc into each of next 17ch, 1sc into each of 15sc that were left.

34sts.

Work 8 rows more.

Next row Sl st over first 6sts, *1sc into next sc, rep from * to last 6sts, turn.

22sts.

Work 8 rows more in C, then 2 rows E, 1 row C.

Fasten off.

Using C and with RS facing, work 1 row sc up front edge around neck and down other front, then 1 row of crab st (sc worked from left to right).

Skirt back

Using size G hook and C, with RS facing, work 23sc across lower edge of bodice back.

Next row 1ch, 1sc into same place, *1sc into next sc, 2sc into next sc, rep from * to end.

35sts.

Work 2 rows.

Next row 1ch, 1sc into next sc, *2sc into next sc, 1sc into each of next 2sc, rep from * to end.

46sts.

Work 22 rows more in C, then 6 rows E, 2 rows C.

Fasten off.

Skirt front

Using size G hook and C, with RS facing, work 8sc across right front bodice, hold the two sections of the bodice together and work 1sc into the double thickness of the two edges together, 8sc across left bodice front.

17sts.

Next row 1ch, 1sc into same place, 2sc into each of next 5sc, 1sc into each of next 5sc, 2sc into each of next 6sc.

29sts.

Work 2 rows.

Next row 1ch, 1sc into next sc, *2sc into next sc, 1sc into each of next 2sc, rep from * to end.

38sts.

Work 22 rows more in C, then 6 rows E, 2 rows C.

Fasten off.

Join side and underarm seams.

Apron

Using size G hook and B, ch 76.

1st row 1sc into 3rd ch from hook, *1sc into next ch, rep from * to end. 75sts.

2nd row 1ch, *1sc into next sc, rep from * to end.

Break off yarn and turn.

3rd row Skip 31sc, rejoin yarn to next sc, 1ch, 1sc into each of next 12sc, turn.

13sts.

4th row 1ch, *2sc into next sc, 1sc into next sc, rep from * to end.

19sts.

Work 2 rows.

7th row 1ch, 1sc into same place, *1sc into each of next 2sc, 2sc into next sc, rep from * to end.

26sts.

Work 19 rows without shaping.

Break off yarn.

With RS facing, work 1 row sc down right front edge, along bottom and up left front edge, then 1 row crab st.

Fasten off.

Hat

Using size G hook and B, ch 7 and beg at back.

1st row 1sc into 3rd ch from hook, *1sc into next ch, rep from * to end. 6sts.

2nd row 1ch, *1sc into next sc, rep from * to end.

Continue in sc, inc one st at each end of next 2 rows.

Work 10 rows without shaping.

15th row Sl st into first sc, 1sc into each of next 8sc, sl st into last sc, turn.

16th row Sl st into first sc, 1sc into each of next 6sc, sl st into next sc.

Fasten off.

With RS facing, rejoin yarn to beg of work and work 14sc up side of back, 10sc across top, 14sc down other side.

38sts.

Continue in sc, inc one st at each end of next and every alt row until there are 52sts, ending with a RS row.

Continue in sc across bottom edge of hat.

Work 1 row crab st all around.

Roll the wings of the hat as illustrated and catch-stitch in place.

Catch-stitch hat to doll's head.

Crochet puppet pets

*Here's a little menagerie of puppets to keep the children
entertained on a rainy day—or a sunny one.*

Finished size
7½in (length).

Techniques involved
Simple crochet; embroidery stitches.

Tools required
Size F crochet hook; basic sewing tools.

Materials
For cat:
1oz of washable sport yarn in each of these colors: blue, maroon, gray, and white
short length of black yarn for embroidery
2 buttons
For dog:
1oz of washable sport yarn in each of these colors: yellow, green, beige, and medium-brown
short lengths of black, pink, and maroon yarn
2 buttons
For pig:
1oz of washable sport yarn in yellow and pink
short lengths of white, black, and maroon yarn
For rabbit:
1oz of washable sport yarn in each of these colors: black, maroon, and white
short length of blue yarn
4 buttons

Gauge
20sc and 22 rows to 4in worked on a size F hook.

Basic hand puppet
Ch16.
Base row 1sc into 2nd ch from hook, 1sc into each ch to end. Turn. 15sc.
Next row 1ch to count as first sc, 1sc into each sc to end. Turn. Rep last row 13 times more.
Next row 1ch, 2sc into first sc, work to last sc, 2sc into last sc.
Turn.
Next row 1ch, 1sc into each sc to end.
Turn.
Rep last 2 rows until there are 27sts, ending with an inc row.

First arm
Next row Work across first 6sts. Turn.
Next row 1ch, (insert hook into next st and pull yarn through) twice, yo and pull through all loops on hook—

called dec 1—, 1sc into each sc to last sc, 2sc into last sc. Turn. 6sts.
Next row 1ch, 1sc into each sc to end.
Turn.
Rep last 2 rows twice more.
Next row 1ch, (dec 1) 3 times.
Next row Dec 2.
Fasten off.

Second arm
Skip center 15sts, rejoin yarn to next st, 1sc into same st, 1sc into each of last 5sts.
Turn.
Next row 1ch, 2sc into first sc, 1sc into each of next 3sc, dec 1 over last 2sc.
Turn.
Next row 1ch, 1sc into each sc to end.
Rep the last 2 rows twice more. Complete as given for first arm.

Head
Rejoin yarn to first of 15sc at center.
Work 9 rows in sc. Dec one st at each end of next 5 rows. 5sts rem. Fasten off.
Make another section in the same way. Place sections tog and work in sc around outer edge in appropriate color.

Cat
Using blue, work first 15 rows of lower body. Change to maroon and work 11 rows of increasing for arms.
Work first 5 rows of arms in maroon, then remainder in white. Rejoin maroon to upper body and work 2 rows, then change to gray to complete head.

Ears (make two)
Using gray, ch 10.
Base row 1sc into 2nd ch from hook, 1sc into each sc to end. Turn. 9sc.
Work 5 more rows in sc.
Fasten off.
Fold corners over to make a point and sew to top of head.

Features
Using black, embroider eyes, eyelashes, nose, and mouth. Thread five short lengths of white behind nose to form whiskers.

Collar
Using white, sew around neck in blanket stitch. Return in opposite direction, working blanket stitch

over top to form a link patt.

Straps (make two)
Using blue, ch 30. Attach to top of blue "skirt" at front and back. Sew buttons to end of front straps.

Dog
Using green, ch 16.
Base row 1sc into 2nd ch from hook, 1sc into each ch to end. Turn.
1st row 1ch, 1sc into each of first 3sc, changing to yellow on last st, (3sc in yellow, 3sc in green) to end. Turn.
2nd row (3sc in green, 3sc in yellow) to last 3sts, 3sc in green.
3rd-4th rows (3sc in yellow, 3sc in green) to last 3sts, 3sc in yellow.
5th-6th rows As 2nd.
7th-8th rows As 3rd and 4th.
Cut off green. Cont in yellow, working first 5 rows of arms in yellow, then remainder in beige.
Rejoin yellow to upper body and work 2 rows, then change to beige to complete head.

Ears (make two)
Using medium-brown, ch 10.
1st row 1sc into 2nd ch from hook, 1sc into each of next 7ch, 3sc into last ch, then working along other side of ch, work 1sc into each of rem 8ch. Turn.
Next row 1ch, 1sc into each of first 8sc, 2sc into next sc, 1sc into next sc, 2sc into next sc, 1sc into each sc to end. Turn.
Rep last row twice more. Fasten off.
Gather up flat end and attach ears to head.

Features
Using black, embroider eyes and nose. Using pink, embroider mouth.

Suspenders (make two)
Using maroon, ch 30. Attach to top of patterned "trousers" at front and back. Sew buttons to suspenders.

Pig
Using yellow, work up to last 12 rows except arms, which have first 5 rows in yellow, then rest in pink. Work remainder of head in pink.

Ears (make two)
Using pink, ch 3. Join with a sl st into first ch to form a circle.
1st round Work 8sc into circle.

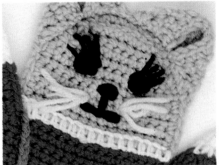

One basic pattern, with suitable variations, makes all four of these hand puppets.

Attach collar around neck.

Using a short length of maroon yarn, make a bow at neck.

Rabbit
Using black, ch 16.

Base row 1sc into 2nd ch from hook, 1sc into each ch to end. Turn.

1st row 1ch, 1sc into each of first 3sc, changing to white on last st, (3sc in white, 3sc in black) to end.

2nd row (3sc in black, 3sc in white) to last 3sts, 3sc in black.

Rep last row 4 times more.

Change to maroon for rest of body.

Work first 5 rows of arms in maroon, then complete arms in white.

Rejoin maroon to upper body and work 2 rows. Complete head in white.

Ears (make two)
Using white, ch 11.

1st row Work 1sc into 2nd ch from hook, 1sc into each of next 8ch, 3sc into last ch, then working along other side of ch, work 1sc into each of 9ch. Turn.

2nd row 1ch, 1sc into each of first 9sc, 3sc into top sc, 1sc into each of rem 9sc. Turn.

3rd row 1ch, 1sc into each of first 10sc, 3sc into top sc, 1sc into each of rem 10sc.

Fasten off.

Fold base of each ear to center, sew down, then attach to head.

Features
Using blue, embroider eyes. Using black, embroider nose and mouth.

Work a row of blanket stitch in black up center front for "jacket" opening. Sew buttons to "jacket."

Thread black yarn around neck for "tie." Make bow at center front.

2nd round Work 2sc into each sc. 16sc.

3rd round (1sc into next sc, 2sc into next sc) all around. 24sc.

4th round (2sc into next sc, 1sc into each of next 2sc) all around. 32sc.

Fasten off.

Fold ears in half and attach to head.

Features
Using black, embroider eyes.

Snout Using needle length of double pink, place needle between and just below eyes. Wind yarn several times around needle, then secure at each end. Using black, embroider the nostrils.

Collar
Using white, ch 31.

Next row 1sc into 2nd ch from hook, 1sc into each of next 2sc, *3ch, sl st into last sc worked, 1sc into each of next 3ch, rep from * to end. Fasten off.

WOODEN TOYS

A few scraps of leftover lumber are all you need to construct many of the wooden toys in this section. They are well-designed, simple to make, and sturdy enough to withstand the most energetic play. There are toys to suit boys and girls of all ages, including boats, a railroad engine, a super truck, also a lovely dollhouse. The cost of the materials is easy on your billfold too.

Basic know-how

Tools

There is a wide range of tools for making wooden toys and some of them have only one purpose. Each technique section explains what tools are available and how they are used. In each case, the tools discussed are the best or most convenient for the job in hand.

Certain basic tools are almost indispensable, but these are relatively cheap, and will probably already form part of even a modest tool kit.

At least one saw is essential, and a crosscut saw is probably the most suitable for general use. It is useful to have a coping saw as well for cutting curves. A saber saw is a very versatile power saw as it can make straight or curved cuts, also bevels if it has a bevel adjustment.

A trimming knife is invaluable for all sorts of odd jobs and for shaping parts.

You will need a drill of some kind and a selection of bits for drilling holes for screws and other fasteners. A hand drill is good for holes up to $\frac{1}{4}$in diameter, a bit brace for larger holes. A $\frac{1}{4}$in power drill can take bits from very small to more than an inch. It is a good choice.

Screwdrivers of different sizes, and perhaps different types, will be needed to drive screws.

A claw hammer will also be needed to join parts which are nailed together. A lightweight type is the most useful.

A steel rule and some type of square are essential for marking and cutting out parts.

Pliers can be used for holding all sorts of parts that are difficult to

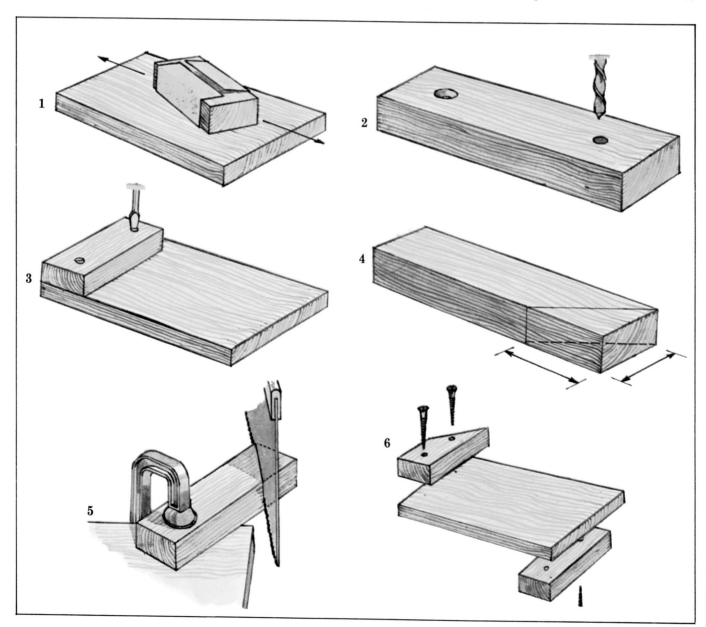

Right: *When scribing cutting lines around a piece of lumber, it is important to work in the correct order, with the try sqare in the right place. After scribing a mark, turn the lumber in the direction of the red arrow, and line your try square with the 'nick' left by it to continue the line around.*

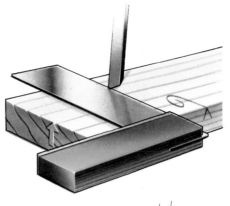

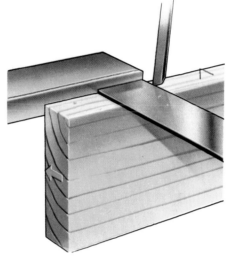

Left: *Making a bench hook. The instructions are as follows:*

Tools required
Pencil; rule; try square; 45° set square; sandpaper and block; tenon or back saw; C-clamp; hand drill and bits (also countersink bit); screwdriver.

Materials
One piece pine ¾in × 7in × 9in
Two pieces pine 1in × 2in × 6in
Four No. 10 1¼in flathead screws
PVA woodworking adhesive

1. *Smooth all wood surfaces with a sandpaper block.*
2. *Using a C-clamp, hold one of the short pieces in place on the larger piece (across the grain). Drill the pilot holes. Remove the short piece and drill out the pilot hole to make the shank hole. Countersink using the countersink bit.*
3. *Apply glue to both surfaces, and rub together to force out excess glue. Screw on the short piece.*
4. *Take the other short length of wood and check that the ends are square. Draw a diagonal line from one corner, and, using the try square, continue around the lumber. Check the diagonals on both sides with the set square.*
5. *Clamp the piece to the bench and crefully saw off the triangular waste, then smooth the cut surface with the sandpaper block.*
6. *Turn the large work piece over and glue and screw the mitered short length in a similar way to the first. If you are left handed the short pieces will be attached to the opposite sides of the board.*

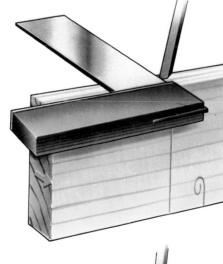

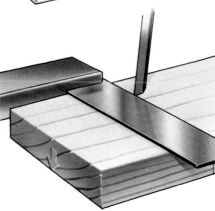

hold in your fingers, and can also be used for bending metal parts or cutting wire and rods.

A hacksaw will be needed to cut parts that are made from sheet metal.

For shaping wood parts, a file or a rasp is the most versatile tool, but it is sometimes possible to manage with just sandpaper and a sandpaper block. These will be needed in any case for finishing parts.

To apply the finish, you will need at least one paintbrush, and preferably a range of small to medium sizes.

Some kind of sturdy work surface will also be necessary, and a bench hook is invaluable for holding parts. This, however, is easy to make from waste cuts and scrap pieces of lumber (see opposite, page 136).

Lumber and boards
The majority of toys involve three basic materials—softwood, plywood and dowels. Other materials occur less frequently.

Softwood covers most of the solid wood used. The term does not mean that the wood is particularly soft, although it often is. It designates the type of tree from which the boards were cut. Pine is the most familiar generic name for this type of wood.

Softwood is sold in various lengths and can often be bought cut to order. It is sold in a variety of sizes described as width and thickness, e.g. 1in × 2in. It can be bought rough-sawed to this size, but the normal way of buying it for these toys is to obtain lumber which is planed all around, which leaves a smooth finish on all four faces and edges. It is important to remember when buying lumber in this form that it is measured when sawed, not when finished. This means that lumber of the nominal size given above will actually be smaller than this in each dimension, because of the material removed in planing it smooth. If a part has to be, for example, exactly 1in thick, do not buy that nominal size as this will be appreciably less. Instead, buy lumber of a larger size and have it "milled" down to size.

Because it is a natural material, the quality of softwood varies considerably and it is often graded for sale. Avoid poor quality lumber that is split or badly warped, has a large number of knots or is watermarked or damp.

Veneers are very thin sheets of wood—generally hardwood—used to give a decorative finish over cheaper woods. They are not often available except from craft shops or cabinetmakers' suppliers.

Plywoods are man-made boards produced by gluing several cross-grained veneers together under heat and pressure with the grain of alternate layers at right angles. They are very stiff and strong, although the thinner varieties can often be bent to form curved shapes. They are sold in standard 4ft × 8ft sheets.

Special materials

Apart from wood, which is the major component of these toys, some toys need parts made from other types of material, generally from metal. Where other materials are used, they are detailed more fully in the individual instructions.

Metals are used in the form of sheet, tube and rods, and usually in quite small pieces. The best source for tubes and rods is usually model shops, although you may have to go to a metal dealer for the sheet metal. Specify the kind of metal required (brass, mild steel, aluminum), and the dimensions. Thickness of sheet metal, and diameters of rod and tube may be given as a measurement or as a gauge number. Check by direct measurement if in any doubt.

Marking from measurements
Check the measurements from the diagram or the text, and note the material used. If the part is made from plywood or board, the size used is identified in terms of its thickness only, e.g., $\frac{1}{4}$in plywood. You should select a piece of the appropriate material and make sure that it is big enough to accommodate a panel of the size required.

If the part is made from softwood, the size required will be given in terms of two measurements—the thickness and width of the lumber, e.g., 1in × 2in pine. Bear in mind that the actual measurements of the lumber will be slightly under these dimensions as explained in the **Materials** section. Select a piece of lumber of the appropriate size and

make sure that it is long enough to make the part required. Take note also of any special requirements, such as that the lumber have no knots in it.

Where parts are made from dowel, this will be identified in terms of its radius, e.g., $\frac{3}{8}$in hardwood dowel. Select a rod of this type, making sure that it is long enough.

Similar rules apply where the part is made from another material, such as metal sheet or tube, and detailed instructions are given where appropriate.

You should always try to use your materials as economically as possible. In the case of solid lumber, this means cutting the parts from one end; with boards cutting them from an edge or corner. If several parts are to be cut from one piece, you should fit them up against one another as far as possible. This also simplifies cutting, since one cut will do for two parts. However, bear in mind that any cut will remove a small amount of material, so mark one part first, cut it, and then mark the second. If you mark them together and then cut, the second part will be undersize by the amount wasted in the saw cut.

Start your marking from a true straight line. You should never assume that the edge of the board or the end of the lumber is straight unless you have checked it. It may have been cut wrongly at first or damaged later.

To check the edge of a board, use the longest straightedge possible. Lay it along the edge and check that it touches at all points. If it does not, the edge is not true.

To check the end of a piece of lumber, use a square. Hold the stock against the edge of the lumber and try to align the blade with the cut end. Do this across the width and down the thickness of the material. If the blade does not align in either direction, the end is not true. You should also inspect even a square end for any damage, such as dents or splits.

If the end or edge is true, proceed with the marking. If not, move a short distance in from the edge of the board or along the lumber, far enough so that the new line will clear the old, and mark a new straight line.

Where the positions of holes in the middle of a part have to be marked, you can use a similar method, on either board or solid wood. Hole positions are given in terms of two measurements—their distances from two edges. Measure these distances along the two edges and mark the points. Square lines across the board from these points. The hole position is where the two lines cross. Mark it with a cross.

Where a part is rounded, use a compass to mark it. Set the compass against a ruler to the radius required. If a full circle is needed, mark this as close as possible to the corner of the board. If only the corner of a part is to be rounded, mark the radius distance along the two edges, working down from the corner (you can use the compass for this as they are already set to the correct distance). Square these two points into the board until they meet. Put the point of the compass on this point and mark enough of a circle to meet the two edge lines.

In a few cases it is necessary to find the center of an existing circle, such as on the end of a piece of dowel. To do this, use a simple jig.

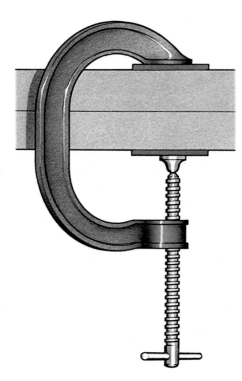

This C-clamp is ideal for holding smaller pieces of lumber as the glue sets.

Fit the circle into the angle of the jig and mark a line across it along the edge of the guide rule. Turn the circle around through 90° and mark another line. The center is where the two lines cross.

Measure materials other than wood (e.g., metal or plastic) as for wood. To mark them, use a scriber, which has a hardened metal point, to scratch a line.

Where two parts are the same size, or have to fit accurately together, it is more accurate and often quicker to measure them against one another, rather than marking each individually. You can also clamp the pieces together and cut through them as one. Where a large number of parts must be cut to the same size, use the first one only as a master pattern—do not cut out each and use it as a pattern for the next, since any errors will also be passed on, getting worse each time.

Marking from patterns
When you have your full-size pattern, transfer it to the material required for that part. You can do this by pinning it to the surface with a piece of carbon paper underneath and going over all the lines with a ball-point pen. Alternatively, if the pattern is not needed for marking another surface or part, paste the pattern onto the material and remove it after cutting. You may have to do this when cutting out parts in metal.

Holding the work
For easy, accurate work, it is essential to be able to hold the workpiece securely. The most important thing is to have a sturdy work surface. The ideal is a heavy, fixed carpenter's workbench but this is expensive and not essential. A portable, collapsable bench is a very good substitute, and has the advantage of a built-in clamp. You can even use a sturdy kitchen table, but you should cover this with a piece of plywood or particle board to protect the surface.

You must be able to hold the work in place. For sawing, the simplest solution is to make a bench hook, which can be done easily as shown on page 136. With this hooked over the edge of the bench, hold the workpiece into the angle formed by

the batten on top to lock it in position.

A vise is very useful for holding work in all kinds of situations. The clamp-on type is the cheapest, and quite adequate. C-clamps are a good alternative to a vise, and can be used to hold two pieces together while they are being joined. Very small modelers' clamps are cheap and convenient for holding small pieces together, but you will need larger clamps to hold work down to the bench.

When you use clamps, you should always pad the workpiece with scraps of wood to prevent the clamp from marking the work. If you are using a Spanish windlass, pad the edges of the work with scraps of heavy cardboard to prevent the cord from cutting into it.

Hold very small pieces of work with pliers. Use long-nosed pliers for the smallest parts. Self-locking pliers will avoid the need to maintain pressure on the handles.

To hold small parts in place, particularly while gluing them, rubber bands and adhesive tape make very useful clamps for light pressure. They can also be used where the parts are an awkward shape.

A temporary support, particularly where small parts require shaping, can often be provided by screwing them to a larger block or directly to the work surface. Insert the screws from below, making sure they do not protrude into the work area, and fill the screw holes after shaping.

Sawing
Sawing is the most convenient way of cutting out parts from most materials. It can also be used to produce slots or grooves in some cases. There is a great variety of saw types to cope with different materials and different types of cutting, but all work in much the same way. The blade has a series of sharpened teeth, each of which takes a small bite out of the material as the blade passes through it. Depending on the size of the teeth and how they are set (bent out from the blade, first to one side, then the other), this means that any saw cut forms a groove (called the kerf) and wastes some of the material as sawdust. For this reason, it is essential that cuts be always

made slightly to the outside of the marked line so that the kerf falls in the waste material and not on the part. If that happens, the part will be slightly undersized.

Also, depending on the type of saw used, the cut line will be rough to a greater or lesser extent. If a smooth finish is important, cut oversize and finish to the marked line with sandpaper or a plane.

The finish achieved, and also the ease of sawing are governed by the sharpness of the teeth. If the blade is replaceable, change it when it becomes blunt. Fixed saw blades can be sharpened by a professional saw sharpener when they lose their edge.

In general, modeling work may be done with hand saws, although power saws are extremely useful, and take much less effort to use. They can also be controlled very accurately for fine work.

In all types of sawing, it is impossible to do accurate work unless the material is adequately supported and firmly held. This is covered under **Holding the work**.

1. *Hand saw (straight back blade).*
2. *Tenon or back saw.*

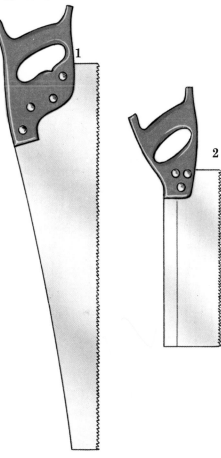

Making straight cuts

In wooden parts, straight cuts are required in two types of material—solid wood and panel materials. Two types of saw are needed to handle the different cuts required, a hand saw and a saber saw.

Hand saws have a long tapering blade. There are many kinds, classified by the type of teeth and their number in points per inch (ppi). The most generally useful is a panel saw, which is suitable for cuts with or against the grain and with about 10ppi. Use the panel saw for making long cuts in panel materials or for cutting larger pieces of softwood.

Support the work firmly so that the cutting line is just over the edge of the work surface with the waste to the outside. Start the cut by putting your free hand down on the workpiece with the back of the thumb aligned with the cut. Using your thumb as a guide, position the saw so that it is just to the outside of the cutting line. Hold it at an angle of about 45°. Draw it up toward you once or twice so that the teeth make a small notch in the edge of the board, just their width. Use your thumb to keep the saw from running off-line. This will start the cut accurately. Continue sawing by pushing and pulling the saw alternately, holding it at an angle of about 60°. Work smoothly and evenly, using the whole length of the saw and not trying to force it through the wood. Watch the marked line all the time to make sure that the cut is running true. Blow sawdust away from time to time as it accumulates. As you near the end of the cut, support the waste with your free hand to prevent it falling under its own weight, breaking free and tearing the wood. Slow down as you reach the very end of the cut.

When you are cutting very thin boards, there is a danger that the saw will tear rather than cut the board. You can cut very thin boards by repeated scoring with a knife. Alternatively, clamp a piece of scrap board (hardboard is ideal) on each side of the workpiece along the cut line. Then cut through the complete sandwich.

Back saws are for more accurate cutting than panel saws. The blade is shorter and is stiffened by a solid metal back to keep it rigid. There are more and finer teeth. The heaviest back saws are called miter box saws. One around 10 to 12in long and with about 16 to 17ppi is good for most purposes. Back saws for finer work are called dovetail saws.

Use a back saw for cutting smaller sections of solid wood or short cuts in panel materials. They are more accurate than hand saws but cannot be used on very large pieces, because the back limits the depth of cut. They also cut more slowly because of the finer teeth.

Start the cut in the same way as with a hand saw. If you are cutting right through a piece of wood, proceed as above. Back saws are also used to cut horizontally when a cut only has to pass part of the way through the material.

Making curved cuts

Curved cuts in solid wood and panel materials are made with saws with very fine narrow blades that can follow the curve without binding in the cut. These are quite prone to damage and cannot be sharpened, but are replaceable. The coping saw, a hand saw type consists of a frame in which the blade is held taut, and a handle. The frame curves so that it does not restrict the blade when work is being done away from the edge of a board. The two most common curve-cutting saw types are the coping saw and the electric saber saw.

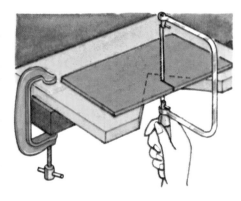

How to use a coping saw.

Use the saber saw on thin boards or on thicker boards a long way from the edge. It has very narrow blades for fine cuts and tight curves, and larger ones for heavier work. It is used from above the workpiece, cutting on each up-stroke. The teeth point upward, tending to hold the saw down on the work.

Support the workpiece over the edge of your work surface with the cutting line just beyond it. Hold the saw with the blade vertical to start it into the work. Keep it vertical as you continue, working just outside the marked line. Turn the work and move it over the edge to keep the saw working in the same position while following the line, or turn it to follow the cutting line, but don't cut into the support. Continue in this way to the end of the cut.

If you have to start a cut in the middle of the board, drill a small hole in the waste near the cut line

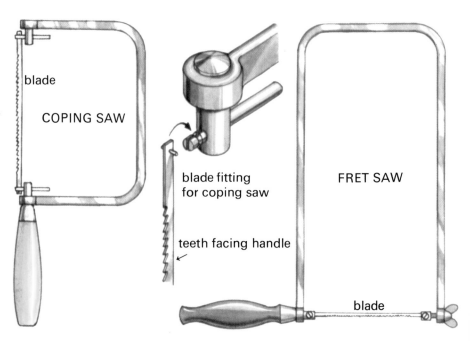

blade

COPING SAW

blade fitting for coping saw

teeth facing handle

FRET SAW

blade

and insert the blade through it. Work over to the cut line, then proceed as before.

If you have to cut a sharp point in the line, you must proceed differently. Instead of working around the point, start two cuts, working into each side of the point. This will result in a sharp angle which is not possible in a single cut.

Coping saw blades are tensioned by a screw in the handle. The blade is mounted so that you can swivel it around. This means that you can work around a line which follows the edge of a board by turning the saw blade around and cutting sideways with the frame over the edge of the board.

You can use a coping saw with the work held vertically or horizontally, but it must be held securely. Both saber saws and coping saws are limited for working on very heavy material. If this is necessary, it can be done with a box saw or a power band saw, or in some cases, with a power jig saw.

Making slots

To make slots on the end or edge of a part, cut both sides with a back saw. Work the blade of a coping saw or saber saw into the cut and use it to cut across the bottom, removing the waste. Wider slots can be cut across the bottom with a chisel narrower than the slot.

Slots in the middle of a part which go all the way through can be cut by drilling holes the width of the slot at each end and joining them with saw cuts using a coping saw or saber saw.

Cutting special materials

Materials other than wood generally need a special-purpose saw. Some types of plastic can be cut with wood cutting saws, but others, and all metals, need special blades. In general, these can all be treated in the same way and cut with a hack saw or coping saw, or a saber saw with a metal-cutting blade.

Hack saws have a metal frame and replaceable blades tensioned with a screw and fitted facing away from the handle, the opposite of those of the coping saw. They are available in two basic sizes and with a range of blade lengths, but for most purposes, the smallest—called a

junior hack saw—is quite sufficient. They will cut straight lines or mild curves, and the smaller blade of the junior type will follow a tighter curve. Clamp the work very securely and proceed as for the coping saw. Work slowly and smoothly. A little light oil on the blade will make cutting easier.

For cutting very tight curves in metal, use a jeweler's saw, which is similar to a coping saw for wood and takes fine blades, or work as close as possible with a hack saw and finish with a file.

To cut thin, flexible metal sheet, use standard snips if possible. You can cut sheet metal with a saw by supporting it on both sides with scraps of hardboard and cutting through the complete sandwich.

Knives

At least one knife is essential for modeling work, as they have literally hundreds of uses. The two most useful types are the trimming knife and the craft knife.

The trimming knife usually has a handle shaped to fit the palm of the hand. The blades can be sharpened to prolong their useful life, but are intended to be discarded and replaced when they become blunt. Some types have blades scored with a series of notches so the point can be snapped off, presenting a new cutting edge. The blade is quite short and stiff, so it can be used for heavy cutting. You can get different blades for various uses, including a hack saw blade and a pad saw blade for light work in metals and wood.

Craft knives are similar, with replaceable blades fitted into a

handle. The handle is smaller and lighter, so that it can be controlled even between finger and thumb for precise work. You can fit it with a wide variety of differently-shaped blades to suit different purposes— with straight edges, curves and points.

Using a knife

Knives can be used to cut parts out of very thin materials, such as plastics or thin plywood, which a saw would damage. The cut edge is cleaner than a saw cut. Use them also to cut card and paper, as they will produce a better edge than scissors. The trimming knife is more suitable for heavier materials than the craft knife.

Support the work on a sturdy working surface. You should cut onto a firm but resilient surface that

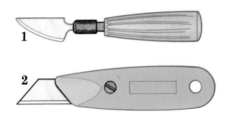

1. *A craft knife can be fitted with a variety of different blades.*
2. *Trimming knife. Some have retractable blades.*

3. *Drill access holes either on the line, or well into the waste area of lumber.*
4. *One large hole, or two or more smaller ones makes cutting awkward shapes easy.*

3

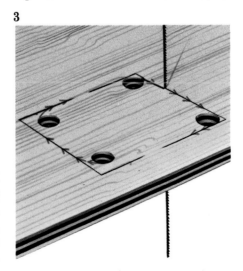

4

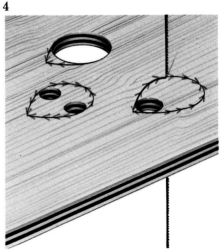

will not blunt the blade if it should cut in, and which will protect the worktop below. A piece of heavy-duty linoleum is ideal.

Straight cuts are much easier than curves. Use a straightedge as a guide to keep the knife on line. Hold it in place on the work with your free hand, pressing firmly to keep it in place. Do not let your fingers overhang the edge. Cut toward yourself, keeping the hand holding the straightedge behind the blade and standing out of the direct line of the cut. Keep the knife in line with the straightedge, and press the point up against the edge. Run the knife along the cut line, pressing down firmly, but not forcing the cut. If you are cutting hard or very thick material, do not try to cut through in one attempt, but make several shallow cuts along the same line until you are through. You can score materials for bending by cutting through to only half their depth to create a fold line.

Curves must be cut freehand, unless you can find a suitable template with the right radius to act as a cutting guide. When you are cutting materials like plywood that have a grain, the knife will tend to follow the grain, so cut the curve along and across the grain in such a way that if the knife does get pulled off line by the grain, it will run outside the curve into waste material. Steady the work with your free hand, but never hold it in front of the blade.

Knives can also be very useful as carving tools, especially where you want to trim the corner or edge of a part. Use them to round off sharp points or edges, and for tapering dowels, with a whittling technique. Holding the part in a vise or with your free hand, use the knife to remove small shavings of the material as if sharpening a pencil. Always cut away from yourself. Do not try to remove too much material at one time, but work down gradually to the required shape. Always cut along or across the grain direction—never into it or it will pull the knife off line and may well split.

If you do not have a special marking knife, you can use an ordinary knife in its place when scribing a line with a square or straightedge. This is better than using a pencil, as the line will be finer and more accurate, and because a knife scores the surface, will make it less inclined to split or splinter.

Always change a blade whenever it becomes blunt during the course of work. A blunt blade will not cut cleanly, and because it will require more force, there will be a greater risk of it slipping off line.

Chisels

Chisels are one of the most important tool groups in general woodworking, although they have less uses in model- and toy-making. They are available in a wide range of widths, and special shapes that include gauges.

They are really a special form of knife, in which the cutting edge is set square to the handle. This concentrates a cutting force on the edge, and makes it possible to reach points that are inaccessible to knives.

Their main use in toy-making is as shaping and carving tools, and it is quite possible to use alternative tools for most of the toys in this book.

Planes

The plane is another tool that is invaluable in general woodworking, but has far fewer uses in toy-making. A form of precision knife, its purpose is to remove accurate, thin shavings to produce a smooth surface on wood or to shape or fit it. The basic plane is available in a wide range of sizes, and there are many special-purpose planes for particular shaping work, including the spokeshave, which can be used to shape curved surfaces.

Planes are not essential for most of the toys in this book, although they, or a wood file, are needed to finish wood blocks to thickness in a few cases. The spokeshave can also be used for shaping the boat hull, although it is not essential.

Using a plane

To cut efficiently, a plane blade must be very sharp. Sharpen it on an oilstone, sharpening it first to an angle of 25°, then finishing the very edge at an angle of 30°. Use the coarse side of the oilstone first, then finish on the smooth side. Use plenty of light machine oil as a lubricant. Fit the blade to the plane and adjust it so that only about a shaving's thickness is visible below the sole (base) of the plane.

Mark the workpiece to show the finished line clearly on all sides. Support it firmly and clamp in position, but make sure that the plane will have an unobstructed run over it.

Study the grain direction before you start. You must always plane in the "uphill" direction of the grain, and with it running upwards along the line of planing, otherwise the blade will dig in and not cut cleanly.

Plane smoothly and evenly along the whole length of the work. The blade should remove a thin, even shaving. If it does not, check that you are planing in the correct direction, and check that the blade is set correctly.

Continue in this way until you reach the finished thickness shown

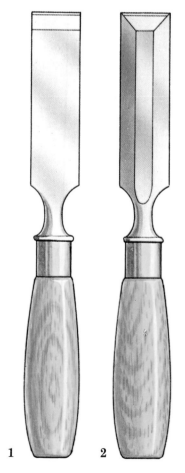

1. *This chisel is firm enough to hit with a mallet.*
2. *A bevel edged chisel for awkward corners.*

by your marked line.

If you have to plane end grain, use a block plane, which is adapted for the purpose. Work in from both corners to the middle, not across the whole width as this will tear the grain at the corners.

You can use a plane to chamfer or round off an edge. Hold it at an angle to the face and edge of the wood (45° in the case of a chamfer) and plane along the edge until you have a chamfer of the desired width. To round the edge, vary the angle of the plane between strokes.

Use spokeshaves for curved surfaces. A flat-based spokeshave is for convex surfaces, a curved base for concave ones. Hold the spokeshave by both handles and draw it towards you along the grain, varying its angle to suit the curve. This is best judged by eye. Remove thin shavings until you have reached the desired shape.

Rasps, files and wood files

This group of tools is generally useful for most shaping and finishing work. Although each type of tool works in a slightly different way, their method of use is virtually the same.

Each tool has a large number of very small teeth which cut or abrade the surface to remove material. Depending on the size, number and angle of the teeth, they can have a fine, medium, or coarse cut. The classification of cut varies depending upon the type of tool. These tools are made in a range of different flat and curved shapes to enable them to tackle different shaping tasks.

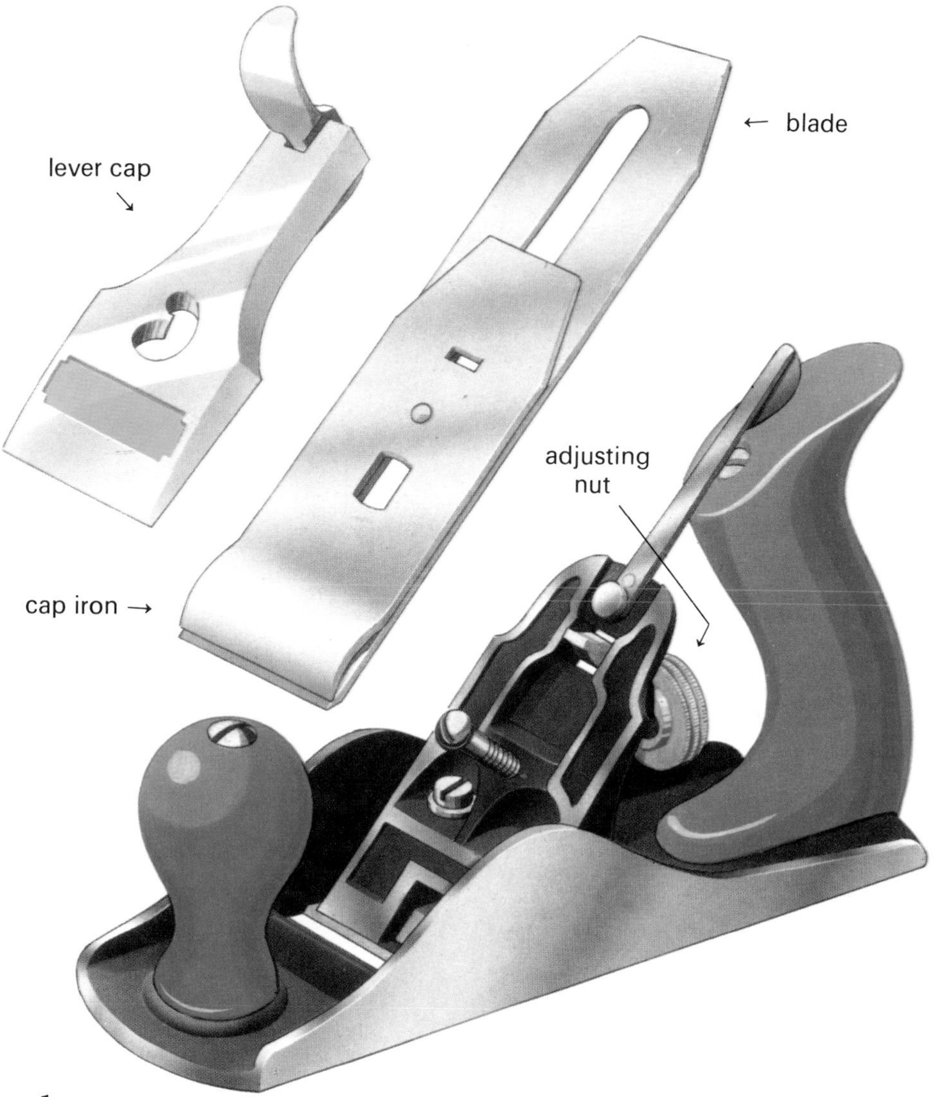

lever cap

← blade

cap iron →

adjusting nut

1

2

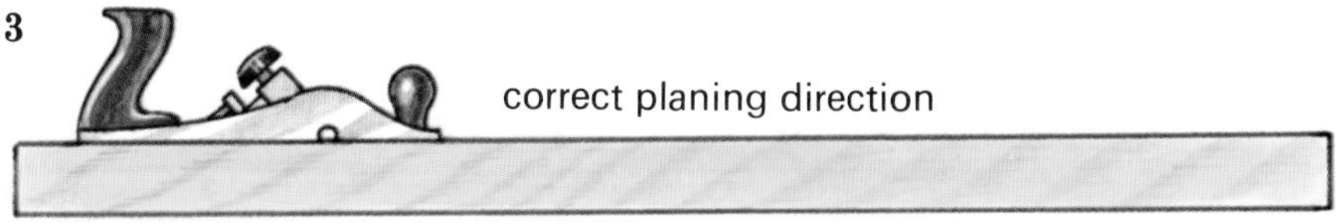

3

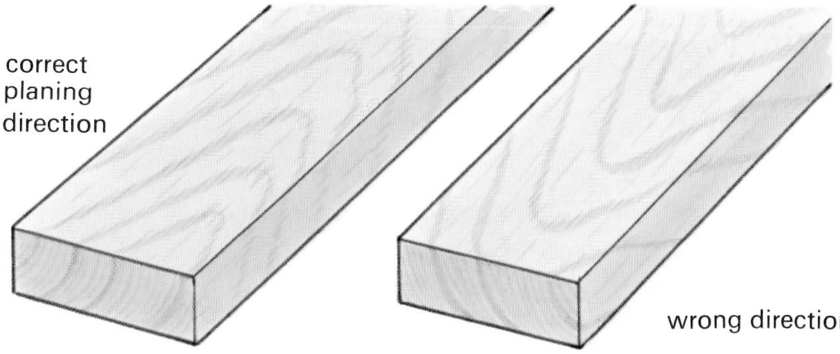

correct planing direction

correct planing direction

4

wrong direction

1. *The parts of a bench plane.*
2. *Two ways of planing end grain in order to avoid breaking and splintering the ends.*
3. *Grain along the edge shows the planing direction.*
4. *Grain on facing surface.*

Rasps

These tools are normally half-round in shape. The flat side is used for flat or convex surfaces, the curved side for concave ones. The teeth are very coarse and set quite widely. They will remove material quickly without clogging. Rasps are usually supplied without handles, and you should fit one before use.

Support the work firmly, preferable at about elbow height. Hold the rasp by its handle. You can use the other hand to hold the tip if necessary for greater accuracy.

Run the tool along the work, using the whole length of the blade if possible. Hold it level with a flat surface, or tilt it as you pass over a curved one. The tool can be used with or across the grain, or on end grain, but will tend to tear the surface more. On end grain, use it from both sides and avoid using it across the corners as they will tear.

Because of the relatively rough surface left by the teeth, you should stop well before you reach the desired profile and finish shaping with another tool, or with sandpaper (see **Finishing**).

Files

Files can be used for finishing and shaping both wood and metal. Their blades have a large number of very fine teeth, shaped in different ways to give a finer or coarser cut. They are shaped in many different ways—flat, half-round, round or triangular plus many special shapes—to enable them to cope with various tasks. Very fine files (called needle files) can be used for fine shaping and piercing work.

Always fit a file handle before use. Needle files have their own shaped handles. Because of the relatively fine teeth, files tend to clog, especially when they are used on soft materials. You can clean the teeth with a wire brush, or on a special cloth which has wire bristles, called a file card.

Use a file in much the same way as a rasp. It can be used in any direction on wood or metal and will leave quite a smooth surface depending on the cut of the teeth. In general, unless very little material has to be removed, start with the coarsest cut and work through to the finest.

Support the work firmly at about elbow height. Hold the file at an angle to the direction of cut and take smooth strokes forward, applying pressure on the forward stroke only. For a smoother finish on metal, hold each end of the file, lay it across the surface, and draw it straight back towards you. When working over a curved surface, tilt the file as you make the stroke.

Sanding

Sanding is the final shaping process. It is a relatively slow way to remove material, even when the coarsest grades of abrasive are used, but this is an advantage when the work is nearing completion. Because sanding leaves the smoothest finish of all the shaping processes, it is used before the finish is applied. For this reason, details of sanding are included in the **Finishing** section.

Drills

There are several types of drill, and all of them can be used in some part of toy-making.

One of the most useful is a hand drill. This is easy to control in making the majority of small holes. A power drill is useful, however, for making large holes and for saving effort, and is essential for using a hole saw, which is used when making very large holes, also some types of wheel. You can also use a brace and bit for making large holes. An archimedean, or push drill, is also quite a useful tool for very small holes. Simply push it against the work to spin the bit and drill the holes.

Use a hand drill by holding it over the work with the handle, pressing down lightly. Turn the handle smoothly and evenly working clockwise.

The bit brace should be held with the palm on the handle to steady it and push down lightly. Rotate the handle in a smooth clockwise sweep.

The power drill needs only a guiding hand on the handle and a finger on the trigger. Be careful to keep the cable out of the way and avoid wearing loose clothing. Be prepared for the drill to work very quickly.

Though not strictly a drill, the bradawl is a useful tool for making small holes and starting smaller

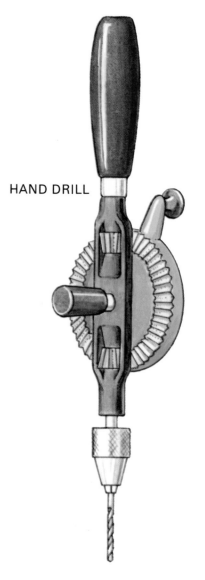

HAND DRILL

screws. Hold it against the wood with the blade at right angles and apply pressure while twisting it from side to side about a quarter turn.

Drill bits

For drilling holes around $\frac{3}{4}$in diameter in wood or metal, you can use twist drills in both a hand or power drill. A set ranging from $\frac{1}{16}$in to $\frac{1}{2}$in will cover most jobs. The best quality are made from high speed steel.

For larger holes in wood, use a power drill fitted with a power bit of the size that you need.

Hole saws are specialized drills designed to remove a core of the material. They are suitable only for use on thin materials. They consist of a central pilot drill, with, around it, a length of saw blade bent into a circle. The pilot drill serves to start the hole and keep it centered. The saw then works around the surface of the material, cutting through it until the center falls free. Hole saws are made to specific diameters. Perhaps the most useful type is one which has a range of interchangeable blades to cut circles of several sizes. They are used in toy-making for cutting very large holes in plywood, and for making wheels.

You will also need a countersink or rose bit, for making countersunk holes for flathead screws.

Drilling pointers

In all types of drilling, accuracy is essential. You should start by fixing the work firmly. Where possible, try to arrange this so that you are drilling vertically. For angled holes, try to clamp the work at the angle, rather than clamping it flat and holding the drill at an angle. Support the work adequately underneath the hole. When the hole is going to pass through the part, place a piece of scrap wood behind it to take the point of the drill as it breaks through. This is particularly important on thin materials.

Mark the position of the hole with a cross, then make a small starting hole with a bradawl. This helps to position the drill bit initially. When drilling metal, mark the hole with a center punch and a hammer.

Select a drill within the size range and fit it into the chuck of your drill. If a hole has to be drilled only partway through a part—to a certain depth—measure this length along the drill bit and mark it. The easiest way is to wrap a piece of masking tape or insulating tape wrapped to mark the depth.

Position the drill bit over the mark, and hold the drill square to the wood (unless drilling an angled hole). You can check that it is square by holding a try-square against it.

Start to drill, not forcing the drill but allowing the cutting edge of the bit to do its work. The weight of the drill alone should be sufficient in most cases. If you are drilling metal, a little light lubricating oil will help the cut.

Continue in this way until the drill reaches the marked depth or the point breaks through. Lift the drill gently out of the hole at this point, but do not stop it rotating until it is almost free. An exception to this is when drilling stopped holes with a brace and bit. They should be rotated counterclockwise for removal.

Opposite: *A hand drill.*
Below: *Ratchet brace and a selection of bits.*

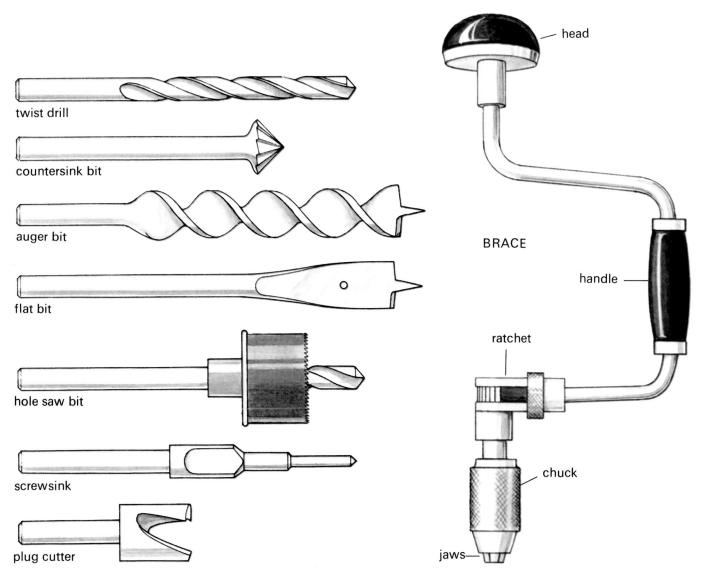

twist drill

countersink bit

auger bit

flat bit

hole saw bit

screwsink

plug cutter

BRACE

head

handle

ratchet

chuck

jaws

Hole saws should be used in much the same way. Use them as slowly as the drill will go and do not force the cut. Stop from time to time if the saw shows signs of overheating. The saw will make a cleaner cut if you stop before it breaks through. Turn the wood over and inset the pilot drill from the other side. Continue drilling until the two cuts join up.

This double-drilling method can also be used for cleaner cut holes with power bits and brace bits that pass right through the wood. Watch the underside of the workpiece for the moment that the center point of the drill breaks through, then remove it and drill through from the other side until the holes join up.

Hammering

Because most of the work is relatively light, the basic tool is the smallest, lightest hammer—called a tack hammer. This is light in weight, often with a small head that has one flat face and which is drawn to a point set at right angles to the handle—and magnetized. It may also be a claw (nail pulling) type.

Use the tack hammer when you have small nails. Hold it well down the handle and strike the nail squarely and evenly. The magnetic head is used for starting tacks into the wood. Hold the tack between your finger and thumb and give it a tap with the hammer to start it. Reverse the hammer and continue driving with the flat face.

When working with larger nails or into hard lumber, you will need a larger hammer. Choose a medium-weight claw hammer. Use it the same way, but carefully because of its greater weight.

Avoid striking the work with a hammer. You should continue nailing until the head is almost flush with the surface of the work. Stop hammering at this point and use a nail set to drive the head below the surface. The type to use is ground concave on the small end so it will not slip off the head of the nail. Choose one with a head of about the same diameter as the head of the nail. Strike it evenly with the hammer until the head of the nail has just sunk below the surface. You can then cover the small hole with some filler and sand it flush for an invisible nailed joint.

If you do have the misfortune to bend a nail, which usually occurs because it was not struck straight, or because it has hit a hard obstruction, stop at once. Remove the nail with a pair of pincers or a claw hammer. Grip the nail between the jaws and lever the handles over to pull out the nail. You should protect the work with a scrap piece of lumber or board under the jaws or the hammer head to prevent them from marking the surface.

To insure that the work is positioned correctly, drive some or all of the nails through the part to be joined first. Work on a piece of scrap board and drive them until the point just starts to protrude. Position on the other part so that the points just bite in when it is correctly aligned and drive the nails right home. When it would be very difficult to hold the part in position while nailing, hold it temporarily with clamps or adhesive tape. You can use light taps from a hammer to drive components together, such as when a rod is to be fitted into a socket that is a little tight. Do not use a hammer when it is likely that it will damage the parts—use a mallet or soft-headed hammer (with rubber or plastic faces) instead. Always use a mallet rather than a hammer for striking a chisel.

Nails

There are many different types of nail, but those often used for toy-making are classified as finishing nails. They are described in terms of their length.

Also used occasionally are round wire nails. These are larger, with a plain round shank and a flat round head. They are classed by length.

Other special-purpose nails, where used, will be described in detail.

Always discard any misshapen or bent nails as they will almost certainly damage the work. You can minimize the risk of the nail splitting the work by blunting the point

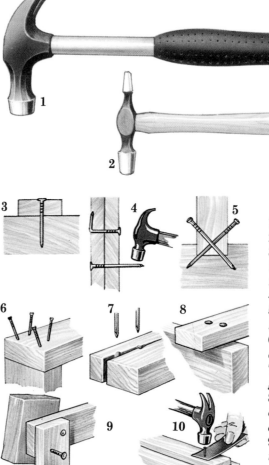

1. *A claw hammer.*
2. *A tack hammer.*
3. *Nails should be 3 times length of workpiece. Always nail smaller to large.*
4. *Clench-nailed joints.*
5. *Skew-nailing is best for housing joints.*
6. *Drive nails in at opposing angles for end grain.*
7. *More than one nail along grain line risks splitting.*
8. *Nail small battens overlength and saw off waste to avoid splitting.*
9. *Place a block under the work to avoid 'bounce'.*
10. *Position small nails with a cardboard holder.*

slightly with a hammer before driving.

Nail in the positions shown in the diagrams. If nail positions are not shown, space them out evenly. Try to nail through the center of narrow parts and avoid nailing very close to the edge.

Screws and screwdrivers
Screws of various kinds provide a strong mechanical fastening between two parts. There are different kinds of screws for different kinds of material, but in this book, all the fastenings are made into wood, and all screws used are types of wood screw.

Screws
Most types of screw have three parts—the thread, which bites into the wood to provide the hold, the shank, which is an unthreaded part passing through the part to be joined; and the head, which is wider than the rest of the screw to draw the parts tightly together.

The head can have various different shapes, according to its use. The ones used in this book are all either flathead, which is flat on top with angled sides designed to drive in flush with the surface, or roundhead, which is shaped like a half sphere and designed to stand out on the surface. In addition, screws have a slot in the head so that they can be driven with a screwdriver, and are classed according to the type of slot. This can be a plain single slot cut right across the head, or a double slot arranged in a cross. The latter type are called cross-head screws. The most familiar are Phillips.

The shank of the screw is the widest part of the screw that goes into the wood and it is this that denotes its size. However, some types of screws are threaded along their whole length.

The different types of screw have different types of thread. Slotted-head screws (the traditional type) taper through their whole length and have a thread with a single helical twist set below a plain shank. Cross-head screws are threaded through their whole length and may only taper at the tip. The main advantage of the different types for toy-making is that the screws that are threaded for their whole length

have a much better holding power when they are screwed into the end grain of softwood.

In addition to being classed by their type, screws are classified by their length and thickness. The length is given simply in terms of inches. The thickness is normally given in terms of a number (No.), called the gauge, which relates to the thickness of the shank and the diameter of the head. The larger the number, the greater the thickness. The most common sizes in this book are No. 8 and No. 6, although others may be encountered.

The final classification of screws is according to the material from which they are made. This is generally steel (which may be painted or plated to prevent rust), or brass.

Screws are thus classified in terms of all these qualities, e.g., 1in No. 8 flathead brass woodscrew.

Screwholes
Although a screwhole might seem quite simple, the relatively complicated shape of a screw means that a screw if it is to drive easily and provide a strong fastening needs a carefully drilled hole.

The first point is that the screw should not bite into the part which is being fastened—only into the part it is being fastened to. This means that it needs a clearance hole that is slightly bigger than its thickest part, so that it can pass through without binding.

The screw must bite into the part into which it is fastening, but will not drive in easily unless it has a hole to follow. This hole is called the pilot hole and should be smaller than the thread—to allow it to grip, but large enough for the screw to drive easily. The pilot hole size is determined by the gauge of the screw.

Clearance and pilot hole sizes for the screws used in this book are given in the diagrams, but in general a No. 8 screw needs a $\frac{9}{64}$ in clearance hole and a $\frac{7}{64}$ in pilot hole. A No. 6 screw needs a $\frac{7}{64}$ in clearance hole and a $\frac{5}{64}$ in pilot hole.

The combined length of the clearance and pilot holes should be the same as the overall length of the screw.

Countersunk heads need a further

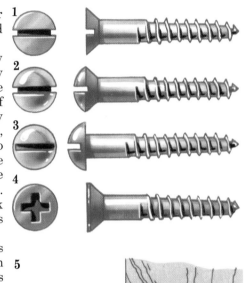

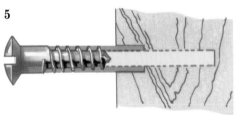

A selection of screws suitable for woodworking.
1. *A flathead screw is flat on top with angled sides. It is designed to lie flush on the work surface.*
2. *A roundhead screw with angled sides lies above the surface.*
3. *A flat-sided roundhead screw.*
4. *A patented Phillips screw.*
5. *Inserting a wood screw. The yellow section shows the first hole, the red the second.*

refinement to the hole. The top should be drilled out with a countersink bit to allow the head to sink into it and sit flush with the surface.

Special screws and fittings
Related to screws, the screw eye and screw hook are used in several types of application. Instead of a head, the end of the shank is bent around to form a loop, which can be a ring or a hook. They are classified by one measurement alone.

Drive them into a very small pilot hole made with a fine drill or a bradawl. They can be turned with the fingers, with pliers or with a screwdriver run through the loop.

Some screws are used to act as axles for wheels. To make sure that the wheels run smoothly and do not bind against the head or on the chassis, these screws are fitted with washers.

Driving screws

The correct tool is a screwdriver, but there are several different types and sizes.

Slotted-head screws need a screwdriver with a plain blade. It should be almost as wide as the screw head, but no wider, and should be a tight fit in the slot. If it is too loose, it will damage the slot and the screw will be difficult to drive and remove.

Cross-head screws need a cross-head screwdriver. There are various kinds, but the familiar Phillips-type is suitable for all applications. The tip size and angle also vary to suit screw sizes. The correct one to use is one that just fills the recess in the head.

Handles have many different shapes—choose the most comfortable. In general, the bigger the handle, the more driving force you can apply.

Screws will drive more easily into a tight hole if you apply a little wax or soap to the threads. Brass screws are relatively weak and can snap if driven hard. To prevent this, drive a steel screw of the same size and type first, remove it and replace with a brass one.

Where screws have to take a heavy load and need not be removed, the hold will be firmer if you apply a little woodworking or epoxy adhesive to the threads before driving. This is particularly useful when fastening the end grain and attaching wheels to a chassis.

If you have the misfortune to snap a screw or damage the head so that it cannot be driven, you should remove it and replace with a sound one. If it cannot be removed with a screwdriver, grip the head or shank with pliers and use these to twist it free.

Adhesives

Where two parts have to be joined permanently, they may be glued together using an adhesive. In many cases this is supplemented with screws, nails or brads, which serve to locate the parts correctly, hold the joint while the adhesive dries and strengthen it when it has set.

PVA woodworking adhesive

This is a general-purpose glue suitable for joining wood to wood or wood to boards. It is available in many container sizes and is applied directly from the bottle. White in color, it dries clear. It is often called white glue.

A relatively cheap adhesive, it is the one to use for most general assembly work involving wooden parts. It is water-soluble, so you can clean any excess from the work using a damp cloth. You can also thin it with water to make an excellent paste for paper which can be applied with a paint brush.

Apply to one only of the surfaces to be joined. Bring them together and hold with light pressure until set. Do not apply a great deal of pressure as this squeezes adhesive out of the joint. Remove any which does squeeze out using a damp cloth. It sets by evaporation of the water solvent, usually in about half an hour, but reaches full strength over a longer period—a matter of several hours.

The bond produced is very strong and durable, and the adhesive is capable of bridging small gaps between the parts to be joined, but it will not stand up to prolonged exposure to water, so do not use for projects such as model boats.

Water-resistant adhesives

Commonly based on a urea formaldehyde composition, these are the adhesives to use for wood-to-wood joints in projects which will be subjected to dampness or outdoor exposure.

Sold in powder form, mix with water as instructed to form a paste which you should apply to the surfaces to be joined. Bring together under light pressure and clamp until set. Initial curing takes around an hour but full strength is not reached for a period of hours, usually overnight. Clean off any surplus with a damp cloth before it has set. Epoxy resin adhesive is one of the strongest types, and will bond most materials. Use this where metal or rubber has to be bonded to wood. It is unaffected by immersion, and is good for use with toys like boats. Follow the maker's instructions.

Safety note

Many adhesives are more or less toxic. Avoid skin contact as far as possible and keep all such substances away from your mouth and eyes. Read the instructions thoroughly before use, and in an emergency get medical advice. As a matter of course, keep adhesives away from young children.

Finishing

Toys should always be finished thoroughly, so that they have a neat attractive appearance and a smooth clean surface with no roughness or splinters. Good surface preparation is indispensable to a satisfactory finish.

Surface preparation

No surface will take paint or varnish well, or look good when finished, unless it is smooth, clean and dry. The easiest way to achieve this is with thorough sanding and then a final cleanup.

Sanding is quite a slow way to remove material, so you should aim to cut parts as cleanly as possible before assembly. If you have any holes or gaps left, fill them before sanding. You can use cellulose filler, plastic wood or a mixture of sawdust and woodworking adhesive for this. Types that have to be mixed should be of the consistency of a stiff paste. Work them into the holes with a putty knife, leaving a little standing above the surface. If the part is to be varnished, use a filler that matches the wood as closely as possible in color.

After filling, if necessary, you can sand the surface. Various types of abrasive paper are used for this. On wood, the most commonly used are sandpapers, which are crushed abrasive bonded to a paper backing. These are available in a range of grades and also by names—fine, medium and coarse. Graded papers often have grit numbers—the highest grit numbers are the finest.

As the names suggest, the finest grades leave the finest finish and remove the least material. A very rough surface will need treatment with coarse paper first, working down through medium to the finest grades. A substantially smooth surface, like that of good-quality plywood, will often need just a very little treatment with the finer grades.

Always use sandpaper with a sanding block. This will allow you to apply even pressure over a large area and prevent the paper from digging in. You can use a scrap block of softwood. When sanding a concave surface, use a block that is rounded to the same or smaller radius than the curve you are finishing. Scraps of dowel are ideal for this.

Cut off a piece of paper big enough to fold right around your block. Wrap it around and hold it in place with your fingers or tape.

Sand with smooth, even strokes working along the grain, and using no more pressure than is required to allow the paper to bite into the surface and remove a fine dust. On end grain, work from side to side and toward the center.

A well designed working area is ideal for woodworking. Tool storage is arranged so that you can reach equipment easily in the course of the job.

Toys from scrap wood

Odd scraps of wood which have been left over from other carpentry projects should never be thrown away. Pieces of solid wood, dowels and plywood are all useful. Put them in a box or bin—they can become toys that are both fun to make and practical. Many lumber suppliers throw away remnants that could be yours for the asking. These simple toys use a few bits and pieces of leftover wood—an inexpensive way to give a child many hours of pleasure.

Robot

Techniques involved

Sawing; drilling; sanding.

Tools required

Back saw; hand or electric drill and bit to correspond to smallest dowel diameter.

Materials

Leftover pieces of wood and dowel
PVA woodworking adhesive
fine sandpaper

Making the robot

Select pieces of wood that will give the correct proportions. Choose thicker dowel for the legs than for the arms, and a piece of wood for the head which is no more than half the width and thickness of the body. The arm pivot dowel must be no more than half the thickness of the arms.

Cut the block used for the body to length. To position the arms, drill a hole straight through the block near the top. The hole must be slightly larger than the diameter of the arm pivot dowel to allow the arms to swing freely.

Cut the arms to length, slightly longer than the body block. Drill holes through them near the top, the same diameter as the pivot dowel.

Measure the thickness of the body plus both arm dowels and cut the pivot dowel to this size.

Cut the head block to size. Cut the legs to length.

Smooth all of the parts with fine sandpaper.

Assemble as illustrated. Pass the pivot dowel through the hole in the body but do not glue. Put a little glue in the holes in the arms and fit them onto the ends of the pivot making sure that they are in alignment.

Glue the legs to the bottom of the body.

Glue the head in place, slightly toward the back of the robot.

You can vary the design to allow the head to turn around. Drill a hole in the head and in the body and use a length of dowel for the neck, glued into the body but not the head.

These sturdy little robots are fun to make from remnants left over from carpentry work. They are simple toys to construct, and would make an ideal introductory project to teach your child basic carpentry skills.

Train

Techniques involved

Sawing; sanding; painting.

Tools required

Back saw; hand or electric drill with bits; screwdriver; paintbrushes; sanding block.

Materials

Leftover pieces of wood and dowel
PVA woodworking adhesive
screw eye
screw hook
4 woodscrews at least 1in long, No. 8 or No. 6
8 cup washers to fit screws
fine sandpaper
enamel paints
polyurethane lacquer
length of cord for pull

Making the engine

Select suitable pieces of wood and dowel. The base should be about 3in wide and from 7 to 8in long. Make it from $\frac{1}{2}$in plywood or pine between $\frac{5}{8}$in and 1in thick. The cab requires a block of 2in × 2in, about 3in long. The boiler and wheels are made from $1\frac{1}{2}$in diameter hardwood dowel, and the chimney from $\frac{3}{4}$in dowel.

Cut the base to size and smooth with sandpaper. Drill pilot holes to suit the screws you are using (about $\frac{1}{32}$in smaller than the thread diameter), at two points on each side to mount the wheels.

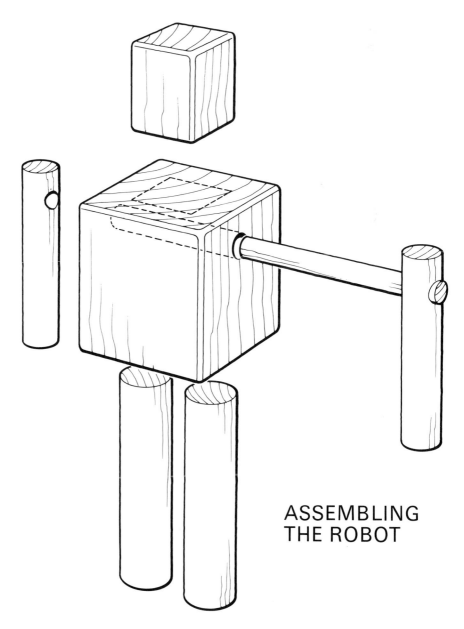

ASSEMBLING THE ROBOT

151

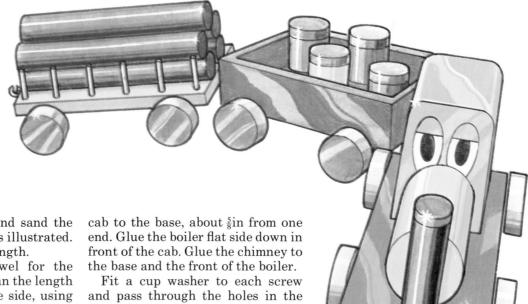

Cut the cab to size and sand the top corners to a curve as illustrated.

Cut the chimney to length.

Cut a length of dowel for the boiler, about 4in less than the length of the base. Flatten one side, using sandpaper or a plane if available.

Also from $1\frac{1}{2}$in dowel, cut four slices $\frac{1}{2}$in thick to form the wheels. Mark the centers and drill clearance holes for the screws you are using.

Sand and varnish or paint all parts.

Assemble as illustrated. Glue the cab to the base, about $\frac{5}{8}$in from one end. Glue the boiler flat side down in front of the cab. Glue the chimney to the base and the front of the boiler.

Fit a cup washer to each screw and pass through the holes in the wheels. Place another washer over the screw, then insert into the holes in the base and screw into place so that the wheels can just turn freely.

Fix a screw eye to the front of the base and a screw hook to the rear. Tie on a length of cord for pulling the toy along.

Make a colorful train like this one from scraps of leftover lumber.

ASSEMBLING THE TRAIN

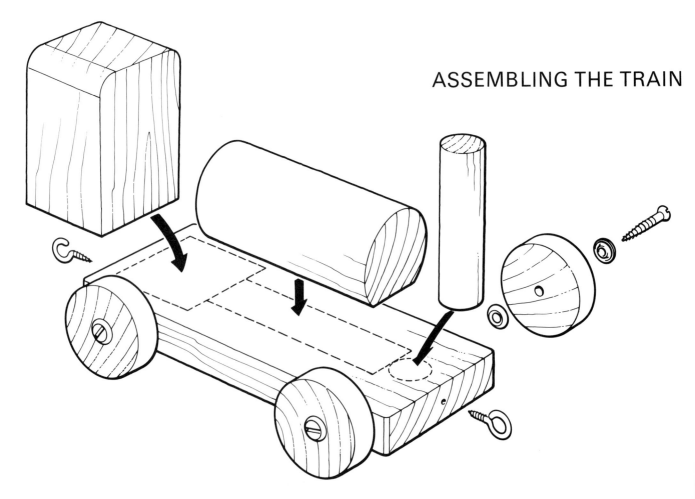

152

Tic-tac toe

This makes an ideal instructional toy for a child. What an entertaining way to learn how to think logically—by placing the chunky wooden pieces in the squares! The game is quite easy to make, and the cutting of the crosses is the only aspect of construction that requires a little extra concentration.

Finished size
12in square.

Techniques involved
Marking; cutting; gluing; finishing.

Tools required
Try-square; saber saw; ruler; pencil.

Materials
$\frac{1}{2}$in × 12in × 12in plywood
$\frac{3}{4}$in × $\frac{3}{4}$in × 44in pine
2in × 2in × 10in pine
$1\frac{1}{4}$in diameter × 10in dowel
PVA woodworking adhesive
sandpaper
varnish or paint

Making the baseboard

Using a try-square and ruler, mark out a 12in × 12in square on a piece of $\frac{1}{2}$in plywood. Cut this to size using a hand saw, and finish the edges smooth with sandpaper. Sand both surfaces lightly.

Make the board dividers from $\frac{3}{4}$in square pine. Cut two lengths 12in long, and six more $3\frac{1}{2}$in long. Following the drawing (fig. 1) arrange these on the board and glue in place with PVA woodworking adhesive to form nine equal squares. Sand the exposed ends and edges of the dividers.

Making the circles

Cut five 2in lengths of $1\frac{1}{4}$in diameter dowel. To insure you make a parallel cut, wrap a piece of broad masking tape around the dowel, putting one edge in line with the cutting position. Overlap the ends and keep the edges even. Saw according to the masked edge. Sand the cut ends of each piece of dowel.

Making the crosses

Cut five 2in lengths of 2in × 2in pine.

Mark the cutting lines with a try-square to ensure that the blocks are cut accurately.

The crosses are formed from these blocks by cutting away triangular wedges from each side. Mark the ends of end block as shown in fig. 2. Start by drawing diagonal lines from corner to corner of the block. Then mark parallel lines on each side of, and $\frac{1}{4}$in away from, the diagonals. Continue the cutting lines over onto the sides.

Clamp each block firmly and make two saw cuts on each face using a saber saw and following the marked lines. Try to position the block so that you can make each cut vertically downwards, then turn the block for the next cut.

Finish very carefully using sandpaper to smooth the cut faces and ends of the crosses. A coat of clear varnish will protect the wood.

2
BASEBOARD

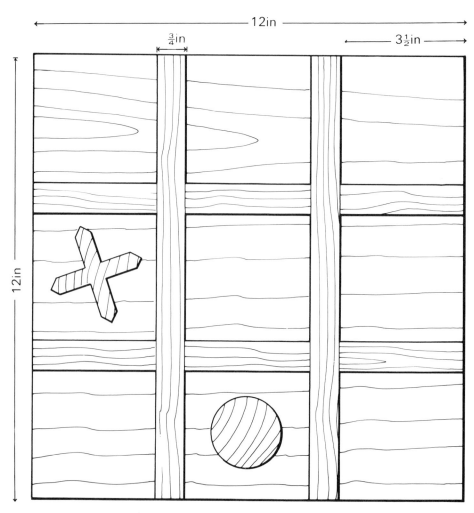

1
TRACE PATTERNS FOR CROSSES

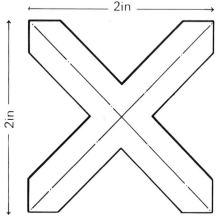

Submarines

There are two versions of this toy. The larger one can be used on a pond or lake or in a swimming pool, while the smaller version can be used in the bath tub. Both work on the same principle. A rubber band motor spins the propeller to power the sub through the water. The ballast weight and the angled vane make the sub sink and move along underwater until the rubber band unwinds.

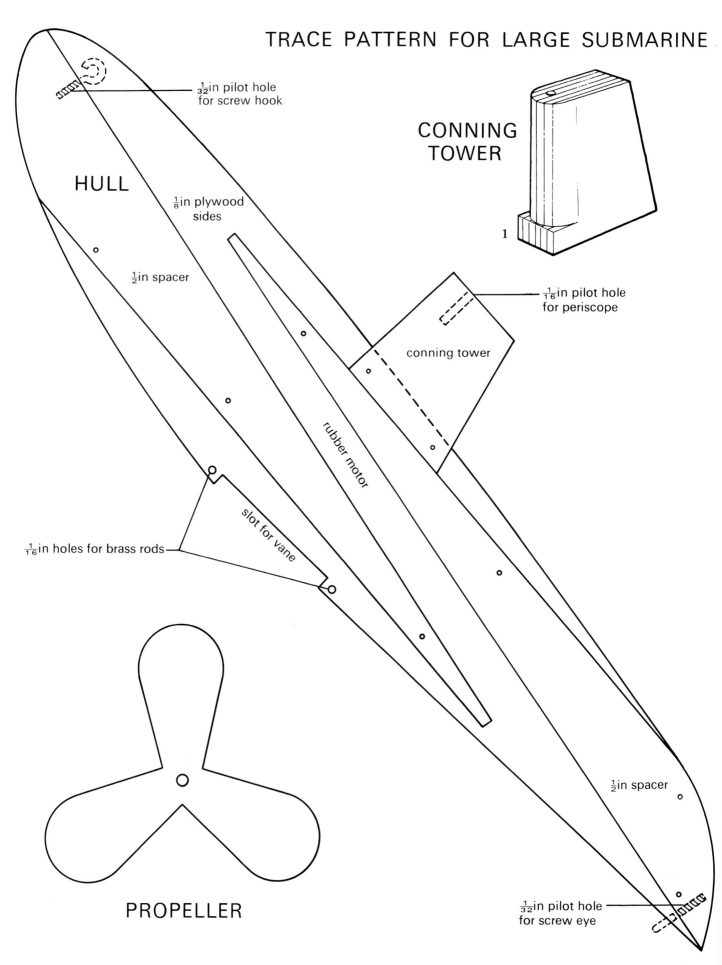

TRACE PATTERN FOR LARGE SUBMARINE

CONNING TOWER

HULL

$\frac{1}{32}$in pilot hole for screw hook

$\frac{1}{8}$in plywood sides

$\frac{1}{2}$in spacer

$\frac{1}{16}$in pilot hole for periscope

conning tower

rubber motor

slot for vane

$\frac{1}{16}$in holes for brass rods

$\frac{1}{2}$in spacer

$\frac{1}{32}$in pilot hole for screw eye

PROPELLER

Finished size
Small sub about 5in; large sub about 12in.

Techniques involved
Sawing; cutting curves; drilling; sanding; working with tinplate; painting.

Tools required
Back saw; saber saw; hack saw; hand or electric drill and bits; craft knife; standard snips or old scissors; C-clamps; vise; long-nosed pliers; side cutters; pencil; paintbrushes; sanding block.

Large submarine
Materials
$\frac{1}{2}$in × 10$\frac{1}{4}$in × 1$\frac{5}{8}$in exterior waterproof plywood
$\frac{3}{32}$in × 18in × 5$\frac{1}{2}$in plywood
$\frac{1}{4}$in screw hook and eye
2 6in round wire nails
3$\frac{1}{2}$in × 3$\frac{1}{2}$in tinplate cut from a can in usable condition
2 $\frac{1}{4}$in diameter glass beads
20 $\frac{1}{2}$in finishing nails
$\frac{5}{64}$in × 5$\frac{1}{4}$in brass rod
$\frac{1}{4}$in × 21$\frac{1}{2}$in rubber band available at stores carrying airplane supplies
$\frac{1}{4}$in screw hook and eye
2 2in rubber bands
modeling clay
fine sandpaper
wood primer
rust-resisting primer
enamel paints
epoxy resin adhesive
paper
cardboard
carbon paper
tracing paper

Warning: Propellers are made of tinplate and should not be handled by small children.

To make large submarine
Trace the full-size patterns for the sides, spacers and propeller.

Using carbon paper, transfer the shapes for the sides from the tracing onto $\frac{3}{32}$in plywood. Cut out with a saber saw or coping saw and smooth the edges with sandpaper. Drill $\frac{3}{64}$in holes in the positions marked on the pattern. Drill $\frac{5}{64}$in holes for the vane retainers in the positions marked on the plans on either side of the vane slots.

Cut a 4$\frac{1}{2}$in × 1$\frac{5}{8}$in rectangle from $\frac{3}{32}$in plywood to form the vane. Sand all the edges smooth.

Transfer the tracings of the spacers and conning tower onto $\frac{1}{2}$in plywood. Cut out with a coping saw. Drill a $\frac{5}{64}$in hole $\frac{5}{8}$in deep into the top of the conning tower in the position shown (fig. 1). Clamp the spacers between the sides in the positions shown and sand the curved portion to the same profile. Shape the front of the conning tower into a smooth curve as shown. Sand all surfaces and edges smooth.

Prime and paint all inside surfaces to prevent them from becoming waterlogged in use. (Do not paint the sides of the spacers or the area on the sides to which they are attached.) Allow to dry.

Glue all parts together using epoxy resin adhesive, and nail through the pre-drilled holes. Punch the nail heads below the surface.

Fill any blemishes and nail holes with plastic resin filler, then sand, prime and finish with enamel paints, adding decorative details. Use several coats of paint to ensure that the finish is waterproof.

Transfer the pattern for the propeller onto a piece of cardboard and cut out the shape. Use this as a template to mark the shape on tinplate, tracing around with a scriber or a compass point. Cut out the propeller with snips or an old pair of scissors. Drill a $\frac{5}{64}$in hole through the center. Bend each blade up at one edge and down at the other as shown in fig. 2.

Straighten a paper clip to make the propeller shaft. Push the end through the center hole and then bend it around the propeller as shown in fig. 2. Make sure that the propeller cannot move on the shaft. Thread two beads onto the shaft to act as bearings, then bend the end into a hook to take the rubber band motor (fig. 3).

Screw a $\frac{1}{4}$in screw eye and hook into the submarine body in the positions shown on the plans. Tie the two ends of the rubber band motor together to form a loop. Pass this down the center of the submarine, hooking one end onto the screw hook. Pass the other end through the eye and hook it onto the end of the propeller shaft. The beads on the shaft are held by the screw eye, thus keeping the propeller clear of the submarine.

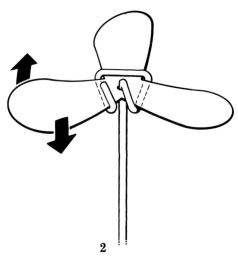

1. Drill hole in conning tower.
2. Attaching propeller shaft.
3. Attaching beads and making hook on shaft. Also included, trace pattern for propeller.

To make the ballast, cut two 3$\frac{1}{2}$in lengths from 6in round wire nails using a hack saw. Paint with rust-resisting primer and leave to dry.

Cut the $\frac{5}{64}$in brass rod into two 1$\frac{5}{8}$in lengths for the vane retainers, and one 2$\frac{1}{8}$in length for the periscope. Glue the periscope into the hole in the conning tower, using epoxy resin adhesive.

Put the ballast in place on the underside of the submarine between the vane slots and fix with modeling clay. Fit the vane retainers through the holes on either side of the vane slot. Fit the vane in place in the slot and hold it in place under the ballast with two rubber bands, criss crossed around the protruding ends of the vane retainers.

Try the submarine in water—its waterline should be where the conning tower joins the hull. Adjust the ballast nails for balance. They slide up and down easily as they are only held in position by the modeling clay and the vane. Wind up the rubber motor by turning the propeller. The submarine should move through the water, then submerge.

Small submarine

Materials

$\frac{1}{2}$in × 5in × 1in plywood
$\frac{1}{4}$in × 1$\frac{1}{4}$in dowel
3 1in finishing nails
2in square piece of tinplate cut from a can in good condition
large paper clip
1 5in nail
$\frac{1}{4}$in screw eye and hook
1 4in rubber band
1 or 2 $\frac{1}{2}$in wooden beads for heads (optional)
fine sandpaper
rust-resisting primer
epoxy resin adhesive
paper and cardboard for pattern and templates

To make small submarine

Trace shape for hull (fig. 5), transfer onto $\frac{1}{2}$in plywood and cut out. Carve and shape ends to slight points as shown in photograph. Drill a $\frac{1}{4}$in diameter hole $\frac{3}{8}$in deep in top of submarine for conning tower if required.

Drill $\frac{1}{32}$in pilot holes at each end of hull for screw eye and hook. Finally drill a $\frac{1}{4}$in hole, 1$\frac{5}{8}$in deep, under the bow for ballast in position shown in fig. 5.

Trace templates for propeller and vane (figs. 6 and 7) and use them to cut out the shapes in tin as for large submarine.

Cut a 1in piece of $\frac{1}{4}$in dowel, chamfer end and insert into hole in hull for conning tower. Insert finishing nail, bending top for periscope. Alternatively, use $\frac{1}{2}$in beads for divers' heads.

Using two finishing nails, nail the tin vane to the underside of the hull with the flaps to the rear. Fold the flaps upwards slightly as shown in the photograph.

Sand and paint hull, conning tower, divers' heads and vane. When

ASSEMBLING THE LARGE SUBMARINE

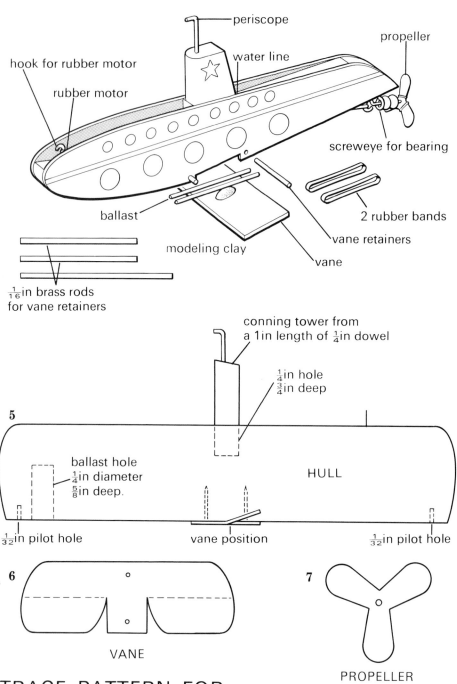

periscope

propeller

hook for rubber motor

water line

rubber motor

screweye for bearing

ballast

2 rubber bands

modeling clay

vane retainers

vane

$\frac{1}{16}$in brass rods for vane retainers

conning tower from a 1in length of $\frac{1}{4}$in dowel

$\frac{1}{4}$in hole $\frac{3}{4}$in deep

5

ballast hole $\frac{1}{4}$in diameter $\frac{5}{8}$in deep.

HULL

$\frac{1}{32}$in pilot hole

vane position

$\frac{1}{32}$in pilot hole

6

VANE

7

PROPELLER

TRACE PATTERN FOR SMALL SUBMARINE

paint is dry, nail divers' heads in place. Screw in screw hook under bow and screw eye at the stern, in previously drilled pilot holes. Cut off 1in from the 5in nail and paint with rustproof paint. When dry, nail into place in $\frac{1}{4}$in hole drilled in bow for ballast.

Bend propeller into shape as for large submarine. Attach propeller shaft and beads and make hook at end as for large submarine.

Fix a 4in rubber band to the propeller hook at one end and to screw hook at the other. Wind up the rubber motor as before.

Truck

This sturdy wooden truck is a smooth-running toy with real wheels that will delight any small child. The body is fully detailed and has headlights made from doorstop bumper tips.

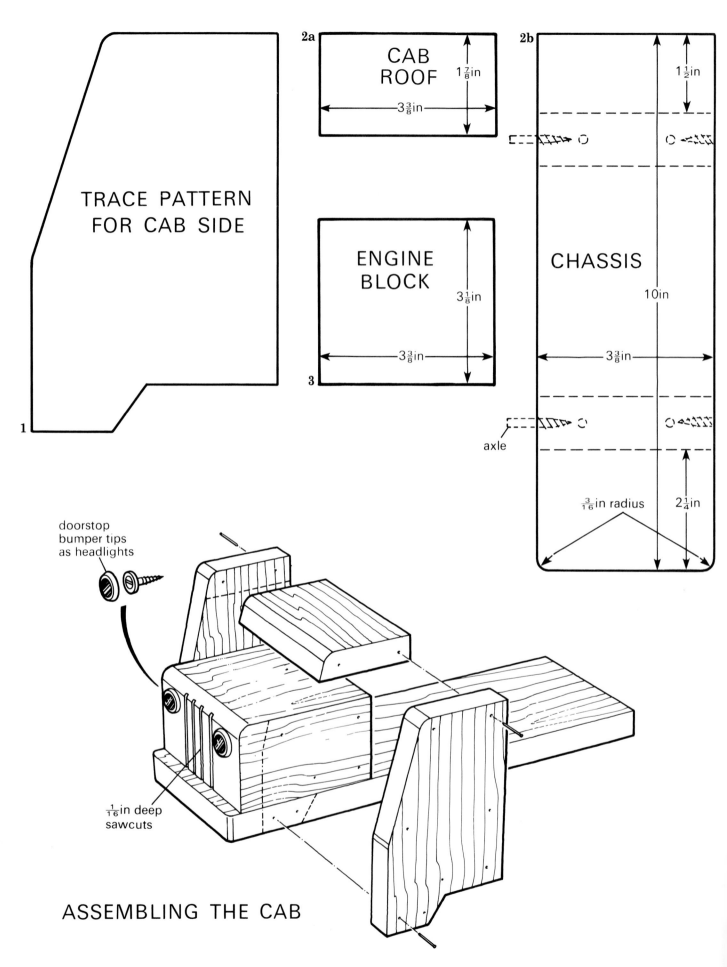

TRACE PATTERN
FOR CAB SIDE

1

2a CAB ROOF

$1\frac{7}{8}$in

$3\frac{3}{8}$in

ENGINE BLOCK

$3\frac{1}{8}$in

$3\frac{3}{8}$in

3

2b CHASSIS

$1\frac{1}{2}$in

axle

10in

$3\frac{3}{8}$in

$\frac{3}{16}$in radius

$2\frac{1}{4}$in

doorstop bumper tips as headlights

$\frac{1}{16}$in deep sawcuts

ASSEMBLING THE CAB

Finished size
Length: 11in; width: 4$\frac{1}{2}$in; height: 8in (including wheels).

Techniques involved
Marking out and measuring; sawing; shaping; screwing and gluing; nailing and gluing; wheels; finishing.

Tools required
Hand saw, miter box saw, try-square, drill and bits, hammer, punch, screwdriver, hacksaw, sanding block, paintbrush.

Materials
$\frac{1}{2}$ × 5in × 5$\frac{1}{8}$in plywood
1$\frac{1}{4}$in × 1in × 6$\frac{3}{4}$in pine
2in × 4in × 3$\frac{1}{8}$in pine
$\frac{1}{4}$in × 3$\frac{5}{8}$in × 2in plywood
2in × 2in × 25$\frac{1}{4}$in pine
1in × 2in × 12$\frac{5}{8}$in pine
4 2in diameter plastic model wheels with hub caps
4 steel washers with $\frac{3}{16}$in internal diameter
4 1$\frac{1}{2}$in No. 8 flathead woodscrews
4 1$\frac{3}{4}$in No. 8 roundheaded woodscrews
2 $\frac{3}{4}$in No. 8 roundheaded woodscrews
2 $\frac{1}{2}$in No. 8 flathead woodscrews
PVA woodworking adhesive
$\frac{3}{4}$in finishing nails
$\frac{1}{2}$in finishing nails
2 $\frac{1}{4}$in doorstop bumper tips
polyurethane lacquer
silver enamel paint
sandpaper

With the truck, a special surprise: the top of the box body slips off easily to reveal a nest of polished wooden building blocks inside. The thirteen blocks are fashioned in a variety of shapes and sizes to fit exactly into the back of the truck. There are eight square and five long shapes in different lengths and widths so that they can be mixed and matched to make different patterns.

Assembly
Cut out all the parts and dry-assemble to check fit.

Making the cab
Trace patterns for cab sides (fig. 1); enlarge plans for the cab roof and chassis (figs. 2a, 2b). Transfer them to $\frac{1}{2}$in plywood and cut out with a hand saw and back saw. Round off the corners where indicated using sandpaper, and sand all the edges smooth. Drill $\frac{3}{16}$in clearance holes for No. 8 screws as indicated in the chassis.

Enlarge the plan in fig. 3 for the engine block. Transfer to 4in × 2in and cut out using back saw. Round off the pine front as shown using sandpaper. Sand the cut ends smooth. Make four $\frac{1}{16}$in deep saw-cuts as indicated to form the radiator grille. Drill $\frac{1}{16}$in pilot holes $\frac{1}{2}$in deep for the headlight screws and $\frac{1}{16}$in pilot holes $\frac{5}{8}$in deep for the assembling screws where indicated.

Cut 3$\frac{3}{8}$in lengths of 1$\frac{1}{4}$in × 1in pine to form the wheel bearers. Sand the cut ends smooth with sandpaper and drill $\frac{1}{16}$in pilot holes $\frac{5}{8}$in deep at the position indicated. Round or chamfer off the two lower edges. Drill $\frac{7}{64}$in clearance holes for the assembly screws at the positions indicated.

Take the engine block and one of the wheel bearers. Glue above and below the front end of the chassis using PVA woodworking adhesive. Screw through the holes with 1$\frac{3}{4}$in roundheaded screws.

Using PVA woodworking adhesive and $\frac{3}{4}$in finishing nails, nail and glue one cab side to the chassis and engine block. Align the back edge of the side with the back of the engine block. Fit the other side of the cab in the same way and nail and glue the cab roof between the tops of the sides. Punch all nail heads below the surface and cover with wood filler. Allow assembly to dry, then sand smooth.

Using 1$\frac{1}{2}$in No. 8 flathead woodscrews and doorstop bumper tips, screw to the front of the engine block to form the headlights. You can paint the centers of the bumper tips with silver paint for more realism.

Making the box
Following the plans in fig. 4, enlarge the patterns for the sides, ends, base and top of the box. Transfer to $\frac{1}{2}$in plywood and cut out using a hand saw. Sand all the cut edges smooth and round off the edges of the top as shown. Drill $\frac{1}{16}$in pilot holes in the base where indicated.

Cut two 3$\frac{3}{8}$in × 1in strips of $\frac{1}{4}$in plywood and sand smooth.

Using PVA woodworking adhesive and $\frac{3}{4}$in finishing nails, nail and glue the ends of the box between the sides, taking care to keep the assembly square. Nail and glue the base in position. Punch all nail heads below the surface. Allow to dry, then sand smooth.

Nail and glue the two plywood strips to the underside of the lid, using $\frac{3}{4}$in finishing nails and PVA woodworking adhesive. Punch the nail heads below the surface, cover with filler and sand smooth when dry.

Position the box behind the cab. Attach with PVA woodworking adhesive and two $\frac{3}{4}$in No. 8 roundhead screws driven through the chassis. Glue the rear wheel bearer in position and fasten with two 1$\frac{3}{4}$in No. 8 roundhead screws.

Sand all surfaces and edges smooth, then finish the entire truck with at least two coats of polyurethane lacquer.

Attaching the wheels
The wheels are 2in diameter truck wheels from model shops. If these are not available, you can use 2in diameter wooden wheels cut from $\frac{1}{2}$in plywood using a hole saw. These should be attached with a domed head screw driven through the center hole.

Drive 1$\frac{1}{2}$in No. 8 screws into the ends of the wheel bearers, leaving the shank projecting. A little adhesive smeared on the thread will provide a more secure attachment. After fitting the screws, cut off their heads with a hack saw. Fit a washer to each, then slip on the wheels. Retain them with snap or fixing hub caps, obtainable with the wheels.

Making the blocks
All the blocks are made from lengths of 2in × 2in or 2in × 1in softwood. In order for the blocks to fit accurately inside the truck, however, these sizes must be trimmed somewhat. This is best done with a plane, but can be done with a surform tool and sandpaper. You will need lumber with a finished size of 1$\frac{9}{16}$in × 1$\frac{9}{16}$in and 1$\frac{9}{16}$in × $\frac{3}{4}$in. Cut to the lengths shown in fig. 5 and sand all edges and surfaces smooth.

Finish each block with at least two coats of polyurethane lacquer and allow to dry.

Fit the blocks together as shown inside the box and fit the lid in place.

ASSEMBLING THE TRUCK

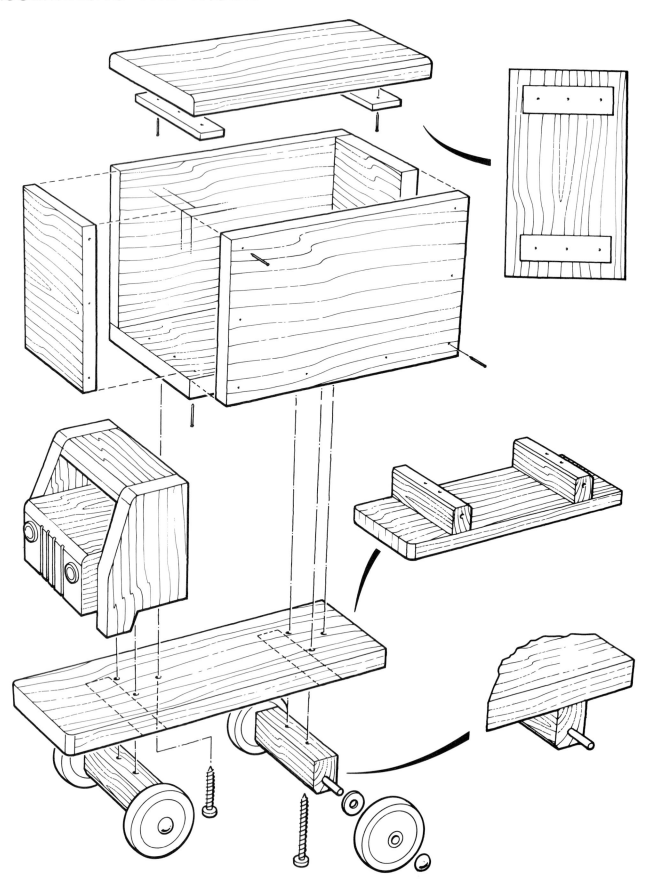

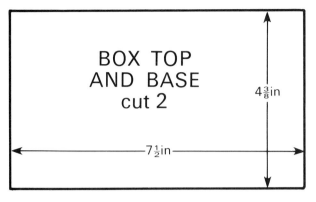

BOX TOP
AND BASE
cut 2

$4\frac{3}{8}$in

$7\frac{1}{2}$in

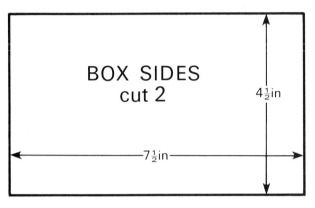

BOX SIDES
cut 2

$4\frac{1}{2}$in

$7\frac{1}{2}$in

FRONT
AND BACK
cut 2

$3\frac{3}{8}$in

$4\frac{1}{2}$in

5 ASSEMBLING THE BRICKS

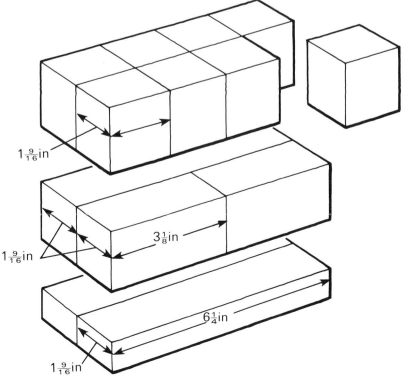

$1\frac{9}{16}$in

$3\frac{1}{8}$in

$6\frac{1}{4}$in

$1\frac{9}{16}$in

$1\frac{9}{16}$in

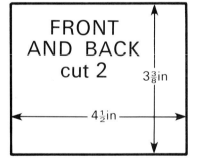

$6\frac{1}{4}$in

4in

$3\frac{1}{8}$in

Railway engine

This combined engine and tender is designed for the under-five age group. By adapting the instructions you can add as many cars as you like. The construction of the boiler is unusual—it is made from a dishwashing detergent bottle.

Finishing length
19in.

Techniques involved
Shaping plywood and dowel; drilling; wheels; painting.

Tools required
Back saw; saber saw; vise; C-clamp; electric drill with $\frac{5}{64}$in and $\frac{1}{4}$in bits, $\frac{3}{4}$in flat bit; countersink bit; hole saws $2\frac{1}{4}$in and $1\frac{1}{4}$in diameter; small hammer; crosshead or slotted screwdriver appropriate to screws; pencil; ruler, try-square, paintbrushes; large plastic funnel; scissors.

Materials
2in × 1in × 50in pine
$\frac{1}{4}$in × 4in × $39\frac{1}{2}$in plywood
$\frac{1}{2}$in × 12in × 12in plywood
$\frac{1}{4}$in diameter × 24in dowel
$\frac{7}{8}$in diameter × $4\frac{3}{4}$in dowel
$\frac{1}{2}$in diameter × 3in dowel
plastic detergent bottle $10\frac{1}{4}$in length
2.2lb plaster of Paris
16 small plastic electric cable clips
16 × $\frac{5}{8}$in No. 1 flathead woodscrews
12 × $1\frac{1}{2}$in No. 6 flathead woodscrews
4 × $1\frac{3}{4}$in No. 6 flathead woodscrews

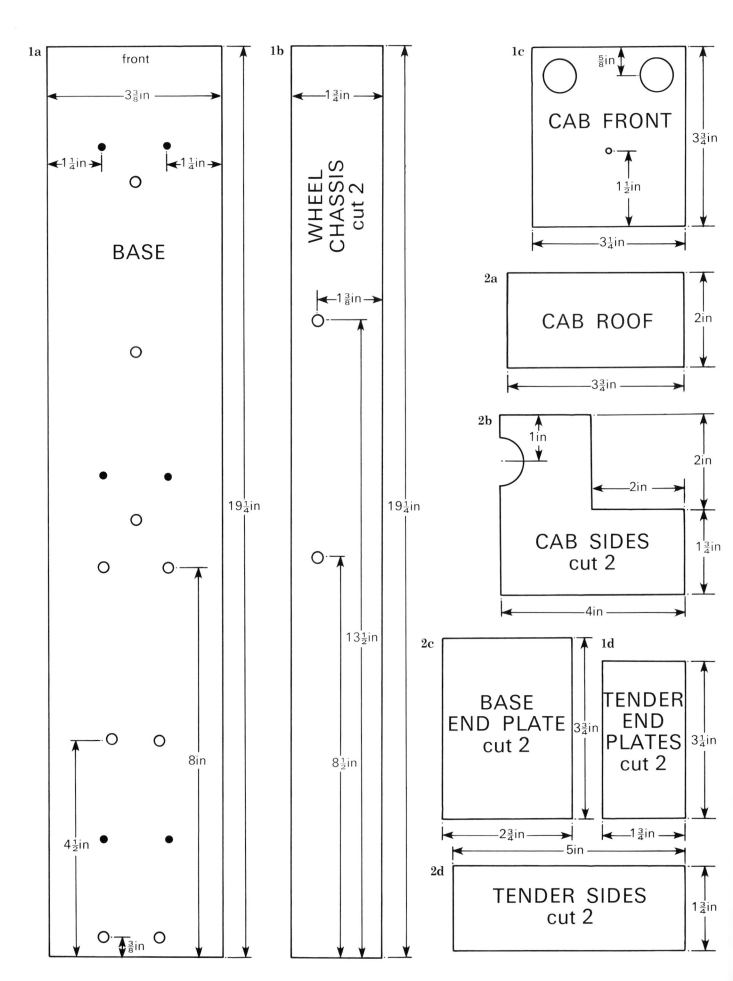

1½oz box ½in finishing nails
1¼in screweye
12⅜in brass upholstery nails
2 discarded plastic lids from coffee
  cans or similar
PVA woodworking adhesive
fine sandpaper
enamel paints

1a,b,c,d. *Measurements for base, cab front, tender end plates and wheel chassis sections.*
2a,b,c,d. *Measurements for plywood parts of engine.*

Construction

Mix plaster of Paris with water to the consistency of thick cream. Remove top from the neck of the detergent bottle and pour in the plaster using a plastic funnel. Pour slowly to avoid a build-up of air bubbles and squeeze the bottle occasionally to make sure that it is completely filled. Leave for several hours to allow plaster to set. When the plaster has hardened, mark a line down one side of the bottle. Measure ¾in and 5⅛in down from top and mark these points. Drill 1in

holes, ½in deep at each marked point.

Following measurements in figs. 1a, 1c, 1d, mark and cut one base, two tender end plates and one cab front from 2in × 1in. Mark and drill six $\frac{5}{64}$in pilot holes (marked A) and countersink on upper side of base. Mark and drill holes B, C and D and countersink on the underside of the base.

Following measurements in fig. 1b, mark and cut out two wheel chassis. Mark and drill the two ¼in holes in each wheel chassis section. These must be carefully positioned

ASSEMBLING THE RAILWAY ENGINE

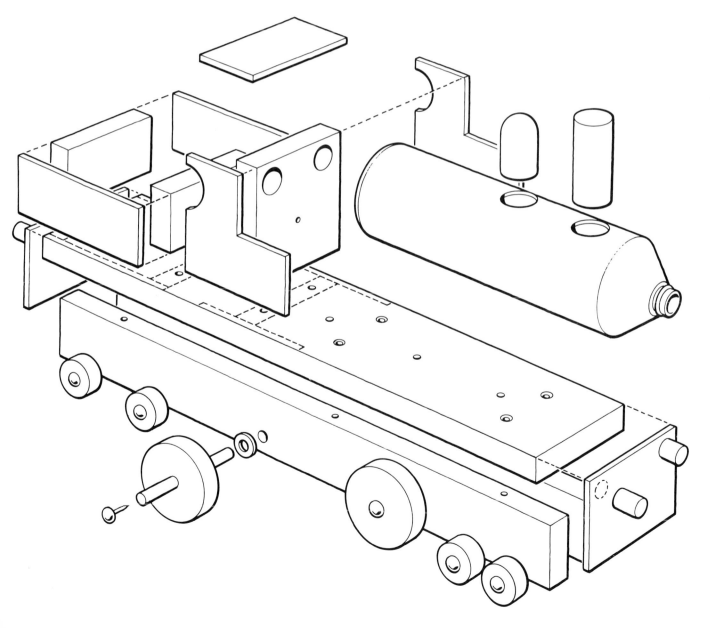

as they carry the axles of the drive wheels.

On cab front mark and drill two $\frac{3}{4}$in holes and one $\frac{5}{64}$in hole as shown.

Sand all pine parts.

Following measurements in fig. 2a, 2b, 2c and 2d mark out $\frac{1}{4}$in plywood and cut two tender side plates, two base end plates, one cab roof and two cab sides. Use a saber saw to cut the curves of the cab sides. Sand all plywood pieces smooth.

Cut wheels from $\frac{1}{2}$in plywood. Using a hole saw, cut four $2\frac{1}{2}$in diameter circles and finish to $2\frac{1}{4}$in. Cut eight circles to an initial diameter of $1\frac{1}{4}$in, and finish to $\frac{1}{16}$in. Drill $\frac{1}{4}$in center holes in all wheels.

Note: If you do not have a hole saw, use a saber saw for wheels, marking circles with compass. Drill the $\frac{1}{4}$in center holes before cutting out wheels. Smooth edges with sandpaper.

From $\frac{7}{8}$in dowel, cut $2\frac{1}{4}$in length for stack and 2in length for dome. Sand top of dome to rounded shape.

Cut four buffers, each $\frac{5}{8}$in long from $\frac{1}{2}$in dowel. Sand smooth.

Cut six axles, each $3\frac{3}{8}$in long from $\frac{1}{4}$in dowel.

Using two $1\frac{1}{2}$in No. 6 flathead screws and PVA woodworking adhesive, glue and screw the cab front to the base, inserting screws through holes marked C in fig. 1a. Attach tender end plates in the same way, using holes marked D in fig. 1a.

Using $1\frac{1}{2}$in No. 6 screws and PVA woodworking adhesive, glue and screw chassis sections to base. Make sure that axle holes in each are aligned, and that the front axle is $5\frac{3}{4}$in from the front of the base as shown in fig. 1a.

Position boiler on base and hold in place with a $1\frac{3}{4}$in long No. 6 screw through the front of cab. Turn assembly over and screw boiler to base using three $1\frac{3}{4}$in long No. 6 screws inserted through holes marked B in fig. 1a. Make sure that the boiler stays centered while the screws are inserted.

Fit cap of detergent bottle onto neck.

Using PVA woodworking adhesive, glue stack and dome into the holes in the boiler.

Using $\frac{1}{2}$in finishing nails and PVA adhesive, glue and nail cab sides to base and cab front. Attach tender side plates and roof in the same way.

Before attaching the larger drive wheels, check that the axles revolve freely in the $\frac{1}{4}$in holes drilled in the chassis sections. If the axles stick, rub down with sandpaper.

Cut twelve plastic washers to fit between the wheels and chassis sections. Cut these from discarded plastic coffee can lids.

To attach drive wheels, turn engine upside down and insert two axles into previously drilled holes in chassis. Thread a plastic washer through each end of axle and then coat dowel tips lightly with PVA adhesive. Press the four large drive wheels into position. Tap a brass upholstery nail into the end of each axle, taking care not to split the dowel. You may find it easier to drill a small hole for the nails first.

Glue the smaller wheels to their respective axles before attaching to engine, including plastic washers and finishing with upholstery nails as before.

Fix axles to chassis with electric cable clips (fig. 3), replacing the nails with $\frac{5}{8}$in long No. 1 screws. Position the front set of wheels $1\frac{1}{8}$in and $2\frac{3}{4}$in from the front of the chassis respectively. Lay each axle in place and fix with cable clips, one on each side of the axle in pairs (fig. 3). Attach the rear set of wheels in the same way, placing them $1\frac{3}{8}$in and $4\frac{1}{8}$in from the rear of the chassis.

Painting
Sand all parts and paint with the colors of your choice.

Freight cars
Various cars can be constructed for the engine by using shortened versions of the base and chassis, which should be reduced to 5in in length. The other dimensions remain the same as for the engine. The wheels should be the same size as the smaller engine wheels and attached in the same way, using electric cable clips. The base can either be left as a flat-bed truck, or have sides and a roof added to form cab and a caboose. Tanker trucks can be made by screwing small plaster-filled plastic bottles to the base of the truck in the same way as for the boiler engine.

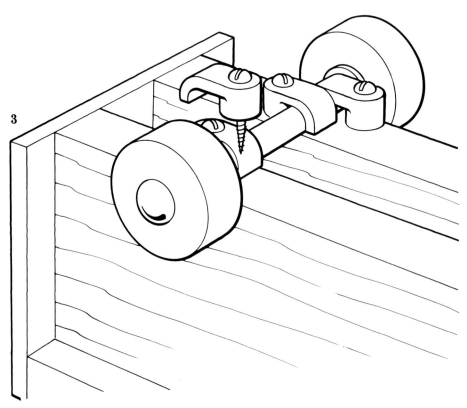

3. *The axles of the smaller wheels, fastened to the chassis with cable clips.*

Toy-box house

This miniature house will brighten any child's playtime, and is a toy with a real practical use. The roof is a lid padded with foam cushioning to make a comfortable seat. It lifts to reveal plenty of space to make a storage box for toys, or even, a giant dollhouse.

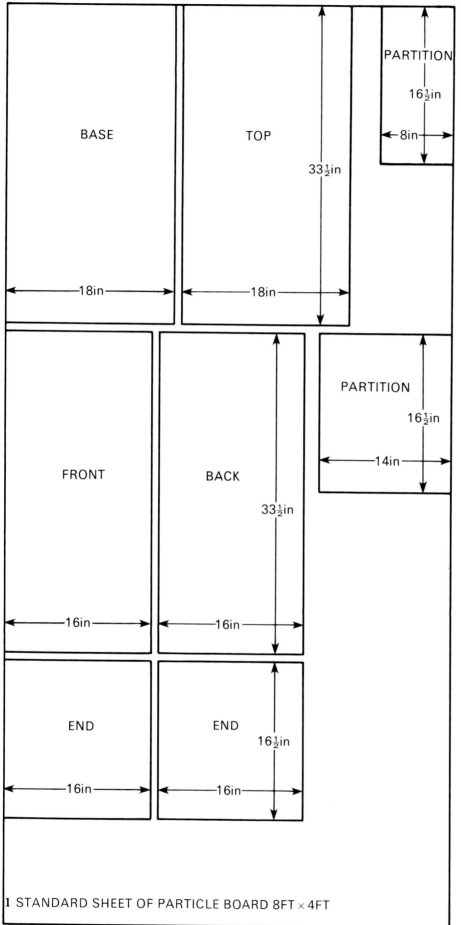

1 STANDARD SHEET OF PARTICLE BOARD 8FT × 4FT

Techniques involved

Sawing; gluing; upholstery; painting.

Tools required

Crosscut saw or power jig saw; keyhole saw; drill; screwdriver; tack hammer; sanding block; scissors; paintbrush.

Materials

$\frac{5}{8}$in × 8ft × 4ft (standard sheet) of particle board
$\frac{3}{4}$in × 180in triangular pine molding
$\frac{1}{4}$in × 1$\frac{1}{4}$in × 48in hardwood dowels
2in × 33$\frac{1}{2}$in × 18in high density plastic foam
$\frac{1}{2}$in × 41$\frac{1}{2}$in × 25$\frac{1}{2}$in plastic foam
42in × 26$\frac{3}{8}$in natural burlap
35$\frac{1}{2}$in × 19$\frac{5}{8}$in natural burlap
24in rope
4 rubber bumpers
2 heavy duty T-hinges or strap hinges as available
$\frac{1}{2}$in No. 6 flathead woodscrews
upholstery nails
$\frac{1}{2}$in finishing nails
2 $\frac{1}{2}$in screw eyes
PVA woodworking adhesive
wood primer
enamel paints
sandpaper

Making the box

Test the assembly before final fitting by assembling without gluing.

Mark out all the panels required on one full standard sheet as shown in fig. 1, or cut from suitably-sized scrap pieces. You will need two panels 33$\frac{1}{2}$in × 18in for the base and top, two panels 33$\frac{1}{2}$in × 16in for the front and back, and two panels 16$\frac{1}{2}$in × 16in for the ends. The two internal partitions are 16$\frac{1}{2}$in × 14$\frac{1}{2}$in and 16$\frac{1}{2}$in × 8in. Cut all the panels using a crosscut saw or power jig saw, taking care to keep the cuts straight.

Following the plans in figs. 3 and 4 mark out the door and window positions on one end panel and the front panel. Cut the holes using a keyhole saw or power jig saw. Drill $\frac{1}{2}$in holes in the end panels where indicated.

Using a $\frac{1}{4}$in bit, drill holes in the edges of the front and back, ends and base at the positions shown in fig. 2 to take $\frac{1}{4}$in dowels for the joints. Mark the hole positions on each joint-face in pairs to insure that their positions coincide precisely.

ASSEMBLING THE BOX

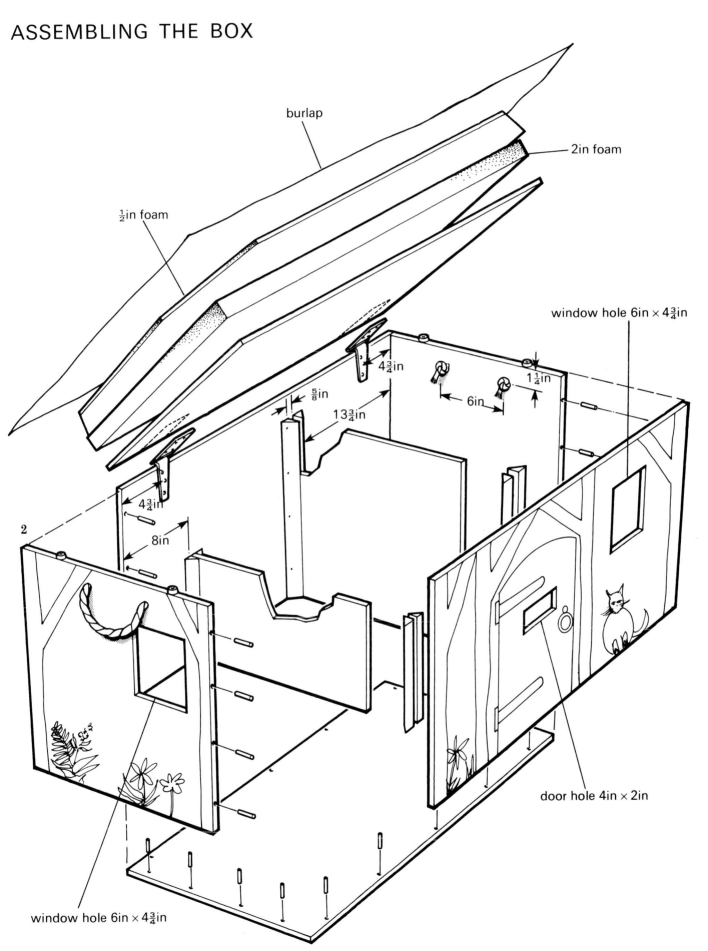

burlap

2in foam

$\frac{1}{2}$in foam

window hole 6in × 4$\frac{3}{4}$in

4$\frac{3}{4}$in

$\frac{5}{8}$in

13$\frac{3}{4}$in

1$\frac{1}{4}$in

6in

4$\frac{3}{4}$in

8in

2

door hole 4in × 2in

window hole 6in × 4$\frac{3}{4}$in

Drill the holes into the edges of the panels to a depth of $\frac{3}{4}$in, and drill the holes into the faces of the panels $\frac{1}{2}$in deep as shown in fig. 2.

Mark the partition positions on the inside of the front and back panels as indicated in fig. 2. Draw two lines separated by $\frac{5}{8}$in at each position. Cut eight 14$\frac{1}{2}$in lengths and eight 8in lengths of $\frac{3}{4}$in triangular molding. Nail and glue on either side of the marked lines, leaving a $\frac{5}{8}$in gap between. Check the gap using the edge of a scrap piece of board.

Putting a little PVA woodworking adhesive on each, inset 1$\frac{1}{4}$in × $\frac{1}{4}$in dowels into the holes in the edges of both end panels. Push in fully. Apply adhesive to the joint-faces on the ends of the front and back panels and apply a drop of adhesive to the end of each projecting dowel. Fit ends, front and back together and apply pressure to each joint. Remove excess adhesive then hold assembly together with a nylon web clamp or bar clamps. Check to be sure the assembly is square.

Insert glued 1$\frac{1}{4}$in × $\frac{1}{4}$in dowels into the holes in the base. Apply glue to the joint-faces and dowel holes on the edges of the sides, front and back, then fit the base. You can hold it in position with a heavy weight until the glue is dry.

After the glue has dried, fill any gaps with wood filler. Sand all exposed edges and corners smooth.

Fit hinges to the inside of the back as indicated in fig. 2. Note that the hinges are set $\frac{1}{2}$in higher than the edge.

Paint the complete box, inside and out, and both partitions with wood primer. Leave to dry.

Making the lid

The lid panel is upholstered with a padded seat in burlap.

Lay the $\frac{1}{2}$in foam on the work surface. Center the 2in foam on top

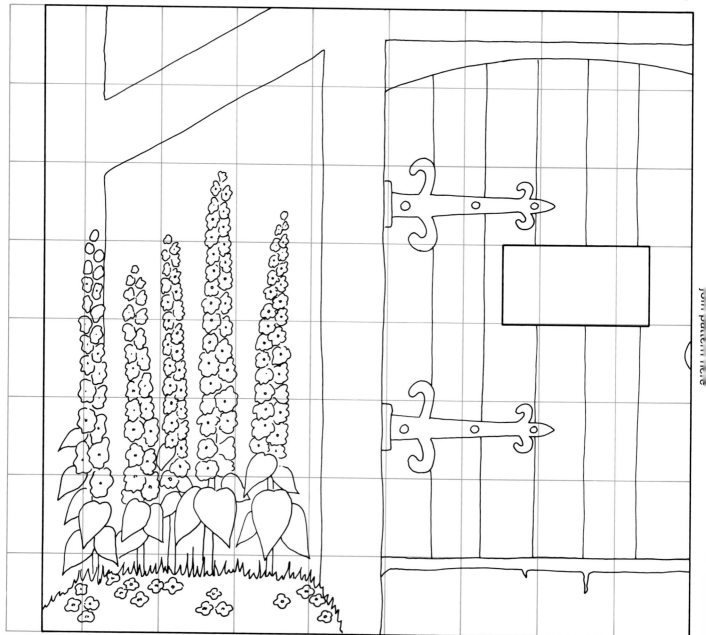

3 GRAPH PATTERN FOR FRONT DECORATIONS

Each Square = 2in

of it. Miter all four projecting corners at 45° to the corners of the 2in foam. Lay the lid on top of the 2in foam and pull the projecting edges of the ½in foam up over it. You can hold the flaps in place temporarily with adhesive tape.

Lay the complete assembly, foam side down, in the center of the larger piece of burlap. Fold the edges of the burlap over the lid and pull into place tightly and evenly, holding them with tacks or staples. Trim excess material at the corners to make a neat finish.

Take the small piece of burlap and turn in 1in all around. Lay this over the lid, with the turnback underneath and tack in place with upholstery nails.

Decorating the box

Trace the patterns for the decorations on the sides and end of the box as shown in figs. 3 and 4. If you wish to decorate the back of the box, use the same pattern as for the front, but leaving out the window, door and cat. Transfer these onto the box using carbon paper. Using enamel paints and following the colors in the pictures, add all the details. Paint the walls white first, then add oak beams. Smaller details can be added with fine artist's brushes, but be sure to let each color dry before adding the next. Allow to dry.

Paint the entire inside of the box and both partitions with any dark-colored paint. Allow to dry, then slot the partitions in place.

Using fabric paints, add streaks of color to the upholstery so the lid resembles a thatched roof. Allow to dry.

Assembly

Screw four rubber bumpers to the top edges of the ends where indicated in fig. 2. These prevent the lid from shutting fully and trapping

join pattern here

Foam should be squashed down
under the burlap.

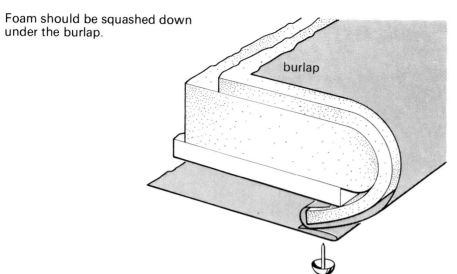

burlap

a child's fingers.

Screw the lid to the hinges and
check that it opens freely. Insert two
screw eyes in the position shown in
the lid and side and join them with a
length of cord to act as a lid stay.
The lid should be free to open to about
$30°$ from the vertical.

Pass the ends of two $11\frac{3}{4}$in lengths
of rope through the holes in each end
of the box, and knot securely to form
two rope handles.

If you wish, the partitions can
be removed. You can cut internal
doorways in the larger one. With a
little ingenuity, you can even cut
out the front door and arrange for it
to open on miniature butt hinges.

4 GRAPH PATTERN FOR END DECORATIONS

Each square = 2in

Sail boat

A boat that really sails is another classic toy that can be made by any reasonably competent woodworker. The instructions given here are for a simple one-masted sail boat that is not an actual scale model but sails well in light winds.

Finished length
$10\frac{3}{4}$in.

Techniques involved
Using coping saw; using spoke-shave; cutting metal; using try square; drilling; painting.

Tools required
Coping saw; hand saw; hack saw; flat spokeshave, surform tool or rasp; vise; drill with $\frac{1}{16}$in, $\frac{5}{64}$in and $\frac{1}{4}$in bits; pliers; small hammer; craft knife; scissors; try square; ruler; pencil; paintbrushes; small bradawl; sanding block.

Materials
4in $\times 2$in $\times 12$in pine or similar softwood without knots
$\frac{5}{64}$in $\times 2$in $\times 2$in plywood
$\frac{5}{64}$in $\times 4\frac{3}{4}$in $\times 3\frac{1}{2}$in steel plate, weight 8oz. (Plywood and lead can be used as a substitute.)
$\frac{1}{4}$in $\times 15$in dowel
$\frac{5}{64}$in diameter brass tube, $3\frac{3}{4}$in long brass collar with set screw with $\frac{5}{64}$in diameter center
10in square nylon or cotton fabric
2 $1\frac{1}{2}$in No. 6 woodscrews
ball household twine
rubber band
$8 \times \frac{1}{4}$in screw eyes
2 small veneer pins
epoxy resin adhesive
fabric adhesive
sandpaper
fast drying enamel paints
polyurethane varnish (optional)
20in $\times 8$in stiff card; carbon paper

1. *Marking a center line.*
2. *Using the try-square to position template lines all around block.*
3. *Overlapping holes are drilled down the center of the keel slot.*
4. *Transferred pattern for the hull on the other side of block.*
5. *Cutting around the shape of the deck with a coping saw.*
6. *Tape the scrap pieces back in their original position.*
7. *Use a hand saw to remove two wedges from underside of block.*
8. *Remove the excess wood on the hull with a rasp.*
9. *The length of softwood screwed in place to hold the hull in a vise.*
10. *The hull block is clamped securely in a vise and carved into shape.*
11. *Using a template to check the curve of the hull.*

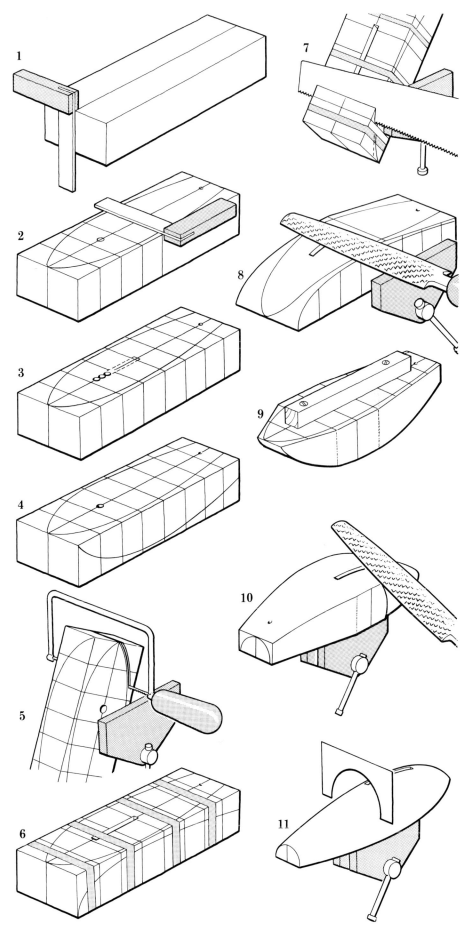

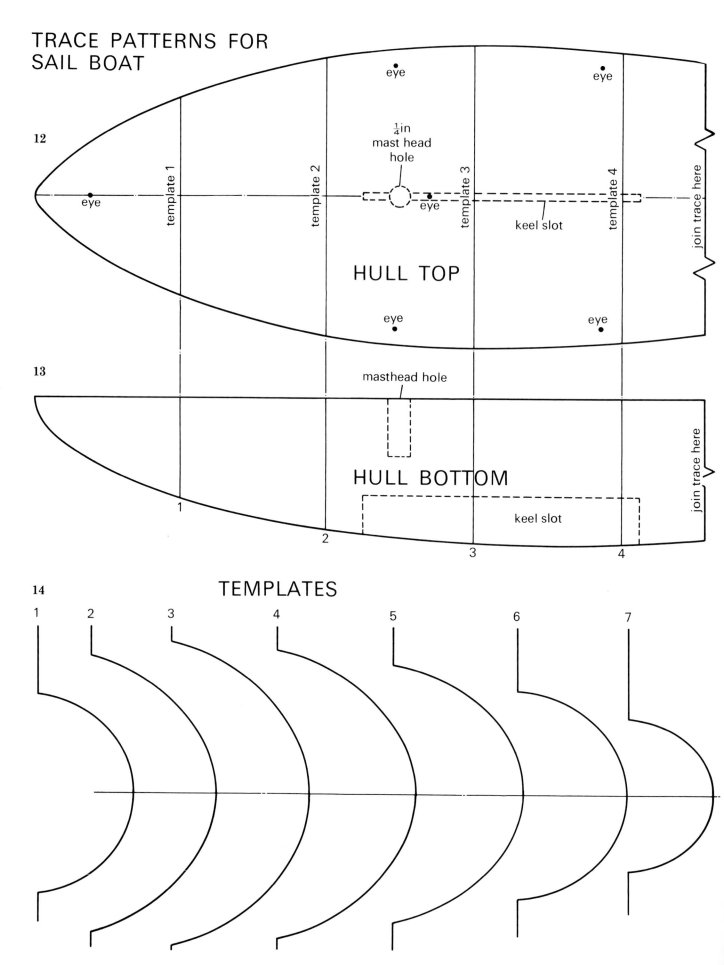

TRACE PATTERNS FOR SAIL BOAT

12

eye

template 1

template 2

$\frac{1}{4}$ in
mast head
hole

eye

template 3

keel slot

template 4

join trace here

HULL TOP

eye

eye

eye

eye

13

masthead hole

join trace here

HULL BOTTOM

1

2

keel slot

3

4

14
TEMPLATES

1   2   3   4   5   6   7

178

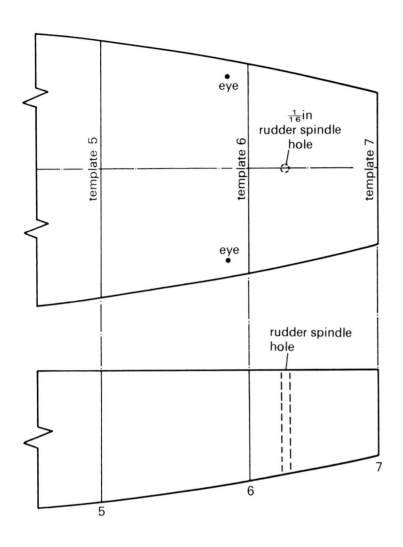

eye

$\frac{1}{16}$in
rudder spindle
hole

template 5

template 6

template 7

eye

rudder spindle
hole

5

6

7

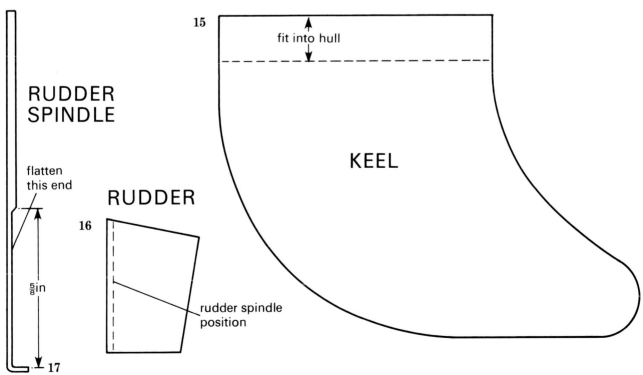

15

fit into hull

KEEL

RUDDER
SPINDLE

flatten
this end

RUDDER

16

$\frac{5}{8}$in

rudder spindle
position

17

12in × 4in sheets of paper
small bolts or lead weights and
    wood filler if needed for
    weighting hull

Carving the hull

Trace full-size patterns for the top
and bottom and profile of the hull
following diagrams in figs. 12 and 13.

Mark the center line along the
length of one wide face of your
softwood block. Using a try-square
and a straightedge, extend this line
down the ends of the block and along
the bottom face (fig. 1).

Lay the block down with the
intended top side uppermost. Using
carbon paper, align your pattern
with the marked center line and
transfer to the block the outline of
the deck. Also mark the positions of
the seven templates and the mast
and rudder holes. Use the try-square
to continue the template position
lines all around the block. Drill a $\frac{1}{4}$in
diameter hole $\frac{5}{8}$in deep at the
position marked for the mast hole.
Drill a $\frac{5}{64}$in hole for the rudder
straight through the block, taking
care to keep it absolutely square to
the surface (fig. 2).

Turn the block upside-down and
mark the outline of the deck on the
underside, including the position of
the keel slot. Make sure that the
pattern is aligned with the center
line, and that the template positions
correspond. Drill a series of overlap-
ping $\frac{5}{64}$in holes to a depth of $\frac{3}{4}$in
down the center of the keel slot. Use
a craft knife to carve out the
remainder of the slot (fig. 3).

Turn the block over on its side and
transfer the pattern for the hull
profile, aligning the deck surface
with the top of the block and making
sure that all the template positions
correspond. Turn the block over and
repeat on the other side (fig. 4).

Clamp the block in a vise and cut
around the shape of the deck with a
coping saw. Take care to cut close to
but not over the line, checking the
outline on the underside as well
from time to time (fig. 5). This is the
first of the two basic shapes of the
hull. Do not discard the two scrap
pieces, but tape them back in the
positions they were cut from. This
restores the outline of the profile of
the hull (fig. 6).

Turn the block over, and using a
hand saw remove two wedges from

the underside of the block as shown
in fig. 7, working close to but not
over the marked line. Using a rasp or
surform tool, remove the bulk of the
remaining wood close to the marked
line. Discard the two cut-off side
pieces. This completes the second of
the basic shapes of the hull (fig. 8).

Trace full-size patterns for the
seven templates in fig. 14. Transfer
these onto stiff cardboard. With a
sharp craft knife, cut out each U-
shape, removing the material within
the curve. These provide guides to
the curvature of the hull at the
positions indicated. Mark the curve
of template 7 directly onto the stern
of your block.

Using two 1$\frac{1}{2}$in No. 6 woodscrews,
screw an 8in length of 1in square
softwood down the center of the
deck. Make sure to avoid the mast
and rudder holes when positioning
your screws. This block will allow
you to clamp the hull securely in the
vise for carving (fig. 9).

Using the clamping block, place
the hull block in the vise. You can
carve it with a wood-file, a flat
spokeshave, surform tool or rasp (fig.
10). In all cases work slowly to avoid
removing too much material, and
work down the curve from the center
towards the bow and stern. As
carving proceeds, check constantly
with the templates at each of their
marked positions to make sure that
you do not cut too deeply at any
point (fig. 11). When the templates
show that you have nearly reached
the correct curve at all positions,
stop carving and finish with sandpaper. If you are using a rasp, you
should stop an appreciable distance
from the templates, because of the
rough surface that the rasp will
leave.

Using a sanding block and working in smooth sweeps, finish the hull
until all the templates fit exactly.
Start with coarse paper and work
down to fine as you near the final
shape. This will leave a smooth
finish.

Remove the hull from the vise and
unscrew the clamping block. Weigh

Above: *The main mast, the
mainsail halyard and the boom.
After these are fitted together, the
rigging and sails are attached.
An extra $\frac{1}{4}$in must be added to all
sides of the sails.*

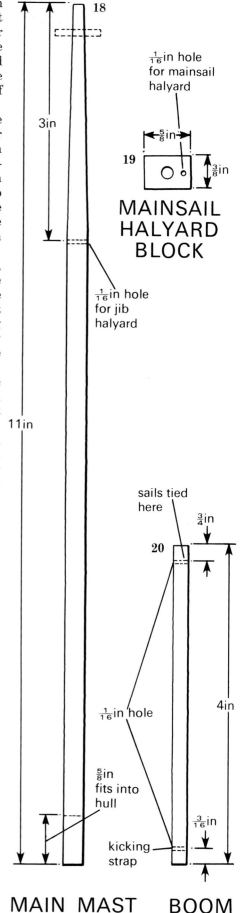

18

$\frac{1}{16}$in hole
for mainsail
halyard

3in

$\frac{5}{8}$in

19

$\frac{3}{8}$in

MAINSAIL HALYARD BLOCK

$\frac{1}{16}$in hole
for jib
halyard

11in

sails tied
here

$\frac{3}{4}$in

20

$\frac{1}{16}$in hole

4in

$\frac{5}{8}$in
fits into
hull

$\frac{3}{16}$in

kicking
strap

MAIN MAST   BOOM

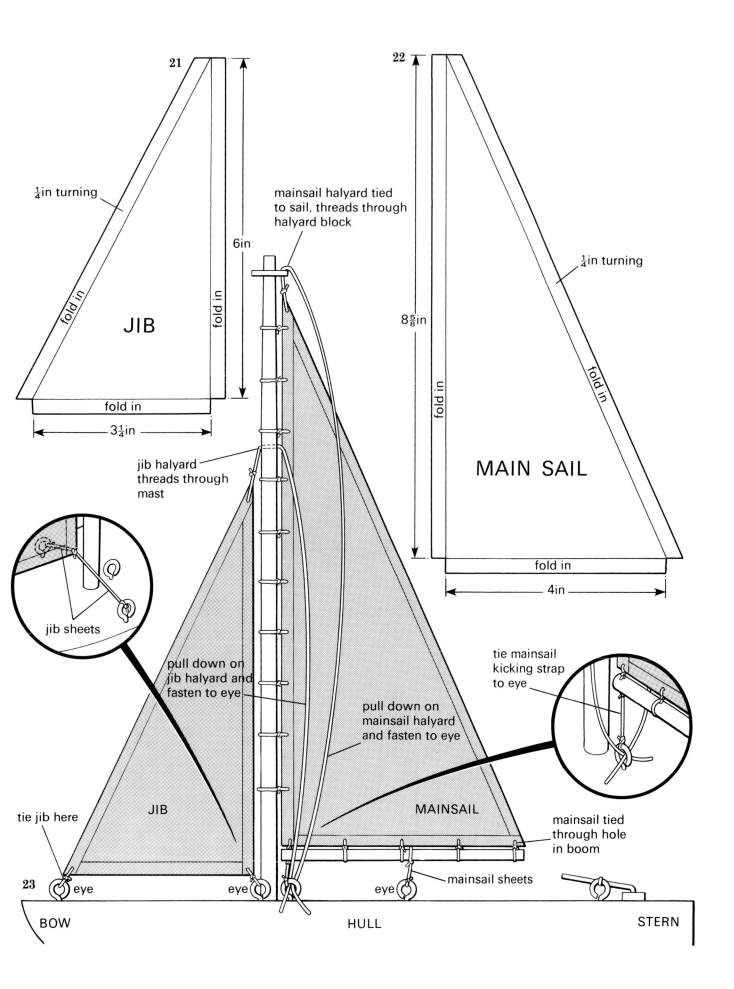

21

$\frac{1}{4}$in turning

6in

fold in

JIB

fold in

fold in

$3\frac{1}{4}$in

mainsail halyard tied
to sail, threads through
halyard block

22

$\frac{1}{4}$in turning

$8\frac{5}{8}$in

fold in

fold in

MAIN SAIL

fold in

4in

jib halyard
threads through
mast

jib sheets

pull down on
jib halyard and
fasten to eye

pull down on
mainsail halyard
and fasten to eye

tie mainsail
kicking strap
to eye

JIB

MAINSAIL

tie jib here

23

eye

eye

eye

mainsail sheets

mainsail tied
through hole
in boom

BOW

HULL

STERN

181

the completed hull. It should be approximately 6oz. If this is the case, fill the screw holes left by the clamping block screws with wood filler and sand smooth. If the hull is appreciably lighter, you will need to add weight. Drill holes into the top surface to take enough fishing lead shot to make up the difference in weight. Cover the weights with wood filler and sand flush. If the hull is too heavy, drill out until it is the correct weight, fill the holes with plastic foam and cover with wood filler as before.

Prime the hull all around and seal with several coats of enamel paint. Alternatively, seal all around with several coats of varnish.

Making the keel

The keel is cut from a piece of $\frac{5}{64}$in mild steel. Substitute plywood if the boat is intended for younger users.

Trace the full-size pattern for keel from fig. 15. Glue the pattern to the steel and cut out using a hack saw (saber saw for plywood version). Finish with a half-round file. The keel is designed to give a weight of 3oz when cut to size. If your keel is lighter or if you use plywood, you will need to add weights to the keel. You can use lead fishing weights for this. Fix them to the tip of the keel using epoxy adhesive, to bring the keel up to the correct weight. Try to fix an equal number on each side of the keel and in the same positions.

Glue the keel into the slot in the hull using epoxy adhesive, with its shape raking back from the bows.

Finish with wood or metal primer as appropriate and then enamel paint.

Making the rudder

Cut out the rudder from $\frac{5}{64}$in plywood, following the dimensions in fig. 16.

Make the rudder spindle from 4in length of $\frac{5}{64}$in brass tube. Flatten $1\frac{1}{2}$in of the end in a vise. Turn up the last $\frac{1}{4}$in of the flattened portion to form a right angle (fig. 17). Position against the leading edge of the rudder with the bent end underneath. Fix in place with epoxy adhesive.

Sand smooth and finish with enamel paint.

When paint has dried, pass the end of the rudder spindle through the

rudder hole in the hull until the rudder is $\frac{1}{8}$in below the hull. Fit the brass locking collar over the top of the spindle and tighten it at deck level to prevent the spindle from slipping through the hole. Bend the end of the spindle over with a pair of pliers until it is parallel to the deck to form a tiller.

Insert screw eyes into the deck on either side of the tiller in the positions shown in fig. 12. Stretch a rubber band between these eyes and twist over the tiller to hold it in position for setting the rudder.

Making the mast

Cut a $10\frac{5}{8}$in length of $\frac{1}{4}$in dowel and taper one end as shown in fig. 18 by whittling with a craft knife and finishing with sandpaper. Drill a $\frac{1}{16}$in hole through the center of the mast 3in down from the tip of this tapered end. Glue the other end of the mast into the pre-drilled hole in the deck, using epoxy resin adhesive. Make sure that the hole through the mast faces from bow to stern.

Cut the mainsail halyard block from $\frac{5}{64}$in plywood as shown in fig. 19. Measure the thickness of the tapered mast at a point $\frac{1}{4}$in down from the tip. Drill the large hole in the block to this diameter, and drill a further $\frac{1}{16}$in hole as shown. Glue the halyard block onto the mast with epoxy resin adhesive, with the small hole directly toward the stern side of the mast as shown in fig. 12.

Cut out the boom, which is a 4in length of $\frac{1}{4}$in dowel. Drill $\frac{1}{16}$in holes through it $\frac{3}{4}$in from one end and $\frac{3}{16}$in from the other as shown in fig. 20.

Finish the mast and boom with several thin coats of polyurethane lacquer. You can support the boom on a wire through the holes while drying.

Making sails and rigging

The sails can be made from any lightweight, close-woven nylon or cotton fabric.

Following the measurements in fig. 21 and 22 make two paper patterns for the sails. Pin these onto the sail fabric and mark the shapes onto the fabric. Add $\frac{1}{4}$in hem allowance all around as shown and cut out the sails.

Fold back the hems and secure by stitching with strong thread or gluing with fabric adhesive.

Using a small awl, punch holes $\frac{1}{4}$in from the three corners of each sail.

Insert a screw eye into the deck directly behind the mast and another $\frac{5}{8}$in from the point of the bow as shown in fig. 12.

Cut about 2in of twine and tie through the hole in the front corner of the jib. Tie the two ends through the screw eye in the bows, as shown in fig. 23.

Cut about 11in of twine and knot to the hole in the top point of the jib. Thread the end of the twine through the hole drilled through the mast. This is the jib halyard. Pull down behind the mast until the jib is taut, then knot through the eye at the foot of the mast.

Use the bradawl to pierce holes $\frac{3}{4}$in apart down the edges of the mainsail as shown in fig. 23. Tie the sail to the mast and boom with short lengths of twine knotted through these holes as shown. Cut the ends of the twine off short and secure the knots with a drop of adhesive. Tie off the twine through the hole in the rear corner of the sail through the hole drilled $\frac{3}{4}$in from the end of the boom.

Tie a 2in length of twine to the hole at the front corner of the sail. Pass the end through the screw eye at the foot of the mast and tie off so that the boom is $1\frac{1}{4}$in above the deck. This is the mainsail kicking strap.

Cut another 11in length of twine for the mainsail halyard. Tie to the hole in the top of the mainsail, then thread through the small hole in the halyard block. Loop over the top and pull down until the tip of the sail almost touches the block. Tie off to the screw eye at the base of the mast.

Insert two screw eyes to secure jib sheets and two screw eyes for mainsail sheets in positions shown in fig. 12.

Cut about 20in of twine. Thread through corner of jib and knot, leaving equal ends on each side. Thread one end through each of the screw eyes on deck and knot ends of twine together. These are the jib sheets, which set the sail.

Cut about $15\frac{3}{4}$in of twine, loop around center of boom and tie. Thread each end of the twine through its corresponding screw eye on the deck and knot ends of twine together. These are the mainsail sheets.

Dollhouse

A dollhouse will give you and your children hours of fun. To make this two-story home, you need only very simple techniques. Most of the construction is of plywood.

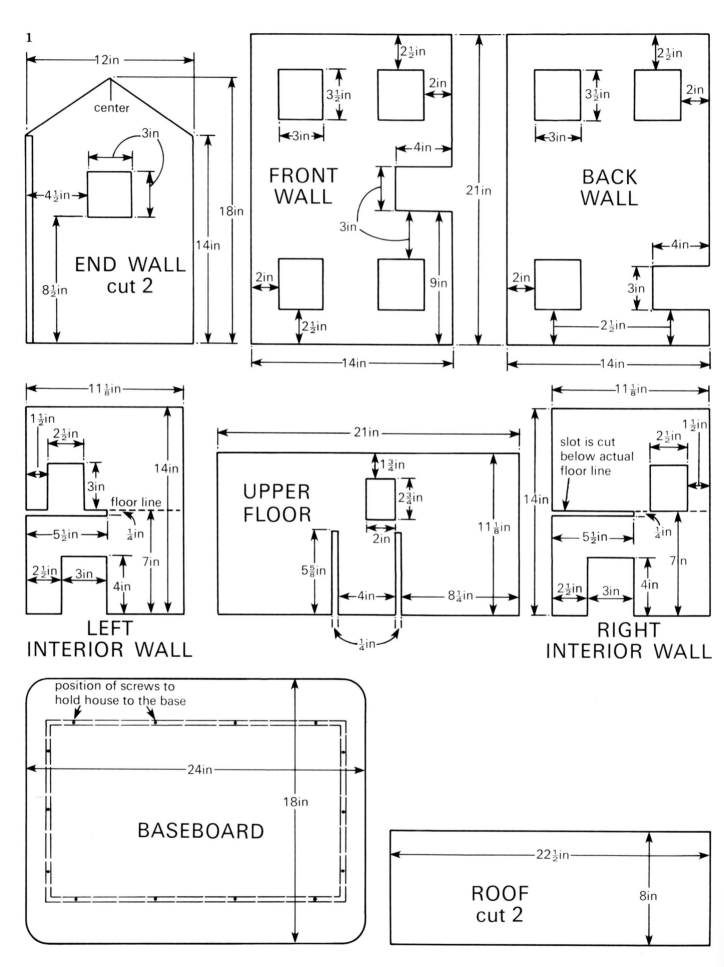

1

12in

center

END WALL
cut 2

3in

4½in

18in

14in

8½in

FRONT WALL

2½in

2in

3½in

3in

3in

4in

21in

2in

2½in

9in

14in

BACK WALL

2½in

2in

3½in

3in

3in

4in

2in

3in

2½in

14in

LEFT INTERIOR WALL

11⅛in

1½in

2½in

3in

floor line

14in

¼in

5½in

7in

2½in

3in

4in

UPPER FLOOR

21in

1¾in

2¾in

2in

5⅝in

4in

8¼in

¼in

11⅛in

RIGHT INTERIOR WALL

11⅛in

slot is cut below actual floor line

2½in

1½in

14in

5½in

¼in

7in

2½in

3in

4in

BASEBOARD

position of screws to hold house to the base

24in

18in

ROOF
cut 2

22½in

8in

184

Finished size

The completed house is about 18in tall, 12in deep, and 21in wide.

Techniques involved

Cutting; sawing; gluing; painting.

Tools required

Drill with $\frac{1}{4}$in and $\frac{1}{8}$in bits; coping saw or saber saw; hand saw; $\frac{1}{4}$in wide chisel; pencil; mallet and small hammer; screwdriver, hand plane and coarse wood file; one fine paintbrush and one 2in wide paintbrush; tape measure; try square; sanding block.

Materials

two pieces $\frac{1}{4}$in × 12in × 18in plywood for end walls
two pieces $\frac{1}{4}$in × 14in × 21in plywood for front and back walls
two pieces $\frac{1}{4}$in × 8in × 22$\frac{1}{2}$in plywood for roof sections
two pieces $\frac{1}{4}$in × 11in × 14in plywood for interior walls
one piece $\frac{1}{4}$in × 11in × 21in plywood for interior floor
one piece $\frac{1}{2}$in × 18in × 24in plywood for base
scrap pieces of $\frac{1}{4}$in plywood
sheet clear plastic
2 rolls of $\frac{1}{4}$in wide adhesive tape—one orange, one yellow—available from office suppliers; or cut larger widths to size.
1in × 23in piano hinge for roof hinge
4 $\frac{1}{2}$in brass hinges and screws
one hook and eye catch
box $\frac{1}{2}$in finishing nails
two pieces corner molding $\frac{1}{4}$in × 14in (cross section looks like a quarter circle)
enamel paints and suitable undercoats
wood filler and primer
scrap of cardboard; plastic tubing
white woodworking PVA adhesive
sandpaper—medium and fine
20 $\frac{1}{4}$in No. 4 screws
10 1in No. 4 screws

The house is designed so that there is easy access to the rooms. The front slides out so that children can play with the furniture inside, and the roof is hinged to open up the top floor.

Each floor is divided up into three sections consisting of a central hallway and stairway with a room on each side.

Each room can be decorated individually and with imagination as you would your own home, with either bought or homemade furniture. Instructions for furniture made from materials around the home are given on pages 216 to 219.

Making the house

Following the plans in fig. 1, mark out and cut the base from $\frac{1}{2}$in plywood. You can cut the basic rectangle with a hand saw, and cut the rounded corners with a coping saw or saber saw. Sand all the cut corners smooth. Mark out the positions of the walls where indicated, and drill $\frac{3}{32}$in clearance holes, countersunk on the underside, for the wall screws.

Following the plans in fig. 1 mark out the basic rectangles for the front and back walls, end walls, interior walls, interior floor and roof sections in $\frac{1}{4}$in plywood. Cut to shape with a hand saw. Mark each piece with the positions of doors, windows and assembling slots, taking care that these are accurately positioned.

Mark the profile of the end gables on the end walls. Cut the gables and slots with the hand saw. You can cut across the ends of the slots with a coping saw or saber saw.

Cut the door openings in the same

1. *Cutting chart for the house.*
Right: *The exterior walls are all ready to be assembled.*
Below: *The finished house with the front wall in position.*

way, cutting the sides with a hand saw, and then across with a coping saw or saber saw.

Cut the windows by drilling a starting hole so that you can insert the blade of your coping saw or saber saw and cut around the outline.

When you have cut out all the parts, sand all surfaces and edges smooth with sandpaper wrapped around a sanding block.

Painting interior

Before assembling the pieces it is advisable to prepare them for painting. Plywood of this thickness has a tendency to split at the edges where it has been sawed, leaving an untidy finish. To avoid this, fill in the splits with wood filler. When the filler is dry, sand the wood down with medium, then fine grade, sandpaper.

To seal the plywood, coat each surface with white primer. At this stage you need only paint the

interior of the house. Also paint the base.

When paint is dry, rub down with fine grade sandpaper before applying an undercoat. Again sand this coat down when dry and finish with a non-toxic enamel paint.

Assembly

The walls can now be assembled and the house attached to the base. Slot the interior walls and floor together and stand them on the base (fig. 2). Next, lay the end walls on the table with the inside surfaces uppermost.

On the left-hand edge of the left end wall, glue a 14in strip of corner molding (see plan). Glue a similar strip to the right-hand edge of the right end wall.

These strips of molding form the

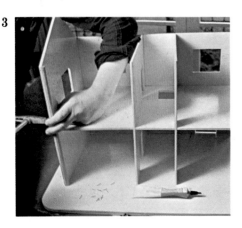

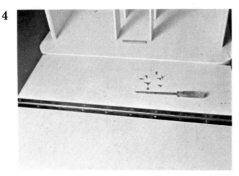

guides that allow the front of the house to slide out.

Lay the back wall on the table, inside surface uppermost. Place the interior wall-floor structure onto this, in the position that it is to be attached.

The rectangle cut for the stairway should be nearest the back wall. Use a try square to check that all the edges are flush.

Draw a line lightly around the interior wall-floor structure where it butts against the back wall. Remove this structure and coat the marked lines with woodworking glue. Coat the edges of the structure, which butt against the back wall, as well.

With the back wall still lying flat, press the two glued edges together and turn the whole structure upright. Tack together with ½in finishing nails.

Hold the end walls in place against the interior wall-floor structure and check that the edges are flush. Draw lines around where the interior wall-floor structure butts against the end wall.

Repeay the gluing and nailing as shown in fig. 3 with the other end wall. The front wall should now fit in between the molding and the inner wall structure.

Doors

The two doors should now be cut from ¼in thick plywood. Use scrap or the cut-outs from the doorways if they were not damaged. Cut them the size of the openings but make them ¼in shorter at the base. This allows a clearance for a small step to be glued to the baseboard. Paint the doors, then hang them with ½in brass hinges.

Attaching house to base

Position the house centrally on the base. Draw around the outer walls, both inside and out, with a pencil. Lift the house off the base and drill holes between the wall lines, as shown in the plan, with the $\frac{3}{32}$in bit. Countersink the holes from underneath the base. Fasten the house to

2. *The interior walls are slotted together on the base as shown.*
3. *Attaching the exterior walls with glue and finishing nails.*
4. *Attaching the piano hinge to the two halves of the roof.*

the base with the 1in No. 4 screws.

Having reached this point, it is advisable to paint the outer surfaces of the house and base with primer undercoat and then with an enamel. Remember to paint the edges of the base.

The roof

The front of the roof is designed to fold back, enabling children to reach the furniture on the upper floor. It also allows the front wall to slide out.

Take two pieces of plywood to be used for the roof and bevel one long edge of each. This is done with a plane and allows the roof to fold upward when you wish to reach inside.

Fill any splits that may have occurred and then sand and paint the inner sides.

Lay the two pieces side by side, beveled edges touching and facing down and screw the piano hinge into position (fig. 4) using the ¼in No. 4 screws.

Place the roof section on the end wall supports. The two sections should lie snugly along the pitch of the end walls with the beveled edge uppermost and the hinge underneath. Make sure the front roof section folds back easily to allow the front section to slide out. Attach the back section of roof to the end walls with finishing nails and finish the roof with enamel paint.

Making the chimney

Cut four pieces of ¼in plywood to the dimensions shown in fig. 5a on the plan. Glue together.

Glue a small piece of cardboard onto the top of the chimney. Chimney pots, which can be cut from short lengths of plastic tubing, are attached to the cardboard.

When the chimney is assembled, paint it and glue to the roof 8½in along from the left-hand end of the house (fig. 5b). The back of the chimney should be level with the edge of the bevel that you made on the apex of the roof.

Porch, stairway and windows

The final components of the house can now be made and fitted. The porch and stairs are cut from ¼in plywood.

Porch

This should be made from three pieces of ¼in plywood, 1in wide. Cut two pieces 4¼in long and a third 4in long. Smooth with fine grade sandpaper, paint and glue to the area around the front of the door. The two longer pieces should be flush with the edges of the door opening, while the third piece forms the lintel with a slight overlap at each side.

To finish off the doors, screw small screws into them to form handles.

Making the stairs

Cut two pieces of ¼in plywood, 8¼in long and 1in wide (fig. 6a).

Measure ⅜in from the top left-hand corner and bottom right-hand corner of each. Draw a line from this point to the adjacent corner and saw along this line. The steps must be set parallel to this sawn edge.

Cut seven steps from a piece of ¼in plywood, 1in × 1½in (fig. 6a).

Fasten to the side pieces with wood glue. Glue the stairway to the inside wall (fig. 6b).

Window glazing

The windows are easily made from clear plastic. The plastic used in packaging is ideal.

Cut the plastic ⅛in larger than the window. Place the plastic flat on the table and, using the yellow adhesive tape, mark out the window panes. For the frames, use the orange tape. The tape used for the surrounds should overlap the plastic slightly in order to fasten the window to the outside of the wall (fig. 7).

Finally, screw a hook and eye catch to one end of the roof so that it will hold the front flap back when the roof is opened (fig. 8). The front of the house can then be slid into position.

ASSEMBLING THE STAIRS

ASSEMBLING THE CHIMNEY

5a. *Making the chimney.*
5b. *Placing the chimney in position.*
6a. *Make the staircase by cutting seven steps and gluing to side pieces.*
6b. *The staircase is moved into position and glued to an inside wall.*
7. *Attach the windows to the outside of the wall.*
8. *Screw a hook and eye catch to one end of the roof.*

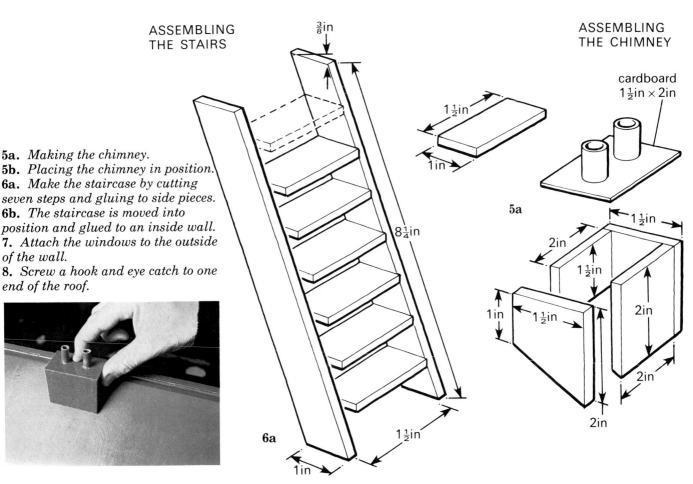

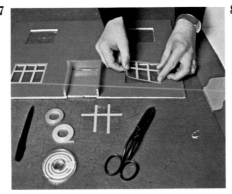

Marquetry chess board

Chess can be played by children well under ten. Your reward is an introduction to the fascinating art of marquetry. The board can be made from plywood or particle board and covered with any two contrasting wood veneers such as mahogany and sycamore. Large sheets of veneer are expensive to buy, but it is possible to obtain lumberyard remnants big enough for this purpose.

Finished size
14in square.

Techniques involved
Working with veneers.

Tools required
Sharp trimming knife; steel rule; combination-square.

Materials
½in × 14in × 14in plywood or particle board for base
1/16in thick wood veneers as follows:
15in × 8½in dark veneer and
    15in × 8½in light veneer for
    squares
15in × 6in dark veneer and
    15in × 2in light veneer for border
15in square of either color light
    veneer for back (plain version)
for patterned back, in diamond
    motif, 4 pieces of identical veneer
    each 10in square
transparent tape
epoxy resin adhesive
fine No. 2 sandpaper
garnet paper grades 4/0, 7/0 and
    9/0
polyurethane lacquer

For making cutting board:
¼in × 24in × 18in plywood or particle board
½in × ¼in × 24in hardwood
2 × ¼in bolts, ⅜in long, fitted with
    nuts and washers.

Cutting board

Great accuracy is needed for cutting and assembling the veneers used on the chessboard. For this the cutting edge of your knife should be kept very sharp; replace the blade as soon as it is blunt. The veneer strips can be cut more quickly and accurately by using a straightedge and a cutting board. The board is made from ½in thick plywood or particle board with a strip of perfectly straight ½in × ¼in strip of hardwood molding nailed and glued along one edge to act as a guide face as shown in fig. 2a and 2b. The bolts form adjustable stops that should be set to give a uniform distance between the

How to use the cutting board:
1. *The bolt is adjustable and can be set to the required width.*
2a. *The molding acts as a guide face. Cut veneer along a steel rule.*
2b. *Cutting the checkered strips.*

guide face and a steel rule placed firmly against the stops (fig. 1). Make sure that the slots in which the bolts slide are set far enough apart to fit your piece of veneer between them.

To cut veneer strips trim one edge of the veneer straight and set both stops to give the desired width between the guide face and the straightedge. Position the veneer against the hardwood strip, place the steel rule over the veneer and firmly against the stops, and then cut cleanly against the rule. Do not

try to cut directly through the veneer at one stroke; make a series of lighter cuts to avoid splintering or tearing the veneer.

Making the chessboard
Checker assembly

Using the cutting board and stops set to 1½in, cut four strips of dark veneer, each 15in × 1½in. These lengths are trimmed later. Keep them together in the order in which they were cut. Now cut four strips of light veneer the same size. Using

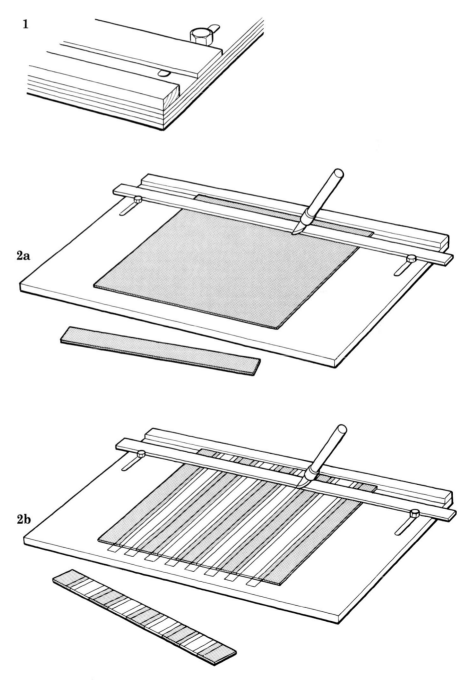

1

2a

2b

strips of transparent tape, fit the strips of veneer together in alternating sequence (fig. 4). Note that the strips should be assembled in the order in which they were cut and with the grain running in the same direction. Check that all strips fit tightly against one another.

Using steel rule and combination squares trim the assembly at one end at right angles to the direction of the veneer strips.

Position the assembly on the cutting board with the trimmed edge firmly against the hardwood face, so that the veneer strips are at right angles to it.

Carefully cut through the assembly so that a new 1½in-wide strip is obtained, comprising nine squares of alternately light and dark veneer (fig. 5). Handle these pieces with care, as the squares of veneer are joined together only by the adhesive tape. In the same way cut seven more 1½in wide strips of nine squares; set aside the remaining veneer. Keeping these strips in the same order, lay

them out on the cutting board and stagger them to form a checkered pattern (fig. 6).

Using tape, join the strips together, again making certain that the joints are tight between adjacent pieces of veneer and checking that the squares meet exactly at the corners. Eight squares of veneer will be left projecting from the assembly. Cut these off and discard them. The result should be the familiar chessboard pattern in a perfect square, with each of the small squares meeting its neighbors exactly at the corners.

Back

Begin with the back of the base board (sand the edges smooth if necessary). The back can be covered with a single sheet of veneer, cut slightly oversize and glued to the back of the base board using epoxy resin adhesive.

A more professional appearance is obtained by using matching quarters of veneer. The four pieces should be

3. *Begin the chessboard by cutting the light and dark veneers into 1½in strips each at least 12in long. The cutting board enables this task to be carried out quickly and accurately. With the veneer placed against the hardwood strip and the steel rule held firmly against the stops the strips are cut.*

4. *Taking care to keep the veneers in the order in which they were cut, the strips are taped together with the colors alternated.*

5. *Strips consisting of nine 1½in squares are cut.*

6. *The strips are kept in the same order, but with alternate ones offset to form the checker pattern.*

7. *Composite strips form the borders, and these are taped to the trimmed assembly with edges overlapping at the corners.*

8. *The taped assembly is ready to be fixed to the baseboard.*

9a. *Making the mitered corners.*

9b. *Finished corner.*

10. *Attaching strips of veneer all around the sides of the baseboard.*

cut from similar leaves of veneer.

Trim the edges flush and sand with sandpaper.

Border

Using the cutting board with the stops reset as appropriate, cut four 15in × ¼in strips of dark veneer, four 15in × ½in strips of dark veneer and four 15in × ¼in strips of light veneer. To highlight the corners 2½in lengths of ¼in wide strips of dark veneer can be inserted along the edges as shown in fig. 7.

Tape the border pieces along the edges of the squared veneer assembly, overlapping at the corners (see fig. 7).

Form miters at the corner by cutting through the two border strips diagonally (fig. 8, 9, 9a, 9b). An easy way to do this is with a chisel held vertically over them and pressed down to cut both together.

Alternatively, use a knife, but take care not to split the veneers. Remove excess veneer and tape the corners together carefully.

Edges

Cut four strips of veneer, slightly oversize for the edges of the board. Using epoxy resin adhesive, stick strips to two opposite edges. Allow to set and sand flush with fine grade sandpaper. Repeat for the remaining edges (fig. 10).

Assembling the chessboard

Make sure that you position the pattern so that the corner square to a player's right is a light square.

Remove all tape from the side of the checkered assembly that will be stuck to the base board. Take care not to pull the pieces apart or to raise the grain of the wood.

Spread epoxy resin onto base

board and then onto back of veneer taking care to cover them fully with a thin even coat, as any bumps or ridges will show through. Leave for about 15 minutes or until the glue is touch-dry, then carefully press veneer assembly into position, making sure that no air is trapped underneath.

Make sure that the assembly is exactly square to the board. Remove all remaining tape carefully.

Sanding and polishing

Using increasingly fine grades of garnet paper, rub down the surface of the veneer. Take care neither to round off any corners nor to rub through the surface of the veneer. Continue until the whole surface of the chessboard is absolutely smooth. You can finish the entire board with polyurethane lacquer, applying at least two thin coats.

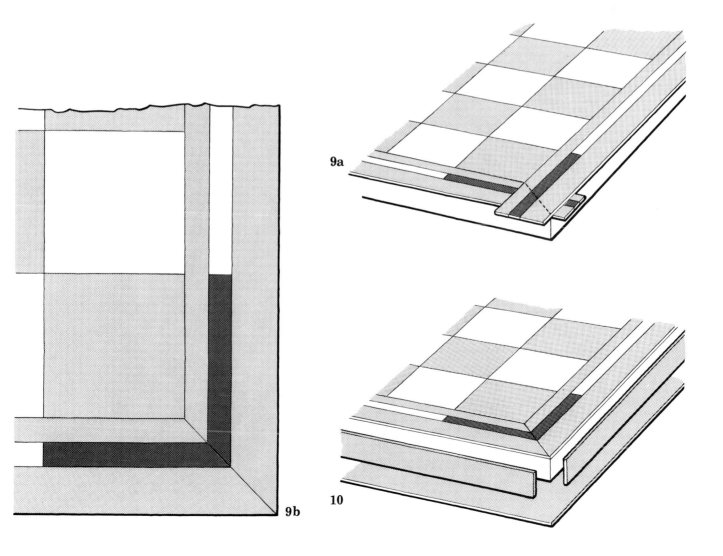

9a

9b

10

Laying hen

This amusing and novel toy will charm adults as well as children. A hole in the back of the hen's body lets you fill her with wooden eggs. Press the body down, and the eggs are released one at a time from a trapdoor underneath.

Techniques involved
Sawing; cutting curves; drilling; sanding; gluing; painting.

Tools required
Pencil; ballpoint pen; graph paper; tracing paper; carbon paper; saber saw; craft knife; hand or electric drill and bits; long-nosed pliers or tweezers; adhesive tape; rubber band.

Materials
$\frac{1}{8}$in $\times 10\frac{1}{4}$in $\times 10\frac{1}{4}$in plywood
$\frac{3}{8}$in $\times 10\frac{1}{4}$in $\times 10\frac{1}{4}$in plywood
$\frac{1}{16}$in $\times 22$in $\times 2\frac{3}{8}$in plywood for bending (grain of outer plies must run across width of the panel)
$1\frac{1}{4}$in $\times 1\frac{1}{4}$in $\times 12$in pine (note that this is the *finished* size)
$\frac{1}{4}$in diameter $\times 16$in hardwood dowel
1in diameter $\times 3$in hardwood dowel
5×1in diameter wooden balls, for eggs
$\frac{1}{4}$in screw hook
2 1in finishing nails
1 $1\frac{1}{4}$in finishing nail
2 $\frac{1}{2}$in No. 4 flathead woodscrews
$1\frac{1}{2}$in $\times \frac{1}{4}$in extension spring (medium tension)
PVA woodworking adhesive
fine sandpaper
wax polish
enamel paints and varnish

List of parts
Before beginning work, study the list of parts below. Each part is numbered as shown in the cutting plan.

Part	No. needed	Part Name
1	2	Inner sides
2	2	Outer sides
3	1	Spacer block
4	1	Spacer block
5	1	Spacer block
6	4	Body dowels
7	1	Outer skin
8	1	Neck
9	1	Head
10	1	Tail
11	2	Tail sides
12	2	Legs
13	1	Feet
14	1	Trapdoor base
15	2	Egg tray sides
16	1	Locking dowel

The moving mechanism inside the body is quite intricate, and must be accurately made if the hen is to lay her eggs properly. So although none

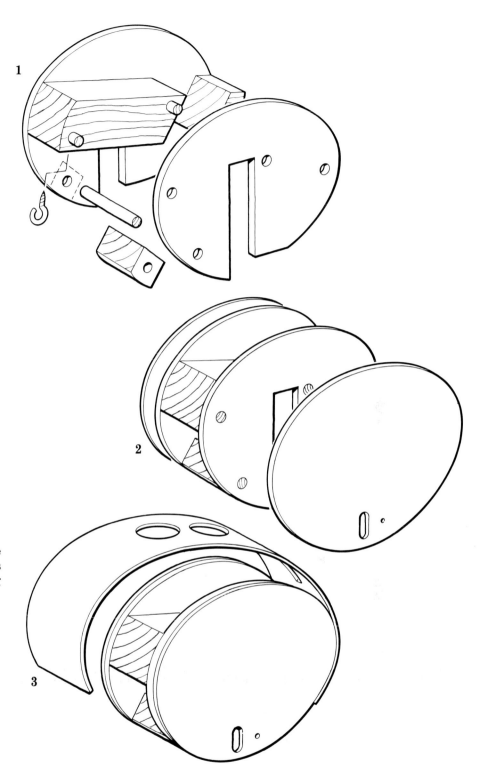

of the individual woodworking skills needed is particularly advanced, construction must be meticulous.

Making the hen
The parts should be cut out first and assembled without glue before final assembly to be sure that they fit properly.

First trace all the full-size patterns.

Then use carbon paper and a ball point pen to transfer all the pattern parts to the appropriate lumber as indicated on the pattern.

Cut out the plywood parts with a saber saw. Cut the slots in 1 by drilling two $\frac{1}{4}$in holes and joining

193

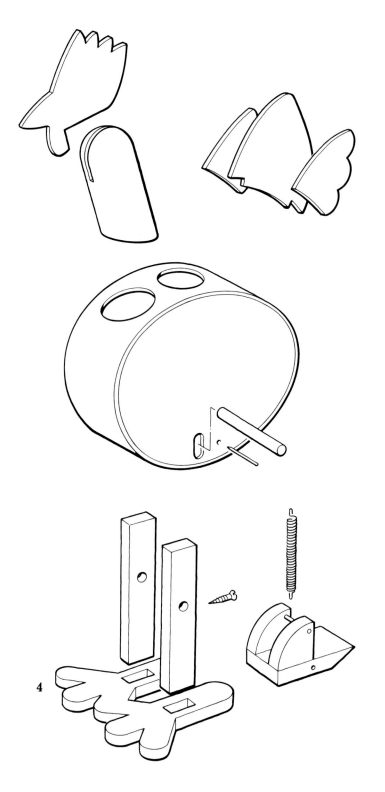

4

diameter dowel using a saber saw.

Cut the 1in dowel for the neck (8) to length using a saber saw to make the angled cut at the end. Cut the other end off square and make two cuts with a saber saw to form the sides of a $\frac{1}{8}$in slot into the end. Remove the waste material with a saber saw. Use sandpaper to round off this end to a smooth dome.

Check all the parts for fit. Lay the softwood blocks (3, 4 and 5) on the sides (1) in the positions shown by the dotted lines and check that the drilled holes align. Check that the legs (12) fit into the slots in the feet (13.) Make sure also that the legs will slide into the large rectangular slots in sides (1). Check that the trapdoor (14) is at least $\frac{1}{16}$in narrower than blocks 3, 4, and 5.

When all these points have been checked and adjusted, assemble as illustrated. Glue dowels (6) into the holes in the pine blocks 3, 4, 5, leaving an equal projection of $\frac{3}{8}$in on each side.

Glue the blocks to the sides 1 in the positions shown by the dotted lines, inserting the projecting dowels into the holes (fig. 1). Allow to dry, then sand off any projections.

Glue sides 2 to the outsides of side 1 (fig. 2).

Wrap the outer skin (7) around the assembly. Make sure that the holes and slot are the right way around, and that the wrap starts and finishes at the points indicated (fig. 3). Glue and hold in place with rubber bands and adhesive tape until glue sets. Sand the edges smooth.

Glue the tail (10) into the slot in the skin and glue sides (11) to it. Insert the neck (8) into the front hole until it touches the block. Glue in place, making sure that the slot faces front and rear. Glue the head into the slot (fig. 4).

Sand the completed body smooth and decorate with enamel paints.

Assemble the legs and egg tray mechanism. Glue the legs (12) into the feet (13). Use a scrap of 1$\frac{1}{4}$in softwood to ensure that they remain parallel throughout (fig. 5). Glue the sides of the egg tray (15) to the trapdoor base (14) as shown (fig. 6). Pass a 1$\frac{1}{4}$in finishing nail through the holes in the sides and cut the end off flush. Hook one end of the spring to it.

Sand the completed assemblies.

them with a saber saw. Cut the chamfer on the end of 14 with a saber saw or plane, and finish with sandpaper. Drill holes in all the positions indicated. Cut the slots in 13 with a saber saw after drilling a starter hole. Take care to keep the corners square. Cut the holes and the slot in 7 with a saber saw after drilling starter holes. Sand all edges

smooth, but do not round them off.

Cut out all the pine parts with a saber saw. Note that the material used should be exactly 1$\frac{1}{4}$in thick; buy oversized and plane down if necessary. Drill the indicated holes in all these pieces. Screw a $\frac{1}{4}$in screw hook in to 3 in the position shown (fig. 1).

Cut the dowels (6 and 16) from $\frac{1}{4}$in

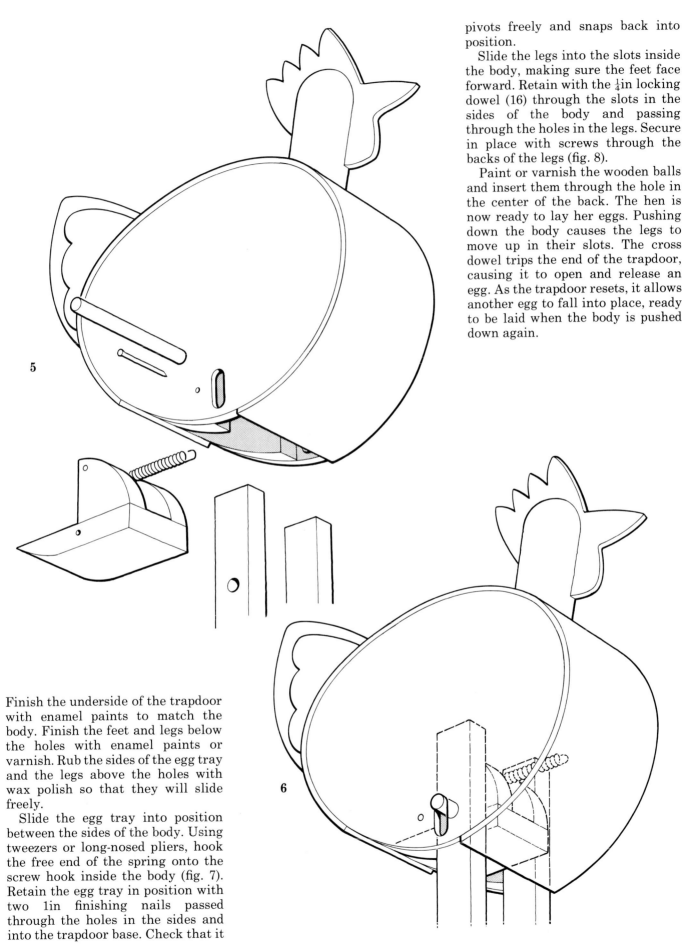

pivots freely and snaps back into position.

Slide the legs into the slots inside the body, making sure the feet face forward. Retain with the $\frac{1}{4}$in locking dowel (16) through the slots in the sides of the body and passing through the holes in the legs. Secure in place with screws through the backs of the legs (fig. 8).

Paint or varnish the wooden balls and insert them through the hole in the center of the back. The hen is now ready to lay her eggs. Pushing down the body causes the legs to move up in their slots. The cross dowel trips the end of the trapdoor, causing it to open and release an egg. As the trapdoor resets, it allows another egg to fall into place, ready to be laid when the body is pushed down again.

5

6

Finish the underside of the trapdoor with enamel paints to match the body. Finish the feet and legs below the holes with enamel paints or varnish. Rub the sides of the egg tray and the legs above the holes with wax polish so that they will slide freely.

Slide the egg tray into position between the sides of the body. Using tweezers or long-nosed pliers, hook the free end of the spring onto the screw hook inside the body (fig. 7). Retain the egg tray in position with two 1in finishing nails passed through the holes in the sides and into the trapdoor base. Check that it

TRACE PATTERN FOR HEN

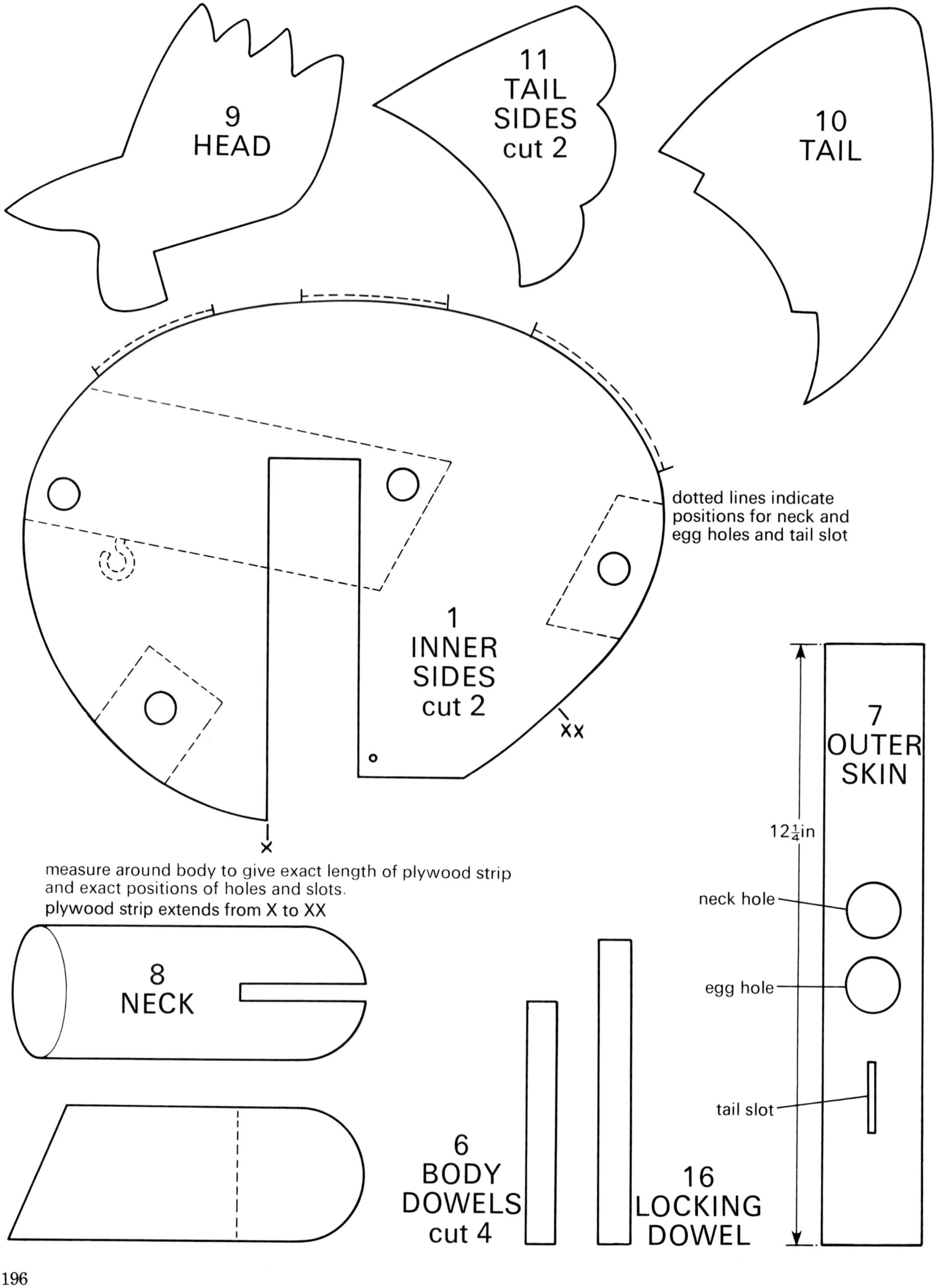

9
HEAD

11
TAIL
SIDES
cut 2

10
TAIL

dotted lines indicate
positions for neck and
egg holes and tail slot

1
INNER
SIDES
cut 2

xx

7
OUTER
SKIN

$12\frac{1}{4}$in

neck hole

egg hole

tail slot

measure around body to give exact length of plywood strip
and exact positions of holes and slots.
plywood strip extends from X to XX

8
NECK

x

6
BODY
DOWELS
cut 4

16
LOCKING
DOWEL

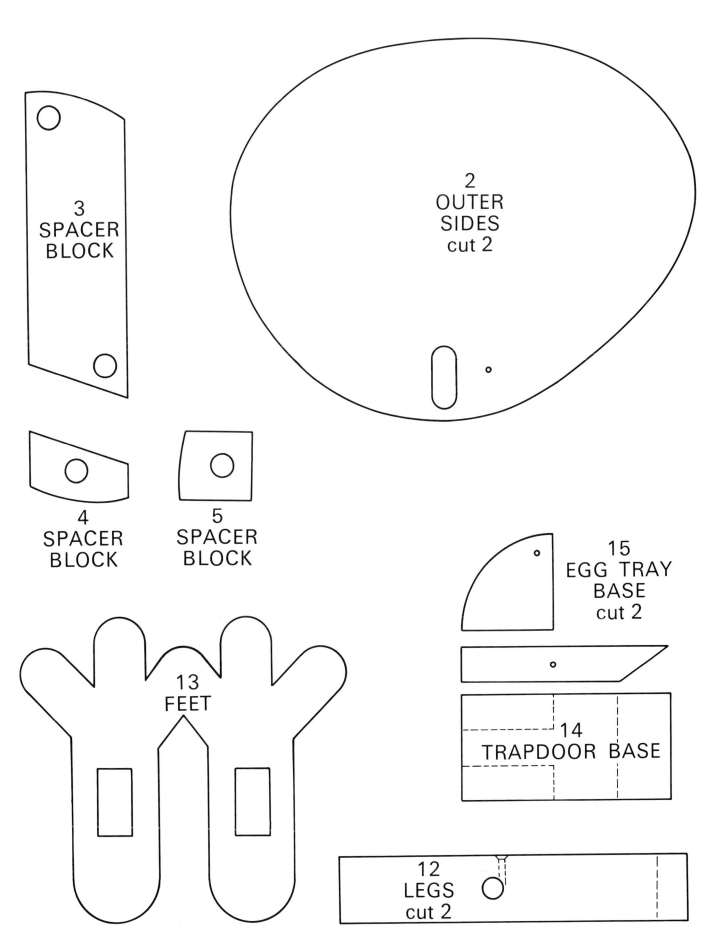

3
SPACER
BLOCK

2
OUTER
SIDES
cut 2

4
SPACER
BLOCK

5
SPACER
BLOCK

15
EGG TRAY
BASE
cut 2

13
FEET

14
TRAPDOOR BASE

12
LEGS
cut 2

MIXED MEDIA TOYS

You'll be truly amazed to see how many amusing and colorful playthings you can make from leftover scrap materials. Papier mâché is cheap and durable, and can be modeled into traditional puppets. Kites are easily constructed from lengths of wood and scraps of paper, and they provide hours of fun and exercise outdoors. We've also included ideas for dollhouse furniture made from odds and ends of everyday materials, plus some ingenious toy tidies.

Basic know-how

General techniques

Apart from those toys that are made from papier mâché, the following projects do not require any special expertise. The kites are basically constructed from paper mounted over a frame—either made from light wood such as bamboo, or medium gauge wire. Cutting, folding and gluing the paper onto the frames should be done on a clear surface, with plenty of work space.

Some projects in this section, such as the dollhouse furniture and the miniature four-poster bed are excellent ways of using up bits and pieces of household materials in an enjoyable and creative way. The only craft skills needed for these are cutting, gluing and painting—plus a certain amount of imagination and ingenuity.

Three projects in this section are ideas for tidying and storing toys, and are therefore not technically playthings in themselves.

Making papier mâché

Papier mâché is a modeling material consisting of pieces of paper bound with paste or glue and molded around a shape to make functional and decorative objects. It is a cheap and easy material to use and has the advantage of drying naturally to a hard and durable substance, without having to be baked like clay.

The craft of making objects from papier mâché is an ancient one. Soon after the Chinese discovered how to make paper, about 2000 years ago, they began to experiment with ways of molding it by tearing it into pieces, mixing it with glue, and shaping it into useful and attractive objects. Interest in this craft declined for hundreds of years until the French revived it in the 18th century. They called it papier mâché, meaning literally "chewed-up paper". They used it to make trays, boxes and even furniture (particularly chairs) which were often inlaid with mother-of-pearl.

Uses for papier mâché were far more limited then than they are today. The invention of epoxy resin makes the papier mâché object much stronger and more durable than traditional water-soluble glues and pastes could do. Epoxy resin can also be used as a surface finish.

Materials

Most of the materials needed to make papier mâché objects can be found in the average home.

Paper

The main item is, of course, paper; old newspapers will probably be your best source. You can also use paper towels, soft tissues or white tissue paper. It is worth experimenting, too, with other types of paper such as rag paper, which is stronger than ordinary paper because its ingredients include cotton or linen rags as well as wood pulp. Sources of rag paper include used fine stationery, pages from old ledgers and old damaged books, and drawing papers.

You can also use paper to decorate an object built up from several layers of papier mâché, if you wish. Gift wrapping paper, wallpaper, colored tissue paper and colored magazine pictures are all suitable. In fact, almost any kind of paper may be used.

Pastes and glues

You will also need some kind of paste or glue for binding the paper together to make papier mâché. The one traditionally used for the purpose is a paste made from flour and water, which is stirred over a low heat, adding water gradually until enough has been added to make it smooth and creamy. Wallpaper paste mixed with water according to the manufacturer's instructions also makes a strong glue.

However, epoxy resin is the strongest type of glue to use. It will make papier mâché objects virtually unbreakable, waterproof, flameproof and dirtproof. It should always be used for large or complex objects that don't have a base support, since they might otherwise buckle.

Using epoxy resin simply as a surface finish for a smaller piece means that the object will not only be protected as though by a varnish, but it will also be strengthened, since the epoxy penetrates the papier mâché itself.

Molds

Some sort of mold will also be required to support the papier mâché object while it is being made. It can either be removed after the papier mâché has dried, or integrated into the piece for added strength. The mold can be either a rigid shape (a plastic bottle, tin can, cardboard cylinder, a glass or china dish or bowl, fruit or vegetables), or it can be flexible (chicken wire, crumpled newspaper, clay or modeling clay or even a balloon).

Methods

There are three basic ways of making papier mâché. The most common is to cut or tear the paper into small strips or squares and glue them onto a base or mold. Tearing rather than cutting the paper means that it will have rough edges which will blend into a smoother surface than straight edges when glued down in layers. Paper can be torn against a ruler to make fairly uniform strips.

Another method, called lamination, consists of gluing together several sheets of paper to make one strong flexible sheet. This can then be shaped over a base or cut into strips before it is applied.

The third method involves breaking down small pieces of paper into a mash or pulp by soaking them in water for several hours. The water is then squeezed out of the paper until it becomes a pulp, and glue is added to make it bind together. Paper mash is often used to add texture and strength to an object molded from strips of papier mâché, but it can also be molded like clay.

There are several commercial mixes available for making "instant" paper mash, to which only water need be added. These are easy to use and can be bought from art supply stores.

Opposite: *Objects in papier mâché.*

Papier mâché puppets

Because papier mâché is so durable and adaptable, it is highly suitable for modeling the heads of puppets and dolls. Even a beginner will find it easy to make the basic head shape, and with practice, sophisticated creations can be made by using papier mâché pulp as a sculpture medium.

Techniques involved

Making papier mâché; drilling holes; basic sewing; modeling; painting and varnishing.

Tools required

Basic sewing tools; brace with $\frac{3}{4}$in bit, and hammer, or screwdriver; wooden spoon; scissors; pencil; plastic bucket and bowl; cocktail pick or fork.

Materials

For the mold

wooden block about 6in square and about 1in thick
$\frac{3}{4}$in × 8in dowel
piece of closely woven scrap fabric at least 5in × 12in
about $\frac{1}{2}$lb kitty litter
wood adhesive
sheet of newspaper
adhesive tape
tracing paper

For modeling heads

newspapers
wallpaper paste with sizing mixed according to package instructions
coarse and fine grade sandpaper
paints (acrylic or poster) and brushes
polyurethane varnish

For the glove

fabric at least 24in × 12in
tape, braid or strip of hemmed fabric 3in long and $\frac{1}{4}$in–$\frac{1}{2}$in wide
string about 28in long to attach head and hands to the glove

For the hands

piece of cardboard about 2in × 2in or 4 pipe cleaners
newspaper
wallpaper paste solution

The instructions given here are for papier mâché heads that are fairly simple in design but which can be a wide range of characters simply by painting on different facial features. By changing the costume (the glove) that is attached to a head, just a few puppet heads can represent many different characters. You can also make the hands for glove puppets from papier mâché.

Making both heads and hands of these glove puppets involves two methods of using papier mâché: the strip method and the mash or pulp method (see **Know-how** section). The basic head shapes are made by the strip method, where layer upon layer of paper strips are shaped

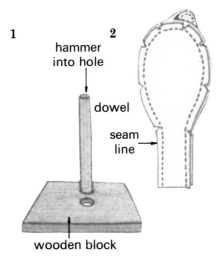

around the mold. Their features (nose, ears, cheekbones) are modeled on this basic head shape with paper pulp and secured with more strips of paper to make a smooth surface.

The mold and stand

The mold consists of a cloth bag, which is filled with cat box granules (commonly known as "kitty litter") and secured to a modeling stand that is a wooden post fixed onto a wooden block.

The granules absorb the moisture from the papier mâché, helping it to dry. The stand makes modeling easier since it provides a steady base on which to shape the papier mâché.

To make the modeling stand

Drill a hole through the center of the wooden block with the $\frac{3}{4}$in flat bit. Spread glue on one end of the dowel and inside the hole, and hammer the dowel into the hole, to the depth of the wooden block (fig. 1). Alternatively, glue the dowel directly onto the block and screw it in place from underneath with 2in No. 8 screw.

To make the mold

Trace the pattern on this page. Use it to cut three pieces from old sheeting or similar fabric. Allowing $\frac{1}{4}$in seams and following the dotted lines on the pattern, sew the pieces together firmly with strong thread (fig. 2). (Machine-stitching is preferable.) Leave the neck edge open. Clip curves and turn inside out.

Pack the bag firmly with cat box granules, to about $\frac{3}{4}$in from the neck edge of the bag. Hold the stand upside-down and push the dowel into the bag, to a depth of about 3in or far

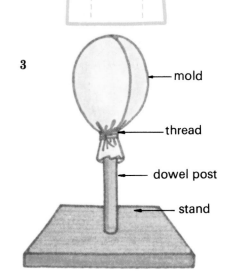

1. *Modeling stand.*
2. *Sewing mold.*
3. *Fix the filled mold to the stand.*

enough that the mold does not wobble on its stand.

Wind strong thread several times around the neck of the bag and the dowel post, just above the filling, and knot securely. Turn the stand and mold upright (fig. 3).

Cover the mold with a single sheet of newspaper, crush it close to the mold and secure with transparent tape at the base of the neck. Tear off any excess paper below the transparent tape. This sheet of newspaper is the base to which the paper strips are applied and keeps the strips from adhering to the mold.

Modeling the head

Tear enough newspaper into small strips to cover the mold with at least eight layers.

Dip the strips, one by one, in the wallpaper paste solution and apply to the mold (for full details of the strip method, see **Know-how** section). Apply strips until you have at least eight layers.

Make up the paper pulp in a bucket according to the instructions given in **Know-how** section, using a little less than ½pt of wallpaper paste solution for one puppet head. Squeeze as much water as possible from the soaked paper and add it gradually to the paste, mixing carefully with a wooden spoon. Enough paper has been added to make a firm consistency when you squeeze out the excess paste from the pulp and it binds together as a lump.

Mold the puppet's features on the basic head shape with paper pulp while the last layer of paper strips is still wet. Mark the positions of the nose, chin, eyes and ears very lightly with a cocktail pick or fork.

Squeeze out a small amount of paper pulp and use it to build up the features, smoothing contours with the fingers. Building up cheekbones and the forehead creates eye sockets. For the face of a child puppet, the features should be rounded, not well defined. Try to compact the paper pulp very firmly, and to make the surface as smooth as possible.

When the features are formed and while the paper pulp is still wet, apply three or four more layers of paper strips to secure the mash to the layers of paper strips beneath it.

Leave the head on the modeling stand to dry for a day or two. The surface will be uniformly pale grey in color and it will feel dry to the touch.

Carefully turn the head and stand upside-down, untie the thread at the neck and remove the stand. Let the granules fall out of the mold into a

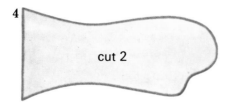

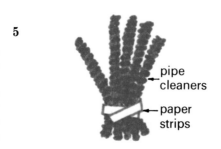

pipe cleaners

paper strips

4. Trace pattern for the cardboard hands. Cut out two shapes.
5. Pipe cleaners are used to make a hand. Bind together with paper strips.

basin or bag, so that they can be used again. Pull out the fabric mold and keep it for another use; it should come away easily.

If the inside of the head is not thoroughly dry, you can put it in an oven at the lowest possible heat and with the door open. Check the head frequently and remove it from the oven as soon as it is completely dry. This may take as long as a few hours.

The hands

To make hands, cardboard hand shapes may be covered with paper strips. Pipe cleaners covered with paper mash make hands that are capable of holding various props, such as a walking stick or baton.

To make a pair of hands using cardboard as a base, trace the pattern for the hands (fig. 4) and draw it twice on the cardboard. Cut out the shapes.

Stick a pin through each cardboard wrist, so that you can hold the cardboard steady while applying the papier mâché. Tear newspaper into very small strips and, using the strip method already described, apply six layers of strips to both hands and wrists. Leave them to dry naturally, away from direct heat; these may curl at the edges if dried in an oven.

To cover pipe cleaners with paper pulp, thus making more capable and expressive hands, cut the pipe cleaners into eight 2in lengths for

the fingers and two slightly shorter lengths for the thumbs. Bind four finger lengths and one thumb together with strips of paper and paste around one end, to hold the pipe cleaners together (fig. 5) before building up the hand shape.

Spread and bend the pipe cleaners to the desired shape. Cover the main part of the hand with pulp, and the fingers with several layers of paper strips. Finally, cover the whole hand with an even, smooth paper strip layer.

Bind the remaining lengths of pipe cleaner together for the other hand, in the same way as you did the others, and cover with papier mâché pulp and strips as described.

Painting and varnishing

Before painting, rub down all surfaces of the head and hands with coarse and then fine sandpaper.

Draw the eye shapes on the head and paint them white. Paint the rest of the head and neck flesh color. While the face is still wet, blend in shading and cheek coloring with a brush loaded with various diluted shades of scarlet lake.

Paint hair with several shades of the same color for a realistic effect. (If you intend to apply fur fabric to represent hair, there is no need to paint on the hair.)

Paint the hands flesh color and, if they are made on a cardboard base,

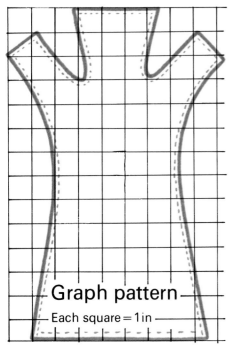

Graph pattern

Each square = 1 in

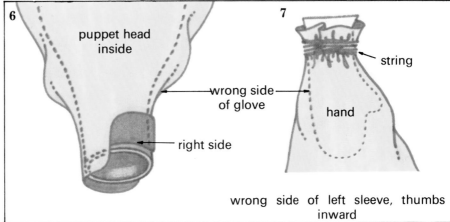

6. *Fitting the neck of the glove over the neck of the head.*

7. *The glove is firmly attached to the hand with string.*

wrong side of left sleeve, thumbs inward

paint lines in red on the back and front of each to indicate fingers. Paint fingernails white; these show up well.

Finally, varnish all the painted surfaces with two coats of clear polyurethane varnish.

The glove

If you have to adapt the graph pattern given, bear in mind that the usual configuration of the fingers is: index finger in the head, thumb in one arm, middle finger in the other arm, and ring and little fingers folded into the body. Make sure that the thumb and index finger just reach the ends of the arms and that there is plenty of room in the body for the other fingers. Adults can use the pattern if they make it $\frac{1}{4}$in longer all around; for very young children it should be made about $\frac{1}{4}$in smaller all around.

The length of the glove is a matter of choice; this pattern allows for a long glove such as professional puppeteers use, so that the puppet can be moved freely without the puppeteer's arm showing above the stage.

Use strong fabrics such as felt, heavy wool or denim, since these do not have to be lined in order to give a substantial body to the puppet. The fabrics used for the back and front of the glove need not be identical.

Trace, enlarge and cut out the

graph pattern. Pin it to the fabric.

Cut out two pieces of fabric from the pattern. With right sides together, sew them together along the stitching lines shown on the pattern, with $\frac{1}{4}$in seams all around. Leave the neck, wrists and bottom of the glove unsewn.

Turn the glove right side out and turn the fabric back $\frac{1}{4}$in inside the neck and wrists of the glove and baste. Turn up and hem the bottom if necessary.

To attach the head to the glove, insert the neck of the head into the neck of the glove. Turn the glove inside out by pushing it up over the head, so that the right side of the neck of the glove faces the neck of the head (fig. 6). Turn up the top 1in of the neck of the glove so that the cloth is double thickness and fits tightly around the neck of the head (see fig. 6). Cut a piece of string about 20in long and wind it around the neck of the head and the neck of the glove several times; then tie securely.

To attach the hands to the sleeves, turn the sleeves inside out and insert each hand into them from the right side of the fabric, up to the wrists, with the thumbs toward the head and palms facing the same way as the face. Fold back about $\frac{3}{4}$in of the fabric from the basted edge and wind one 4in length of string around each sleeve and wrist (fig. 7). Tie. Turn glove right side out.

Attaching the glove to the head and hands with string means that it is easy to remove the glove and fit on another for a change of costume.

Wind a strip of tape, braid or hemmed material around the puppet's neck and stitch the ends together.

Additional dress

Additional costume items such as hats, shawls and aprons can be made from scraps of fabric; pieces of fur can be glued to the head to make the hair; and props such as baskets, frying pans and walking sticks are easy to make from papier mâché. Do not make the props too small for the puppets to grasp and the audience to see.

Doll's head

The doll's head is also made of papier mâché and could be fitted over a stuffed fabric body. The mold used is different from that for the puppet heads, since it must incorporate a neck piece which fits over the front and back of the doll's cloth body.

The head (including neck piece) is first modeled in clay, slightly larger than the desired finished size, to allow for papier mâché shrinkage as it dries.

The clay model is then cast in plaster, which is cut in two pieces (from ear to ear). When dry, the two halves of the cast are pulled apart, washed out with clean water and allowed to dry thoroughly.

The inner surfaces of the cast are then greased with margarine or oil, the paper pulp is firmly pressed against them, and the two halves are then pressed together and the pulp allowed to dry. The cast is then removed.

Finally the head is sanded down, painted and varnished in the same way as the puppet heads.

Kite making

*No one knows who flew the first kite or why. They are supposed
to have been invented in Greece about 400BC, but they were
certainly popular in China some 600 years before that date.
Whatever their origins, kite flying is a most enjoyable pastime.*

Techniques involved
Cutting sticks; gluing.

Tools required
Scissors; craft knife; pencil; ruler.

Materials
two sticks, one 24in, the other 36in
   long
large sheet of paper
small ball of thin string or strong
   thread
curtain ring to act as towing ring
scraps of colored paper or streamers
   for the tail
nylon kite string
glue or adhesive tape
poster paint and brush (optional).

Choosing the materials
Surprisingly, there is no need to bother too much about the weight of a kite unless it is to be flown in very light winds. Choose any paper you like for the cover—heavy papers such as brown wrapping paper or wallpaper; medium weights such as decorative wrapping papers, poster or shelf paper; or lightweight papers such as tissue. Crêpe is probably the only unsuitable paper because of its tendency to stretch.

The sticks for the frame can be garden canes, balsa or pine battens, dowels or even twigs. Split thicker, heavier sticks lengthwise with a sharp kitchen knife to make them lighter.

Balance is more important than weight, so shave off any knots or thicker sections. To test for balance, mark the middle of the stick and balance it across the back of the knife blade. If one end dips, shave a little off it.

A cutter kite
Scale the size of this kite up or down as you wish, according to the size required. The important part is the proportionate length of the sticks; the longer stick should be half again as long as the shorter one.

The frame
First cut two small notches, each about ¼in in from each end of both sticks (fig. 1a). Make a mark at the center of the shorter stick and a mark one-third of the way along the longer one. Lay the sticks across each other at right angles, the marks touching, and tie them together

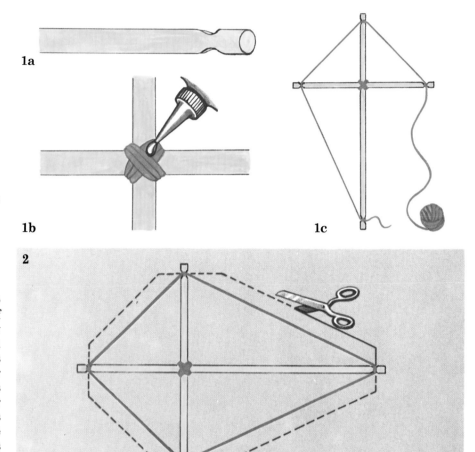

tightly with the thread. Put a dab of glue on the junction for extra strength (fig. 1b). Tie a piece of thread to the notched end of one of the sticks, then run the string tightly through the other notches and back to the first. Wind the string two or three times around each notch as it passes through (fig. 1c). Tie the ends to complete the frame.

The cover
Lay the frame on the wrong side of the sheet of paper and cut around it, leaving about 1in outside the string (fig. 2). Trim off the corners of the paper (see fig. 2). Fold the edges of the paper up over the string and fasten them down with glue or transparent tape.

Decoration
Turn the kite face up, with the frame underneath, and decorate the front by painting it or by pasting on paper shapes. Keep the design simple and the colors bold, because details will be lost when the kite is in the sky. A bold motif from a poster is pretty.

1a. *Cut two small notches as shown.*
1b. *Put a dab of glue on the joined sticks for extra strength.*
1c. *Tying thread around the frame.*
2. *Cut around the edges of the paper, fold over and stick down.*

Bridle
This is the name for the strings that hold the kite at the correct angle to the wind and to which the towing line is attached. The cutter kite has two pieces of string or thread, making a double bridle.

Lay the kite on the table, decorated side uppermost. Take a piece of thread long enough to reach around one short and one long side of the kite with just a little to spare. Tie the ends to the notched ends of the vertical stick where they jut out beyond the cover (fig. 3a).

Tie the second bridle to each end of the horizontal stick. This time the piece of thread should be twice the length of one of the short sides of the kite, with a little to spare (fig. 3b). Loop the curtain ring onto the long bridle (fig. 4) about one-third of the

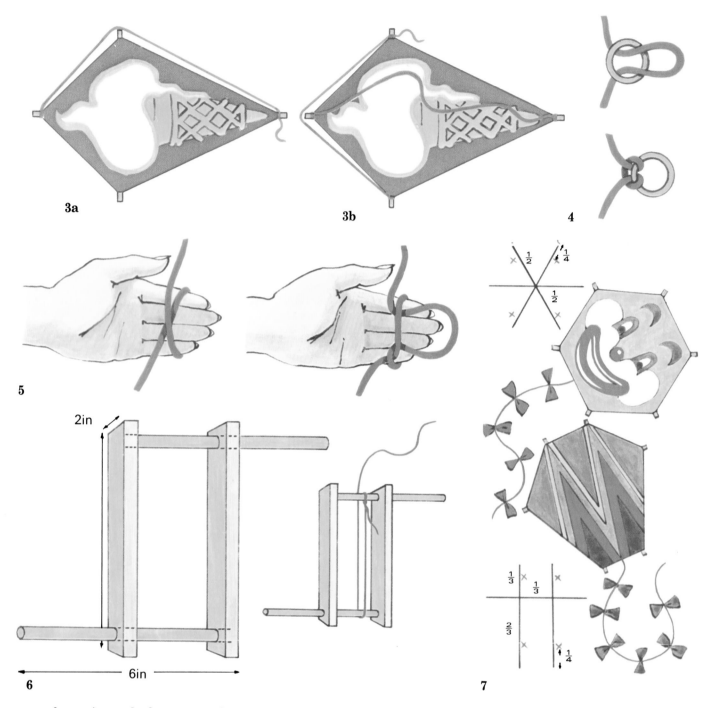

3a

3b

4

5

2in

6in

6

$\frac{1}{2}$ $\frac{1}{4}$

$\frac{1}{2}$

$\frac{1}{3}$ $\frac{1}{3}$

$\frac{2}{3}$

$\frac{1}{4}$

7

way down it, and then onto the center of the short bridle.

Test the balance of the kite by holding it above the table by the ring. The two sides should be equidistant from the table and the kite itself should hang at an angle of about 45° to it. If necessary, adjust the angles slightly by slipping the ring along the bridles.

Tail

Some kites will fly well without any kind of tail, but the cutter kite needs one at least three times its own length. Make it from long paper

streamers, or make the traditional kind of tail by knotting rectangles of paper onto a length of string.

For a traditional tail, use pieces of paper about 6in by 2½in and set them about 3in apart along the length of string. Attach them by means of a slip knot. To do this, wind the string over your hand to form a loop (fig. 5). Make a twist in the center of one of the pieces of paper and then insert it through the loop. Pull the ends of the thread tight. Repeat along the length of the string to form the tail, then tie the tail to the stick at the bottom of the kite.

3a. *Tying the first bridle.*
3b. *Tying the second bridle.*
4. *Attaching the ring to bridle.*
5. *Making a slip knot for the bridle.*
6. *Making a flying line and reel.*
7. *Other kite shapes- X marks bridle position on sticks. Pierce the paper to bring bridle to the right side.*

String and reel

Before you can fly the kite you need a string and reel, which can be bought quite cheaply from hobby shops and some sports equipment suppliers.

To make your own line, use about

200ft of light nylon cord, or fiber-glass fishing-line, and wind it onto a length of strong cardboard to act as a reel.

If you prefer to make your own reel, you will need two rectangles of plywood, about 6in by 2in, two pieces of dowel about 6in long, a drill and strong glue. Drill two holes in each of the two pieces of plywood, to the same diameter as the dowels, and assemble the reel as shown in fig. 6, gluing each dowel into place.

Tie the end of the line firmly to the reel and wind it on tightly. The other end of the line should be tied to the kite's bridle or towing-ring.

Flying a kite

Do not assume that you need to wait for a really windy day in order to try out your kite. On the contrary, a gentle but steady breeze is all you need, and too much wind can damage a kite. If the tree tops are bending, then the wind is too strong for kite flying. Always take a pair of gloves with you to keep the line from cutting into your hands.

Where to fly a kite

Choose a large open space, such as a field or park, and keep well away from trees or telephone poles. It is not at all necessary to fly a kite from a hill, but if you wish to do so, stand on the windward side about 20 yards from the top so as to take full advantage of the steady upcurrent. If you stand right on the summit the kite will be caught in the turbulence of conflicting air streams and will be difficult to fly.

Launching and landing

Stand with your back to the wind and hold the kite by the towing-ring at arm's length. Have the reel on the ground at your feet. Wait until the wind lifts the kite and then release it, letting the line slip out through your fingers.

If you have a helper, ask him to stand a little distance in front of you holding the kite tilted slightly forward until the wind lifts it out of his hands. Do not let him throw it into the air and do not try to run with it yourself. Neither will help to get it airborne. Make the kite rise by pulling on the line. Grip the line at arm's length and bend your forearm back at the elbow, still gripping the line. Straighten your arm again slowly, letting the line slip through your fingers as you do so. Continue pulling and letting out the line until the kite is high in the sky.

Land the kite simply by winding in the line. If it is pulling strongly, walk toward it as you wind. If you have a helper, he can put his hand over the line and walk toward the kite, pulling it down gradually while you wind in the line.

Watch out for any spectators appearing in front of you; a kite can often crash as it comes in low and could be dangerous.

Repair kit

It is a good idea to take along with you some sort of bag to carry a small repair kit: a reel of tape for mending torn paper, several sewing needles that can be taped to broken struts to act as splints, and a pair of scissors for cutting tangles out of the line. Take an extra piece of tail as well in case you lose that part of the kite.

Correcting faults

There are several common faults, all easy to correct, which can hinder successful flying. If the kite will not rise, it is probably flying too flat to the wind. Move the towing-ring a little higher. If the tail is hanging down rather than streaming out behind, shortening it may help the kite to rise.

If the kite flutters and dips, it may be flying too close to the wind. Move the towing-ring down a little. Spinning, diving and looping the loop mean the kite needs a longer or heavier tail. This is a common problem. If the kite keeps falling constantly to one side, tape a small weight—a tiny piece of twig, per-haps, or a small fishing weight—to the back of the kite on the opposite side.

Safety note

Believe it or not, kite-flying can be dangerous. Be sure to remember these two important points:

Kites can act as lightning conduc-tors, so never fly a kite in stormy weather, or with a wire line, or with a wet line of any description. Kites can be a real hazard to aircraft, so be sure to check for any legal restric-tions on kite-flying in your area, particularly near airports.

Oriental kites

In Asia kite-flying is far from being a game for children. It is a serious national pastime for adults and the calendar is filled with festivals and tournaments, many of them with religious significance. Kites can take the form of fabulous birds or beasts which are then imbued with evil spirits in order to float away the harm that might otherwise attack the owner's family. Others are used for fighting, the lines covered with glue and then dipped in powdered glass so as to sever an opponent's line.

Techniques
Cutting sticks; gluing.

Tools required
Scissors; craft knife; razor blade; brush; pencil.

Materials
Carp
two large sheets of tissue or other
 lightweight paper
scraps of colored paper
medium-gauge wire
short length of thread or
 twine
string and reel
poster paints, glue, adhesive tape

Butterfly
3 pieces of bamboo garden cane
 about 24in long
sheet of strong paper about 24in
 square, or tissue paper for
 butterfly variations
curtain ring to act as towing ring
twine or strong thread
poster paints

Bird
bamboo cane
medium-weight white paper
newspaper for papier mâché
modeling clay
flour and water paste
thread or thin twine
watercolor paints

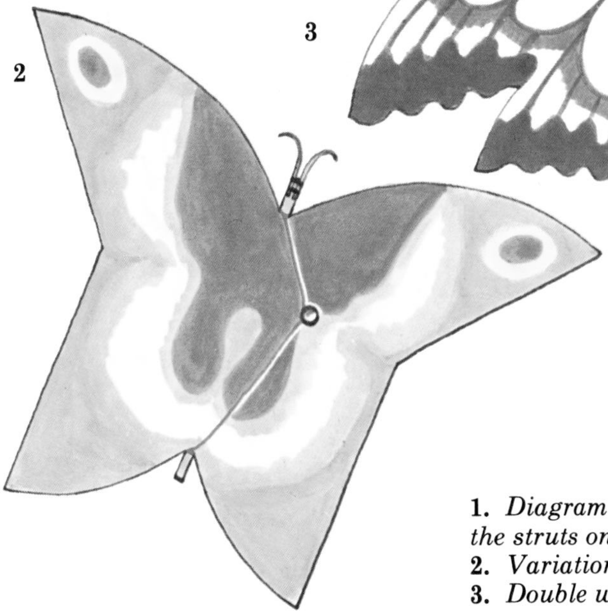

1. *Diagram shows how to position the struts on a butterfly kite.*
2. *Variation on the butterfly shape.*
3. *Double winged butterfly kite.*

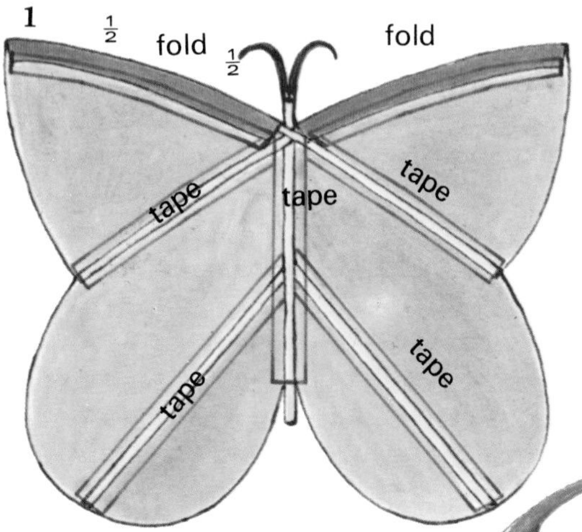

Carp
This fish shape of the carp, shown in the picture, is the simplest of all the Japanese kite designs. On the Boys' Festival of May 5 a carp is flown for every male child in the household in the hope that the boy will emulate the character of this fish, which swims upstream, overcoming all difficulties.

The kite is tubular, rather like a windsock, with a hole at each end. It can be any size you like, provided the hole at the mouth is larger than the one at the tail so that the wind will inflate the body.

Draw the carp shape freehand on the paper and cut it out, cutting through two thicknesses at once. Glue the pieces together along the top and bottom edges. Fold the seams over and glue them down. Paint the carp or, if you have used tissue, decorate it with paper shapes.

Bend the wire into a loop to fit the carp's mouth, fold the edges of the paper over it and glue it in place. Tie the ends of the thread or twine to the wire at either side of the carp's mouth. The line can be attached to this loop.

Although very decorative, this kite is not a good flyer and will only rise if there is a very strong upcurrent.

Butterfly
This is a popular design, perhaps because the fluttering of a kite tends to resemble a butterfly.

Fold the paper in half and draw a half butterfly shape on it so that the fold is along the butterfly's spine. Draw the largest shape the paper will permit and cut out. Open the paper out flat and paint it with any design you choose.

While the paint is drying, split the cane lengthwise with a knife. You will need firm, rigid pieces for the butterfly's spine and lower wing supports and thin, pliable pieces for the upper wing supports: 12in for the spine, two 12in pieces for the lower wings and two 24in pieces for the upper wings. Mark the position of the supports on the back of the butterfly, making sure that one side is the mirror image of the other for perfect balance. (See fig. 1.)

Now enlist the help of a friend. One pair of hands is needed to hold each support in place while the other tapes it in position. Tape the supports on in this order: spine, lower supports, lower half of upper supports. Fold the top edge of the paper over the remaining half of the upper supports and tape them (see fig. 1). Tape two thin bamboo antennae to the top of the spine.

With the right side of the kite facing you, make tiny holes in the kite and tie a piece of thread through them onto the frame at each of the three points marked X in fig. 1.

211

Tie each thread to the towing-line so that the kite hangs at the correct angle.

This kite, which does not need a tail, will fly even better if it offers a convex surface to the wind. To curve the kite, tie a piece of thread to one upper wing tip, stretch it across behind the kite, and tie it tightly to the opposite wing tip, so that the kite is bowed.

Butterfly variations

When you have made a simple butterfly, you may want to go on to a more complex design. The kites in figs. 2 and 3 have rigid spines and pliable wing supports bowed into shape with thread. Figs. 4 and 5 show the design of the frames, heavy lines representing the canes and dotted lines the threads.

Follow the procedure of notching the canes, binding them where they cross, and fitting the cover.

When making the double butterfly (see fig. 5), bow the four wing supports into arcs and bind the sticks where they cross. Add extra thread supports (shown in green) before removing the two longer bow strings (shown in red). Attach a single bridle to the points marked X.

Bird

The body of this bird kite is built on a framework of bamboo slivers rather like the ribs of a row boat, and the head is a thin hollow shell of papier mâché.

Begin by splitting a number of pieces of cane to build the body. Construct a framework and bind the pieces where they overlap (fig. 6a). Try to match the two halves perfectly with joins in exactly the same places.

Following fig. 6b, construct the front of the body with a series of curved canes to form the ribs. Spread glue on the curved ribs and cover the sections of the ribbed framework with strips of paper. Use a razor blade to trim the paper where it overlaps to form a butt joint and trim off surplus paper.

Now shape the head in modeling clay and cover it with a thin layer of papier mâché. When dry, dig out the modeling clay and glue the head to the body.

Make two separate wings and join them together (fig. 7). The wings have bamboo along two sides and a thread (dotted line) to bow the tops of the shape. These threads may be removed later if you wish. Bind and glue the finished wings onto the back of the body. Cut out a tail shape in paper and reinforce this by gluing on a piece of thin cardboard. Attach it to the bird with loops of thread. Finally, tie a single bridle to the body framework at the neck and three-quarters of the way down its body.

Dragonfly

Make this as for the bird, but build up the tail sections on flat bamboo frameworks. Tie the sections loosely together.

Giant kites

There is no limit to the size and complexity of the kites you can make. A giant kite can be imaginatively built up on a rectangle of thin plywood with a decorative lantern hung in the middle. Fabulous birds and beasts can be perched around the frame; make them all on the same principle as the bird already described and you can let your imagination run riot on the tassels, lanterns and other decorations acting as the tail.

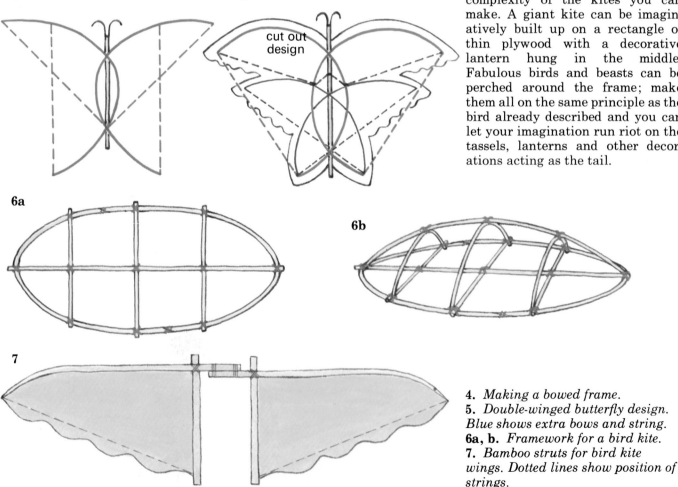

4
5
cut out design
6a
6b
7

4. *Making a bowed frame.*
5. *Double-winged butterfly design. Blue shows extra bows and string.*
6a, b. *Framework for a bird kite.*
7. *Bamboo struts for bird kite wings. Dotted lines show position of strings.*

Dollhouse furniture

Young children love a hideaway to play games in. This charming country cottage is simple to sew and needs no integral supports. Made of tough muslin or sailcloth, the playhouse fits over a table, so that the walls hang down on all sides. The attractive decorations, including flowers, apple tree and bird house, are all appliquéd in place.

Techniques involved
Basic sewing; simple woodworking.

Tools required
Craft knife; sharp fingernail scissors; bradawl; coping saw (optional); basic sewing tools.

Materials
matchboxes of various sizes
wooden matchsticks
toothpicks
cardboard
egg cartons
plastic containers and lids, such as for yogurt
spools
jar lid
cardboard tube from toilet tissue roll
scraps of various fabrics: velvet, corduroy, or fur fabric for rugs; lace for curtains, prints and plain colors (closely woven) for upholstery, etc.
buttons
plastic foam
aluminum foil
pencil
plastic straw
pleated paper candy cups
magazine picture (small)
thread
molded plastic "bubble" container of type used to pack model cars
small piece of acetate film
rubber cement
poster paints

Children can make some of this furniture themselves, with a little parental supervision. You needn't worry too much about scale, though you should try to make the pieces more or less proportional to one another.

All types of materials can be used for the furniture. Make a collection of likely objects to keep on hand. The materials listed above are the ones you'll need for the complete set of furnishings shown here.

Living room
Armchairs and sofa
Use different-sized matchboxes. For armchair use the inside of the box for the base (fig. 1a). Cut away section of the box as indicated. Cut away parts of the inside box as shown in fig. 1b to make the back of the chair. Glue the back to the base, with rounded ends upward, at a

1a. *Use the inside of the box for the base of the armchair.*
1b. *Use the outer sleeve for the back of the armchair.*
2. *Making a simple coffee table.*

1a

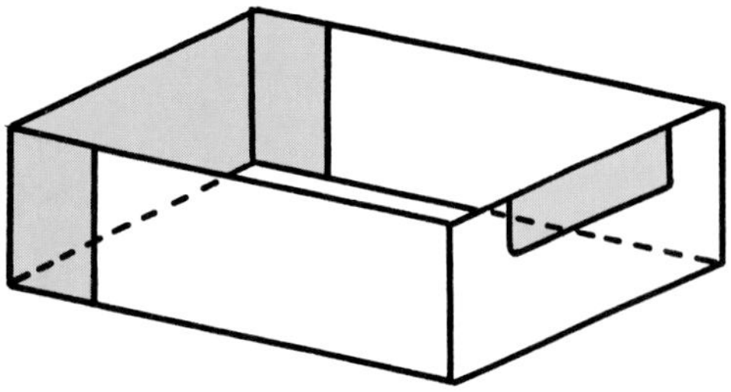

1b

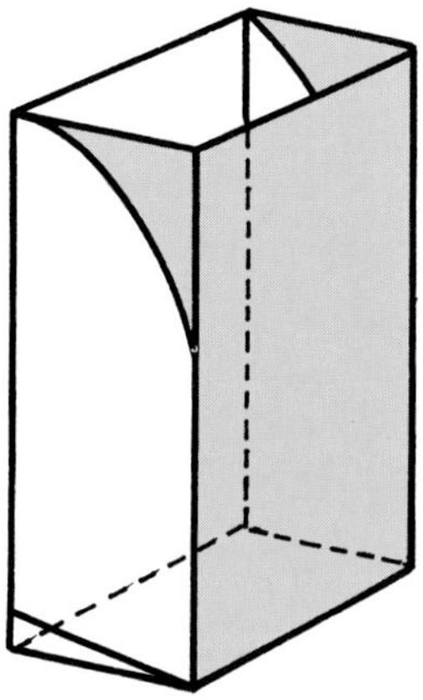

2

slight angle. When chair is dry, paint it with poster paints.

For cushions, cut pieces of plastic foam to fit seat and back.

Coat each piece with glue and then carefully fold a piece of fabric around it. Leave to dry and then glue the cushions into the chairs.

For the legs, make four holes in the base of the chair and trim four burned matches to ½in. Push the matches into the holes, leaving the match heads exposed, then paint the match heads.

Make a sofa in the same way, using a larger matchbox.

Coffee table
Use a plastic yogurt container for this. Using nail scissors, cut away part of the container as indicated in fig. 2. The bottom of the container is

the top of the table. Paint the table with poster paint.

Lamps

For the floor lamp use a button and a plastic straw. Remove the center holes of the button by melting the center or by cutting with a coping saw. Insert the straw into the hole. Make a shade from the bottom of an egg carton cup or from a pleated paper candy cup, painted as you like.

For ceiling lamp make shade as described above; attach it to the ceiling with thread and a dab of glue.

Small cabinet

Cut the inner part of a small matchbox to the desired size; paint exterior with poster paint and place against wall.

Rug

Any fabric with pile will do, but if you want an elegant rug, embroider one, using needlepoint canvas and tapestry wool. The rug in the living room was made in this way. Or you can simply color the canvas with felt-tip markers, as was done for the hall rug.

Dining room/kitchen

Table

If possible, use a very large spool (obtainable from an upholsterer or tailor) for the base. Paint the spool and when it is dry, glue a jar lid to one end. Cover the lid with a circular piece of cloth, glued to the top and sides of the lid.

Chairs

Use a cup section from an egg carton for each chair. Cut away most of the sides, as shown in fig. 3. Paint it or leave it the natural color. Poke four holes in the seat for the legs. Make legs from matchsticks (remove heads first), inserted in holes and fixed with glue. As the chairs are very light, give them a little added weight by making cushions of pennies covered with fabric. Glue the cushions to the seat.

Kitchen cupboard

Cut a large matchbox sleeve (cover) in half across the width. Cut a top from a piece of cardboard slightly larger than the open end of the matchbox. Cut two doors in the front

3. *How to make chairs from sections of discarded egg cartons.*
4. *A dresser made from the sleeve of a large matchbox.*

of the box, leaving the "hinged" sides uncut. Score these sides so they will fold forward easily. Glue the top in place, then paint the entire cupboard with paint and insert small pieces of matchstick in the door fronts for handles.

Stove

Use the remaining half of the big matchbox sleeve for the stove. Cut two pieces of cardboard to cover the sides and another for the top—large enough to accommodate the four buttons used for the burners. Cut the oven door as for the cupboard doors. Cut a window in the oven door. Now glue the cardboard sides and top to the box and paint with poster paint. Glue four buttons to the top and a piece of acetate over the inside of the oven window.

Sink unit

This is also made from half of a matchbox sleeve. Cut three pieces of cardboard as for the stove. Take one cup section from an egg box and cut the top two-thirds away, leaving a shallow cup. Cut a circle at one end of the top cardboard piece to match the upper edge of the cup.

In the front of the box, away from the position of the sink, cut a door, as for cupboard. Glue the cardboard top and sides in place. Paint unit.

Glue a piece of foil to the inside of the cup, then glue the cup in the hole.

Dresser

This is made from a whole matchbox sleeve. Cut away the sections shown in fig. 4, and cut doors as for cupboard. Cut three pieces of cardboard: two to cover the top and bottom and one to form the bottom shelf, allowing $\frac{1}{4}$in extra along the long edges of each piece. Score and fold the extra $\frac{1}{4}$in to one side. Position and glue these three pieces in the matchbox cover.

Cut shelves to fit within the box and then cut matchstick brackets to the depth of the shelves. Glue a bracket to the ends of each shelf. Glue the shelves in place and paint the dresser. Then glue two small pieces of matchstick on the front as knobs.

Hallway

Coat rack

Insert a pencil into a plastic spool. Make little holes with a bradawl along the length of the pencil and glue small lengths of matchstick into each hole. Paint the coat rack with poster paint.

Painting or mirror

Use the lid of a small plastic

218

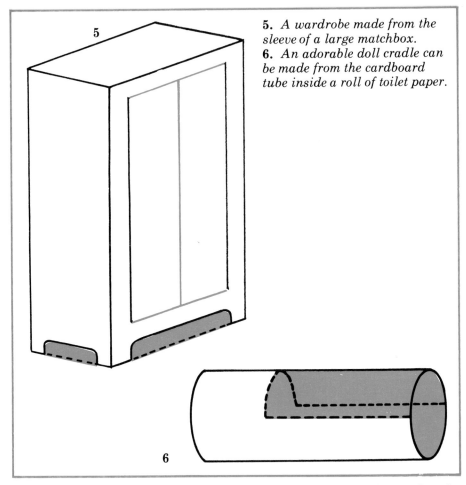

container. Paint the edges and then paste either a magazine picture or a piece of aluminum foil in center.

Master bedroom
Double bed
Cut a piece of cardboard to the size of bed required. Cut a piece of 1in-thick plastic foam to the same size. Cut a small strip of foam to represent pillows and glue it to the mattress piece. Glue the cardboard to the mattress bottom, and cover the whole bed with a piece of fabric, glued in place.

Dressing table
Cut a plastic lid in half and glue this to a spool. Cut a semicircle of fabric large enough to cover the lid and reach the floor and glue this in place over the lid. Make a mirror from a small lid; cut away roughly one quarter of the lid and then paint it to coordinate with the skirt. When the paint is dry, glue a circle of foil to the inside of the lid.

Wardrobe
This is made, too, from the sleeve cover of a large matchbox. Cut the doors as for the kitchen cupboard, scoring the hinged sides so that they open out easily. Cut away the parts of the box shown in fig. 5. The top of the wardrobe and the base are cut to size from the inner part of the box and glued in place. Paint the wardrobe and glue matchstick handles in place.

Chair
Use the lower part of an egg carton for the base and cut another cup as shown in the photograph. Glue this to the base and paint with poster paint. Make a foam cushion as for living room chairs.

Children's room
Cradle
Use the cardboard tube from a toilet tissue roll. Cut away the areas indicated in fig. 6. Cut two strips of thin cardboard $\frac{1}{4}$in wide and long enough to fit the inner circumference of the tube. Glue these in place just inside each end of the tube, with the outer edges flush. Cut two circles of cardboard the size of the tube openings and glue the circles over the ends, attaching them to the cardboard collars fitted inside. Paint with poster paint.

For the bedding, use a small piece of foam cut to fit within the cradle and covered with fabric.

Playpen
For the base use the inside of a large matchbox and a piece of fabric-covered foam for the mattress. For the sides use toothpicks with the sharp ends removed, glued between the mattress and the edge of the box.

Chest of drawers
Glue four small matchboxes one on top of the other. Cover the sides and top with thin cardboard cut to fit. Use matchsticks for handles. Take the inside of another small matchbox and cut away each side so that the corners of the box remain to represent legs. Glue this to the bottom of the drawer unit.

Bathroom
Bathtub
Use the inside of a large matchbox for the exterior of the tub and a molded plastic container of the kind used for a model car. Trim the plastic to fit. Paint the outside of the matchbox and leave it to dry. Then glue the plastic container into the box.

Washbasin
Cut off the bottom of an egg carton cup and glue it to a thin plastic spool. Make a surround for the basin from a square piece of cardboard cut slightly larger than the cup. Cut a hole the size of the cup in the center of the cardboard and round off two adjacent corners to make the front of the washbasin. Glue the cardboard surround to the cup. Paint basin to match the bathtub.

Toilet
This is made from two cup sections of an egg carton, plus a piece of cardboard. For the base cut one cup in half, and for the bowl use the bottom third of another cup. Cut the cardboard to fit the circumference of the bowl, adding a small tab to serve as a hinge. Glue the tab to the back of the bowl and glue the bowl to the bottom of the base piece. Paint toilet to match bathtub and basin.

Four poster bed

This elegant bed can be made entirely of scrap materials. The bedding involves only the simplest sewing techniques, and you can adapt the instructions to make any size bed you wish.

Finished height
10in.

Techniques involved
Basic sewing.

Tools required
Basic sewing tools; paintbrush.

Materials
28 empty spools
epoxy resin adhesive
$9\frac{1}{2}$in × $7\frac{1}{2}$in of $\frac{1}{4}$in-thick plywood
four round wooden beads $\frac{5}{8}$in in
    diameter
enamel paint
1in-thick piece of plastic foam
    $9\frac{1}{2}$in × $7\frac{1}{2}$in
piece of 36in-wide white plain-
    woven cotton about $\frac{2}{3}$yd length
11in square of non-woven
    interfacing
$1\frac{1}{4}$yd of $\frac{5}{8}$in-wide gathered eyelet
    lace
$2\frac{3}{8}$yd of 2in-wide eyelet lace
piece of quilted fabric $12\frac{1}{2}$in × 9in
piece of contrasting lining fabric
    $12\frac{1}{2}$in × 9in
2yd of $\frac{1}{4}$in-wide ribbon
sewing thread

The bed
Strip off labels from spools. Using epoxy resin adhesive, glue spools on top of each other in four groups of six. Glue a wooden bead on top of each column of spools. Put aside until dry.

Paint the four columns of spools; also paint four single spools to serve as feet.

Round the corners of the piece of plastic foam, using an extra spool as a guide in drawing curves. Cut curves along marked lines (fig. 1). This makes the mattress.

To make base of bed, glue the four single spools at each corner of plywood rectangle. Turn base right side up and glue spools to each corner (fig. 2). Leave to set.

Bedding
Cut white cotton fabric into six pieces: two pieces, each $10\frac{1}{4}$in × $8\frac{3}{4}$in, for canopy and base cover; two pieces, each $16\frac{1}{2}$in × $13\frac{3}{4}$in, for sheets; two pieces, each $8\frac{3}{4}$in × $5\frac{1}{2}$in, for pillowcases. Seam allowances of $\frac{1}{4}$in are included.

Pillow
With right sides together and raw edges even, baste narrow gathered eyelet lace all around one pillow piece. Place second piece of fabric on top, sandwiching lace in between. Stitch together around three sides, leaving the fourth side open. Turn right side out.

Fill pillow with scraps of foam and sew open end together. Join the short ends of lace.

Sheets
Stitch a narrow hem all around one sheet piece to make bottom sheet. Similarly hem top sheet, adding gathered eyelet lace to finish one short end.

Base cover and canopy
Stiffen one remaining piece of white cotton with iron-on interfacing. This piece is for the canopy.

Round the corners of both canopy and base cover to fit around bedposts. Hem curved edges. Baste hems along straight sides of both pieces.

Cut 2in-wide eyelet lace into four $8\frac{3}{4}$in and four 11in pieces. Gather raw edges of lace until pieces are the same length as straight sides of canopy and base cover.

Placing right sides and raw edges together, baste and stitch eyelet lace to canopy and base cover (fig. 3). Press ruffles downward.

Cut ribbon into four lengths, each $16\frac{1}{2}$in long. Sew center of each piece of ribbon to center of cut-out corner on canopy (fig. 3).

Quilt
Round off corners of quilted and lining fabrics (fig. 4). Placing right sides together, stitch quilt to lining around three sides as shown. Snip into seam allowances on curves and turn quilt right side out. Turn in seam allowances and slipstitch remaining open side closed.

Assembling the bed
Place base cover on base, then put foam mattress on top. Tuck bottom sheet under mattress. Add top sheet, quilt, and pillow. Tie the canopy to the top of the bedposts.

1. *Cutting a piece of foam for the mattress.*
2. *Assembling bed frame.*
3. *Sewing ruffles and ribbons to canopy.*
4. *Stitching quilt; ends are curved to fit around bedposts.*

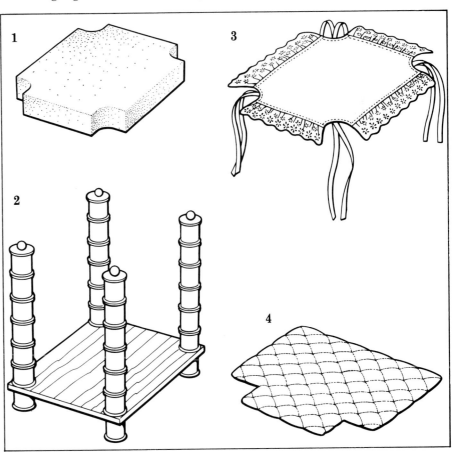

Toy bag

This sturdy toy bag will hang on the back of a door to provide a handy catchall for all kinds of playthings. Its bold appliquéd front will brighten the playroom and may even encourage a bit of neatness!

Techniques involved

Basic sewing; machine stitching; machine appliqué.

Tools required

Basic sewing tools; sewing machine.

Materials

tracing paper
dressmaker's carbon paper
59in × 19¾in of heavy-weight muslin
19¾in × 7⅛in of red heavy-weight poplin or sailcloth
scraps of plain cotton fabric in red, turquoise, yellow, green and purple
matching and contrasting threads
2⅜in of Velcro tape
tissue paper
1 bright-colored button

Trace the motifs from the patterns. A seam allowance of ⅝in is included. Using dressmaker's carbon paper, mark the shapes on the wrong side of fabrics in appropriate colors. Cut out all the pieces.

Fold the muslin fabric in half crosswise. Press and baste along the fold line. This will be the base of the bag. Unfold the muslin.

Mark the window frames on the right side of the turquoise house piece.

Place the two house pieces together, with turquoise on the right side and yellow fabric for windows underneath. Position them on one half of the 2¼in from the base fold. Pin and baste in place (fig. 1).

Put the roof on top of the house so that the lower edge overlaps the top of the house. Slip the lower, slanted edge of the chimney under the edge of the roof on the left-hand side of the house. Pin and baste the roof and chimney in place (fig. 2).

Place the door in the center of the base edge of the house. Pin and baste in place. Mark the position of the small window on the door. Carefully baste all around the outer edge of the house very close to edge (fig. 3).

Set your sewing machine to satin stitch (zigzag stitch) of medium width and minimum length. Place a sheet of tissue paper under the muslin and the house, and satin-stitch along all the raw edges. (The tissue paper helps to prevent the material from puckering as you stitch.)

Begin by stitching the house sides and base edge and the chimney, using turquoise thread to match the house. Stitch around the roof, using red thread, and then stitch around the edge of the door with green thread. Stitch around the window in the door with green thread as well. Finally, stitch around the outlines of the windows, using dark blue thread to make the outer frames. You may find the satin-stitching easier if you topstitch sections in place (fig. 4).

Using sharp-pointed scissors, carefully cut away the top layer of fabric from within the window frames, exposing the yellow fabric that is underneath. Similarly, cut away the green fabric and then the turquoise fabric from inside the window on the door (fig. 5).

With a contrasting colored thread, satin-stitch crossed lines in each of the windows and in the door window. Again using a contrasting color, satin-stitch a line on the door to represent the mail slot (fig. 6).

Place the smoke clouds in a row,

1. *Place the house pieces together and baste them onto the muslin.*
2. *Pinning and basting the roof and chimney into position.*
3. *Baste door into position. Baste around the outer edges of the house.*
4. *Outline the window, door and house shapes in satin stitch.*
5. *Clip away the top layer of fabric in windows to expose yellow fabric.*
6. *Decorate the windows with crossed lines of satin stitch.*
7. *Position smoke clouds in a row above chimney and stitch in place.*
8. *Making the side hems of the bag. Neaten the edges in zigzag stitch.*

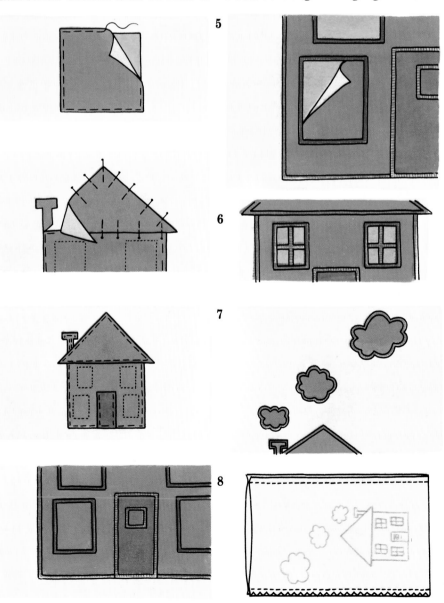

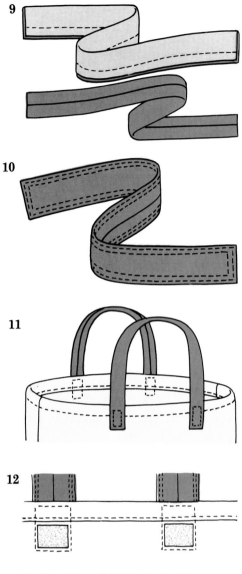

9. *Cut the red fabric in half to make the handle pieces.*
10. *Topstitch around each handle close to the outer edge.*
11. *Position handles, pin and baste. Stitch firmly in place.*
12. *Attaching Velcro tape.*

one above the chimney and the next two slightly to the right, graduating in size (fig. 7). Stitch in place as for the house.

Remove the tissue paper and press the appliquéd area on the wrong side.

Sew the button to the middle of the door, underneath the mail slot.

Fold the calico in half, right sides facing. Pin, baste, and stitch the side seams. Finish the raw edges of the seams with zigzag stitch (fig. 8).

Fold over a double hem $\frac{3}{8}$in wide all around the top edge. Pin, baste

and topstitch around the top edge.

Cut the red fabric in half to make two pieces, each $19\frac{3}{4}$in × 4in, for handles.

Fold each handle in half lengthwise; pin, baste, and stitch long sides. Turn handles right side out. Press the handles flat with the seam centered on the under side (fig. 9).

Tuck the raw edges on each short end of each handle inside; pin and baste. Using a contrasting colored thread, topstitch all around each handle close to the outer edge. Topstitch again, about $\frac{1}{4}$in inside the

first line of stitching (fig. 10).

Pin and baste the handles to the right side of the top edge of each side of the bag. The outer edges should be $5\frac{1}{8}$in from the side edges of the bag, with the short edges overlapping the top edge $1\frac{5}{8}$in. Stitch in place at each handle and over the previous stitching lines (fig. 11).

Cut the Velcro tape in half. Pin and baste one half of each piece on the inside of the bag behind the ends. Pin and baste the second halves of fastening behind opposite handle ends. Topstitch in place (fig. 12).

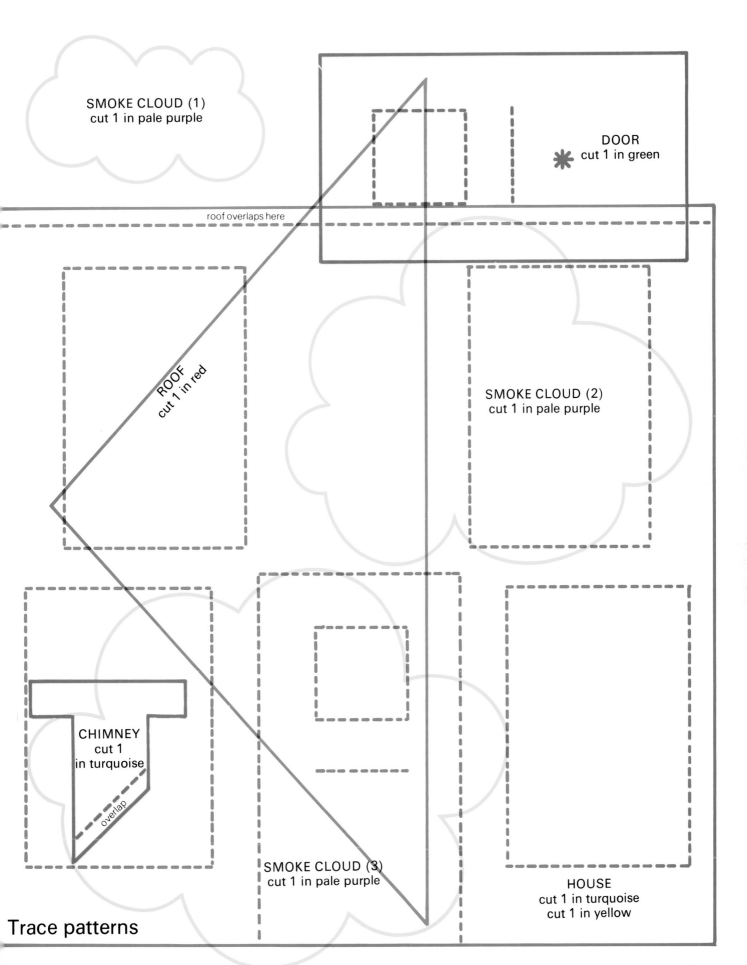

SMOKE CLOUD (1)
cut 1 in pale purple

DOOR
cut 1 in green

roof overlaps here

ROOF
cut 1 in red

SMOKE CLOUD (2)
cut 1 in pale purple

CHIMNEY
cut 1
in turquoise

overlap

SMOKE CLOUD (3)
cut 1 in pale purple

HOUSE
cut 1 in turquoise
cut 1 in yellow

Trace patterns

Wall hanging

A wall hanging that not only provides exotic decoration but storage space as well must be a blessing in any playroom or child's bedroom. Both the elephant and the rhino have pockets for a comb and pencils, and three gusset pockets that can hold books and all sorts of toys, so they can be spotted at a glance. And they are both very simple to make.

Finished size
Elephant 36in × 30in;
rhino 42in × 30in

Tools required
Basic sewing tools; sewing machine;
hammer; sharp knife.

Techniques involved
Basic sewing; machine stitching;
drawing patterns.

Materials
For each animal:
graph paper for patterns
45in × 35in of felt in main color of
  your choice
scraps of felt for the features
matching thread
black buttonhole twist (silk size D)
35in square of strong cardboard
2 large eyelets (available from
  camping suppliers)
fabric adhesive

For elephant only:
12in square of felt in contrasting
  color for blanket
graph paper for pattern

To make the elephant
Using graph paper, draw the main
body section to scale. Mark in the
position of each pocket and all
features and lines. Cut out. Trace
the patterns for the eyes and
features and for the blanket top from
the patterns given, and cut out.

Pin the body pattern piece to the
felt for the body and cut out.
Transfer all markings from the
pattern piece to the fabric.

Cut out the pockets from the
remaining felt as follows: 5¾in × 2¼in
for the comb pocket; 6in × 2½in for
pencil holder; 4in × 1in for pencil-
holder strip; 10in × 9in for one
gusset pocket; 15¼in × 8¾in for
second gusset pocket.

From the scraps of felt cut out the
blanket decoration, the tusk, and
the eye.

From the contrasting square of
felt cut out the blanket top and the
third gusset pocket 14¼in × 6¾in.
Finally, cut a strip 11in × 2¾in for the
fringe of the blanket.

Now pin and stitch the eye and
tusk into the positions marked on
the pattern. Using black embroidery
floss, work backstitch around the
eye pieces.

Thread the bobbin of your sewing

machine with black buttonhole
twist, and from the wrong side
machine-stitch along the lines for
the legs and ear. Add a second or
third line for emphasis, if you wish.

Pin and stitch the comb pocket in
place on the elephant's trunk.

Pin the blanket top into position
and stitch all around the felt as close
as possible to the edge. Press 1¼in to
the wrong side on each short edge of
the pocket. Stitch along each fold
close to the edge.

Pin the pocket into place on the
elephant, overlapping the edge of
the blanket top. Place the side edges
of the pockets on the pocket lines
and stitch down both sides. Fold the
pocket into the gusset and stitch
along the bottom edge of the gusset.
Fasten off all ends (fig. 1).

Draw a line 1½in from the edge of
the blanket fringe and make cuts in
the strip to this line and ½in apart.
Baste the fringe over the bottom
edge of the pocket. Pin and baste
decorations over the join. Stitch
along the center of the circles and
work another row of stitching ⅛in
below the first.

Attach the other two gusset pockets in the same way.

Stitch the right-hand edge of the
pencil holder into position as indicated on the pattern. Place a
pencil under the strip and pin the
strip to the elephant over the pencil.
Baste alongside the pencil (fig. 2).
Repeat five times more. Stitch down
each row of basting and along the
bottom edge of the pocket. Trim off
any excess felt on the left-hand edge
of the pocket. Line up the ends of the
pencil holder strip with the edges of
the holder. Baste and stitch into
position.

To finish, press the elephant with
a damp cloth to remove all creases.
Spread adhesive evenly on the
wrong side of the felt and stick the
elephant to the card, making sure it
is completely flat. Allow to dry.
Mark the positions for the eyelets so
that the pockets will hang straight.
Cut out the holes and insert the
eyelets, using a hammer.

Cut away the excess cardboard.

To make the rhino
Draw the pattern pieces and cut out
the main body felt across the
rectangle of fabric, transferring all
markings.

Cut out pockets from the remaining felt as follows: 5¾in × 2¼in for the
comb pocket; 7in × 2½in for pencil
holder; 5½in × 1in for pencil-holder
strip; 10in × 9in for first gusset
pocket; 15in × 8in for second gusset
pocket; 9in × 5in for third.

From the scraps of felt cut out the
spots, eye, and ear.

Stitch the ear piece and the eye
pieces onto the head where marked.
Sew the spots to the rhino's back.

Using black buttonhole twist in
the bobbin of the sewing machine,
stitch in the lines for the top of the
head, the neck, mouth and chin from
the wrong side of the fabric, stitching over the first lines for emphasis.

Stitch the comb pocket into position on the rhino's back.

Attach three gusset pockets as for
the elephant.

Attach the pencil in the same way,
but making seven loops.

Finish rhino as for elephant.

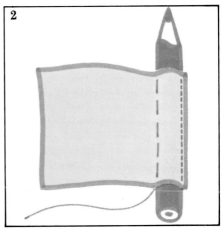

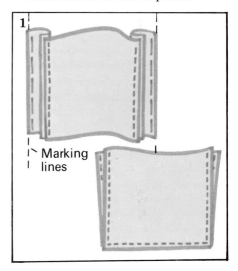

1. *Making a gusset for the pocket.*
2. *Place a pencil under the strip to make slot for pencil holders.*

Trace patterns

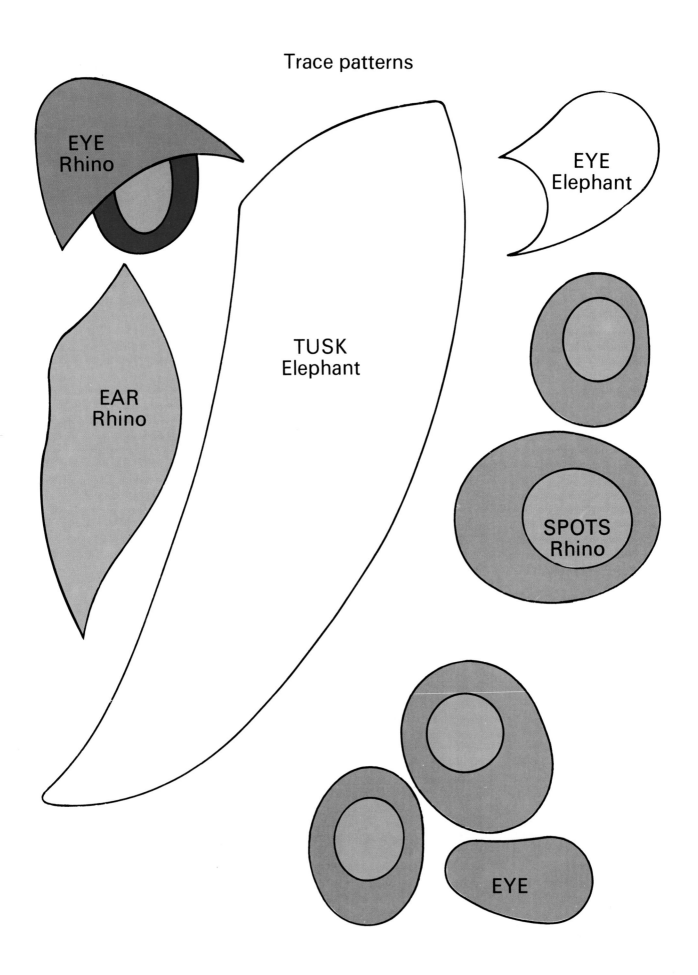

EYE
Rhino

EYE
Elephant

EAR
Rhino

TUSK
Elephant

SPOTS
Rhino

EYE

Graph patterns
Each square = 3in

229

Hanging shelves

These colorful hanging shelves are ideal for storing toys and books. They are made from double-thickness heavy-duty canvas that forms pockets into which pieces of plywood are inserted to provide a strong, firm base.

Techniques
Basic sewing; drilling holes.

Tools required
Basic sewing tools; hand or power drill; drill bit, $\frac{3}{8}$in diameter.

Materials
3yd heavy-duty canvas, 36in wide
5 pieces $\frac{1}{4}$in × 17$\frac{3}{4}$in × 11$\frac{3}{4}$in plywood
sewing thread to match heavy-duty
   canvas
machine needle large enough for
   thread (size 16 or 18)
1yd rope, $\frac{1}{4}$in thick
4 × $\frac{3}{8}$in eyelets
hooks for hanging the shelves

Cut out the canvas pieces as shown in the cutting chart (fig. 1).

Fold the main panel in half across the width and mark the fold line with a basting stitch to indicate the center top of the unit.

Join the short ends of the panel, with right sides together, with $\frac{1}{2}$in seam. Machine-stitch, using strong thread and a heavy needle.

Press the turnings open and machine-stitch them down to the wrong side of the panel.

Make a narrow hem along the raw edge of the panel. If you have a zigzag machine this can be done with a single line of a close zigzag stitch.

Fold the piece for the top pocket in half across the width. Crease lightly.

Open it out and make a narrow hem along one of the longer sides. Turn under a $\frac{3}{8}$in hem along the remaining three sides.

Place the pocket, wrong side down, on the wrong side of the main panel so that the crease line marking the center of the pocket falls exactly over the basted line at the top of the panel (fig. 2).

Measure 2in diagonally from the corners of the pocket and make tailor's tacks, using heavy, double thread through both layers of canvas. Cut through the tacks and open out the layers. Make eyelet holes in the position of the tacks at each corner in both pieces of canvas (fig. 3).

Replace the pocket, matching the holes. Leaving the side with the narrow hem open, pin and machine-stitch the remaining sides of the pocket to the main panel along the folds of the turnbacks. Work a second line of machine-stitching $\frac{1}{4}$in away from the first line (fig. 4).

Fold the piece for the bottom pocket in half across the width. Crease lightly.

Open it out and make a narrow hem along one of the longer sides. Turn under a $\frac{3}{8}$in hem along the remaining three sides.

Place the pocket, wrong side down, on the wrong side of the main panel so that the center crease line falls exactly over the seam line at the bottom of the panel and the hem of the pocket is on the same side as the opening of the top pocket. Machine-stitch the pocket to the main panel along the other three sides.

Attaching the shelves

Make narrow hems along the short raw edges of the three remaining pocket pieces. Fold the pockets in half across the width with the right side out and press.

Measure down the required depth of the shelf from the top pocket on each side of the main panel and mark.

Keeping the opening of the pocket to the same side as the others and with turnbacks up, pin the doubled short sides of the pocket to the main strip along the marks indicated, allowing $\frac{1}{2}$in seams. Machine-stitch twice (fig. 5).

Attach the other shelves in the same way, making sure that the distance between them on each side of the main panel is the same.

Strengthening the shelves

To cover the raw edges of the shelves where they are stitched to the main panel, cut six strips, each $1\frac{1}{2}$in × $12\frac{1}{2}$in, from the leftover canvas. Turn under a narrow hem on the wrong side of each long edge of the strips and press.

Place each strip over the raw edges of a seam joining one of the pockets to the main panel so that the

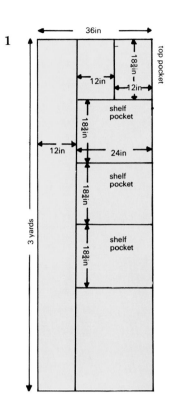

lower edge of the strip is level with the stitch line. Pin in position and machine-stitch around all sides. Repeat with each of the other seams.

Insert the pieces of plywood into the shelves.

Insert the plywood into the pocket at the top of unit and mark the positions of the eyelet holes in pencil. Take out the wood and drill holes at each position. Replace the wood positioning it so that the holes correspond with the eyelets.

Cut the rope in half and tie a double knot at one end of each half. Insert the other end of one of the pieces up through the eyelet hole at the front of the unit and then down through the hole at the back on the same side. Tie a knot underneath. Repeat this with the other piece of rope on the opposite side (fig. 6).

Attach hooks in the required place, adjust the rope to the desired length and hang in position on the hooks, or hang the unit over a horizontal rod as pictured.

1. *The cutting chart.*
2. *Placing pocket onto main panel.*
3. *Making the eyelet holes.*
4. *Secure pocket to the main panel with double line of stitching.*
5. *Attaching shelf pocket to sides of main panel with double stitching.*
6. *Threading rope through eyelets.*

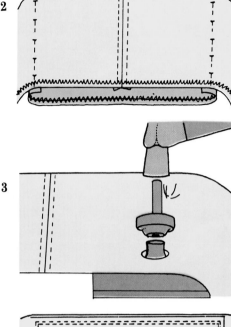

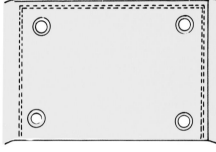

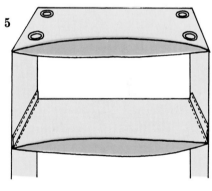

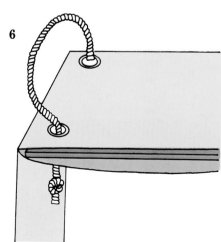

Glossary

BACK SAW Used for more accurate cutting than can be done with a panel saw. The blade is shorter and has a solid metal back to keep it rigid. Also there are more and finer teeth. The heaviest back saws are called miter box saws. Back saws for finer work are called dovetail saws.

BACKSTITCH (Embroidery) Bring thread through on stitching line, then take a small backward stitch through fabric. Bring needle through again a little in front of first stitch. Then take another stitch, inserting needle at point where first stitch came through.

BENCH HOOK A device for holding work in place while sawing. It is easily made by nailing two scraps of batten to a piece of board and hooking it over edge of workbench.

BINDING OFF (Knitting) Closing off the knitting loops. With the yarn and needles in usual working position, work the first two stitches so that they are transferred to right-hand needle. Use point of left-hand needle to lift first stitch worked over second one and off needle. Work next stitch on left-hand needle and repeat process. See page 16 for full working instructions.

BLANKET STITCH A simple looped embroidery stitch. When the loops are worked close together, it is known as Buttonhole stitch.

BRADAWL A chisel-pointed boring tool used for marking screw positions and counterboring for small-size screws.

BRIDLE The name for the strings that hold a kite at the correct angle to the wind, and to which the towing line is attached. The cutter kite has two pieces of string or thread, making a double bridle. See pages 207–208 for working instructions.

BUTTONHOLE STITCH A simple looped embroidery stitch. It is useful for reinforcing both knitted and crocheted buttonholes.

CASTING ON Making the required number of loops onto a knitting needle to supply a foundation for knitted fabric. Subsequent rows are worked into these loops. See page 16 for two-needle method, which gives an especially firm edge. There is also a one-needle method of casting on.

CENTER PUNCH This is used for spot-marking metal to provide a guide for drilling. The drilling point is marked by tapping the wide end of the tool with a hammer.

CHAIN STITCH Embroidery stitch worked from right to left, making a chain of loops on the right side of the fabric. The needle returns to the place where it came out, the thread looping under it. When each stitch is held down separately with the working thread, it is called detached chain, or lazy daisy stitch.

CHAMFER To cut or round off in a sloping manner, as the edge of anything square, so as to form a chamfer or bevel.

CHISELS These tools are really a special form of knife, in which the cutting edge is set square to the handle. This concentrates a cutting force on the edge, and makes it possible to reach points that are inaccessible to conventional knives.

CLAMPS Devices to hold the work in place. C-clamps are used to hold two pieces together while they are being joined. Very small modelers' clamps are cheap and convenient for holding small pieces together. When using clamps, always pad the workpiece with scraps of

wood to prevent the clamp from marking the work. *See also* **VISE**.

CLAW HAMMER Available in various weights, the claw hammer serves a dual purpose: one side of the head is for driving nails; the other side, shaped to a long, curved claw, is for removing nails and pins.

COPING SAW This hand saw cuts curves and shapes in wood. It consists of a frame, in which the blade is held taut, and a handle. The frame curves so that it does not restrict the blade when work is being done away from the edge of a board. Coping saw blades are tensioned by means of a screw in the handle.

COUNTERSINK OR ROSE BITS *see* **DRILL BITS**

CRAFT KNIFE This is similar to a trimming knife, with replaceable blades fitted into a handle. The handle is smaller and lighter, so that it can be controlled between finger and thumb for precise work.

CROSS CUT SAW Used to cut across the grain of hardwoods and softwoods, and for working with the grain on very hard woods. The knife-point shaped teeth give the sharper cuts needed when working across the grain.

CROSS STITCH (Embroidery) For the most even appearance, work cross stitches in two stages: Work the first diagonal all along a row, then work back along the row, adding the second. Stitches should form a perfect square. Whether working this way or one stitch at a time, make sure that top threads of all stitches slant in the same direction.

DOVETAIL SAW *see* **BACK SAW**

DRILL A pointed instrument used for boring holes in wood, metal, etc.

DRILL BITS The boring part of a drill, a whole range is available for use with braces, hand drills and power drills. Each bit is specially shaped to do a specific job, and they are available in a range of sizes. *Twist bits,* often referred to as a twist drill, are for drilling small holes in wood or metal, and can be used in both hand and power drills. A set ranging from $\frac{1}{16}$in to $\frac{1}{2}$in will cover most jobs. *Countersink or rose bits* are used for drilling countersunk holes for flathead screws. *Auger bits* have a clearly defined spiral so that the waste is cleared rapidly from the hole during drilling.

FILES Used for finishing and shaping both wood and metal. File blades have a large number of very fine teeth, variously shaped to give a finer or coarser cut. Very fine files are called needle files and are used for fine shaping and piercing work.

FRENCH KNOT An embroidery stitch made by bringing needle and thread through fabric to right side, winding thread once or twice around needle, and then reinserting needle beside the point where it first emerged and pulling thread through.

FRENCH SEAM A narrow reef-enclosed seam sewed on both sides to conceal raw edges of cloth.

FRET SAW Similar to a coping saw but deeper, to allow work with larger boards.

GARTER STITCH Knitting pattern formed by knitting both right-side and wrong-side rows, producing a horizontally ridged effect.

GAUGE Standard measure of a knitted fabric expressed in terms of the number of rows and stitches that are worked to produce a given measurement. Since individual variations in the tightness of stitches affect elasticity, and therefore size, gauge can be adjusted by changing to a different size needle.

GRAFTING A method of joining two sets of knitting stitches invisibly without first binding them off. See page 19 for working instructions.

HACKSAWS These saws are used for cutting metal. They have a metal frame and replaceable blades tensioned with a screw and fitted facing away from the handle, the opposite of those of the coping saw. Available in two basic sizes and with a range of blade lengths; for most purposes, the smallest, called a junior hacksaw, is sufficient. They will cut straight lines or mild curves and the smaller blade of the junior type will follow a tighter curve.

HARDWOODS Lumber from broad-leaved deciduous trees. Hardwoods are usually more difficult to work than softwoods; they are also heavier and more expensive, but they do last longer. The more commonly available hardwoods include walnut, oak, beech and birch.

HERRINGBONE STITCH This embroidery stitch is worked from left to right, taking a small horizontal stitch in upper layer and then, moving diagonally, a small horizontal stitch in lower layer. See pages 14 and 15.

HOBBY HORSE A horse's head attached to a stick, e.g. a broom handle. For instructions on how to make, see pages 92–94.

HOLE SAW This is a specialized drill designed to remove a core of the material. It is suitable only for use on thin materials. It consists of a drill with, around it, a length of saw blade bent into a circle. The pilot drill serves to start the hole and keep it centered. The saw then works around the surface of the materials, cutting through it until the center falls free. The hole saw is used in toy-making for cutting very large holes in plywood and for making wheels.

INCREASING AND DECREASING (Knitting/crochet) Adding to or subtracting from the number of stitches in a row of knitting or crochet. For knitting techniques, see pages 18–19.

JEWELER'S SAW Used for cutting very tight curves in metal. It is similar to a coping saw for wood and takes fine blades.

KERF Groove formed by saw cut.

KNITTING AND PURLING STITCHES see page 17 for working instructions.

KNITTING IN ROUNDS Using a set of four needles, pointed at both ends, to produce a narrow tubular fabric such as for a sock. Three needles are used to hold fabric; the fourth is the working needle.

LAMINATION Here, a method of making papier mâché, by gluing together several sheets of paper to make one, strong, flexible sheet. This can then be shaped over a base or cut into strips before it is applied.

LAZY DAISY STITCH see **CHAIN STITCH**

LUMBER Timber that is sawed or split for use as boards, beams, joists, etc. For toy-making, you can buy lumber that has been planed all around, leaving a smooth finish on all four faces and edges.

MARQUETRY Work inlaid with *redundant* pieces of variously colored fine woods. See pages 188–191, for making marquetry chessboard.

MITER BOX SAW see **BACK SAW**

NAIL SET OR PUNCH This tool is used for tapping nail heads below the surface of wood. A range of head sizes is available to suit nail sizes.

OILSTONE Used for sharpening the cutting edges of such tools as planes and chisels. Comes in both natural and artificial forms.

OVERCASTING Used on raw fabric edges to prevent fraying, and sometimes to join pieces. Working from either direction, make diagonal, evenly spaced stitches over edge of fabric.

PANEL SAW The most generally useful hand saw, suitable for cuts with or against the grain and having about 10ppi (points, or teeth, per inch, a standard saw specification). The panel saw is used for making long cuts in panel materials or for cutting larger pieces of softwood.

PAPIER MÂCHÉ A modeling material consisting of pieces of paper bound with paste or glue and molded around a shape to make functional and decorative objects. It is a cheap and easy material to use and has the advantage of drying naturally to a hard and durable substance, without having to be baked like clay. The term literally means "chewed-up paper." The invention of epoxy resin makes today's papier mâché object much stronger and more durable than traditional water-soluble glues and pastes could do.

PARTICLE BOARDS Group of man-made boards, the most common of which is chipboard.

PINKING SHEARS Shears with notched blades, used to prevent raw edges of fabric from fraying. Produces a saw-toothed decorative edge.

PLANE This tool is a form of precision knife that pares shavings to produce a smooth surface on wood, or to shape or fit it. The basic plane is available in a wide range of sizes, and there are many special-purpose planes for particular shaping work, including the spoke-shave, which can be used to shape curved surfaces.

PLYWOOD Man-made boards produced by gluing several cross-grained wood sheets together under heat and pressure with the grain of alternate layers at right angles for greater stability. Plywoods are very stiff and strong, although the thinner varieties can often be bent to form curves. They are sold in standard 4ft × 8ft sheets.

POUPARD DOLL Originally a simple plaything—a wooden ball on a stick wrapped in swaddling clothes—the poupard (French for "baby doll") later became very elaborate. Nineteenth-century poupards were richly dressed and often equipped with music boxes or mechanisms for turning their sculpted wax heads.

RAG DOLL Traditionally made from cast-off clothes and odds and ends from the sewing basket.

RASPS These tools are coarser files and normally half-round in shape. The flat side is used for flat or convex surfaces, the curved side for concave ones. The teeth are very coarse and set quite widely. They will remove material quickly without clogging. Rasps are usually supplied without handles, you should fit one before use.

RUNNING STITCH Weave needle in and out of fabric before pulling it through. Several stitches can be taken on needle at the same time. Running stitches, drawn up, are used for gathering, large running stitches are used for basting.

SABER SAW An electric saw that can make straight or curved cuts; also bevels if it has a bevel adjustment. It is used on thin boards, or on thicker boards, at a distance from the edge. It has very narrow blades for fine cuts and tight curves, and larger ones for heaver work. It is used from above the workpiece, cutting on each up-stroke.

SANDPAPER Crushed abrasive bonded to a paper backing. It is available in a range of grades (degree of coarseness). Always use sandpaper with a sanding block. This will allow you to apply even pressure over a large area and prevent the paper from digging in.

SATIN STITCH (Embroidery) Work straight stitches close together, usually to fix a shape. Stitches should be of even tension and not too long.

SCREW EYE AND SCREW HOOK Related to screws, these are useful in several kinds of application. Instead of a head, the end of the shank is bent around to form a loop, which can be a ring or a hook. They are classified by just one measurement.

SCREWS Screws of various kinds provide a strong mechanical fastening between two parts. Most types of screw have three parts: the thread, which bites into the wood to provide the hole; the shank, which is an unthreaded part passing through the part to be joined; and the head, which is wider than the rest of the screw to stop the screw penetrating further and draw the parts tightly together. The head may be a so-called flathead or roundhead in shape and has, additionally, a slot in it made to take the tip of a screwdriver.

SCRIBER A marking tool, one end of which is ground to a chisel-shaped cutting edge for marking lumber. The other end is sharpened to a point and can be used for scribing metal.

SINGLE RIB Knitting pattern in which one knit stitch and one purl stitch are alternated across first row; on the next and every even-numbered row, each stitch knitted in the previous row must be purled alternate and each one purled must be knitted. For double rib, alternate two knit stitches and two purl stitches, then reverse.

SLIPSTITCH Used to join two folded edges, or a folded edge to a surface, as in hemming. Working from right to left, take stitch through fabric, and then pass needle through the turned-in edge opposite.

SOFT-HEADED HAMMER A hammer with a rubber or plastic face.

SOFTWOOD Wood from coniferous trees, usually of an evergreen type. The term does not mean that the wood is particularly soft, although it often is. Rather, designates the type of tree from which the boards were cut. Pine is the most common softwood.

SPANISH WINDLASS Used for clamping, this device is made of a loop of cord or strong string wound around the framework to be held together; a lever, such as a screwdriver or scrap of wood is inserted into the loop and twisted around to increase the pressure. As with any clamps, pad the edges of the work with scraps of heavy cardboard to prevent cord from cutting into it.

SPLIT STITCH A form of backstitch rather like chain stitch in appearance and is ideal for outlining. See page 14 for working instructions.

SPOKESHAVE A cutting or planing tool consisting of a blade with a handle at either end. So called because it was originally used to shape spokes, it is now used for trimming and smoothing round surfaces.

STEEL RULE Pocket-size adjustable measuring device from 6–12ft long. Larger versions extend to 100ft.

STEM STITCH (Embroidery) Work from left to right, taking regular, slightly slanting stitches along line of the design.

STOCKINETTE STITCH Also known as "plain knitting." Knit and purl rows are worked alternately to produce a smooth fabric on the right side and a ridged texture on wrong side. For reverse stockinette stitch, all right-side rows are purled and all wrong-side rows are knitted.

TACK HAMMER This is the smallest, lightest type of hammer. Its small head has one flat face and is drawn to a point set at right angles to the handle. It may also be a claw type hammer.

TRIMMING KNIFE This knife usually has a handle shaped to fit the palm of the hand. The blades can be sharpened to prolong their useful life, but are intended to be discarded and replaced when they become blunt. Some types have blades scored with a series of notches so that the point can be snapped off, presenting a new cutting edge. The blade is quite short and stiff, so it can be used for heavy cutting. You can get different blades for various uses, including a hacksaw blade and pad saw blade for light work in metals and wood.

TRY SQUARE An instrument for testing the accuracy of square work or for marking right angles. It consists of a thin steel blade about 6in long, set into a wooden stock of similar length and securely fastened at right angles to it.

TWIST BITS *or* **TWIST DRILL** *see* **DRILL BITS**

VENEERS Very thin sheets of wood, generally hardwood, used to give a decorative finish over cheaper woods. They are not often available except from craft shops or cabinetmakers' suppliers.

VISE A clamping device that is attached to a workbench, for holding an object to be worked on in a fixed position. It consists of a pair of steel-faced jaws moved by a screw or lever. The clamp-on type is the cheapest, and adequate for most purposes.

YARN The word "yarn" once meant only wool yarn, but now a wide range of synthetic yarns, which imitate wool, is also available.

YARN OVER The term for a basic increasing technique in knitting. It has several applications, all of which involve making an extra loop on needle using the working yarn. See page 18 for working instructions.

Index

Make your home special

Since 1922, millions of men and women have turned to *Better Homes and Gardens* magazine for help in making their homes more enjoyable places to be. You, too, can trust *Better Homes and Gardens* to provide you with the best in ideas, inspiration and information for better family living.

In every issue you'll find ideas on food and recipes, decorating and furnishings, crafts and hobbies, remodeling and building, gardening and outdoor living plus family money management, health, education, pets, car maintenance and more.

For information on how you can have *Better Homes and Gardens* delivered to your door, write to: Mr. Robert Austin, P.O. Box 4536, Des Moines, IA 50336.

Better Homes and Gardens ®

The Idea Magazine for Better Homes and Families